TACTICAL
FLY FISHING

A Guide for the Advanced and Competition Angler

TACTICAL FLY FISHING

A Guide for the Advanced and Competition Angler

JEREMY LUCAS

THE CROWOOD PRESS

First published in 2009 by
The Crowood Press Ltd
Ramsbury, Marlborough
Wiltshire SN8 2HR

www.crowood.com

British Library Cataloguing-in-Publication Data
A catalogue record for this book is available from the British Library.

ISBN 978 1 84797 126 5

Typeset by Jean Cussons Typesetting, Diss, Norfolk

Printed and bound in Malaysia by Times Offset (M) Sdn Bhd

CONTENTS

ACKNOWLEDGEMENTS

I have a very understanding wife! In all our years together she has never once complained about my disappearing with a fly rod. Fortunately we live right by the River Eden and some of the loveliest trout and grayling fishing in England, so most days my fishing forays are just for a couple of hours; but there are times when I travel away for weeks at a time, and this drains both of us horribly. I miss Jennie and our children, Ben and Rachel, just too much. This book is dedicated to them.

I am thankful for the rivers and lakes, the lovely environments where I have practised this wonderful sport, and of course the fish themselves. I should add that all of the fish in the photographs in this book were returned to the water unharmed (with the exception of the fish from Bewl Water in the photograph on page 206, caught by my good friend John White: returning fish is not allowed at Bewl). Catch and release is now firmly entrenched in most countries in the fly fishing world, and as a result we have the survival of wild fisheries. I do not want to imply from this that there is anything wrong with catch and kill, but I firmly believe that this must be in moderation. Indeed, there are so many managed and stocked fisheries that a degree of catch and kill for the table is entirely healthy and sustainable. Anyway, anglers killing fish are almost insignificant as compared with real threats to the freshwater environment, where in almost every case the enemy is one of the many forms of agriculture.

My thanks go also to Hardy Greys, the tackle company – 'Tackling the World' – that endorses me as a guide through the Hardy Greys Academy, and has produced for us absolute state of the art high performance tackle of exceptional quality and beauty. John Wolstenholme of the company and Andy Smith, manager of the Academy, have supplied a few of the photographs in this book, and I have given credit to these in situ.

I am indebted to my colleagues in the Game Angling Instructors Association, GAIA, who in recent years have not exactly made me a better fisherman, but have certainly made me a better teacher and guide. Mike Roden is one of these, and I am delighted that he agreed to give us herein a contribution on float tubing, which is something he is championing in Britain. Gwilym Hughes and Mark Roberts of GAIA have also given me huge support, and frankly without Gwilym's careful mentoring I doubt that I would have made the grade for APGAI level.

My friend Stuart Minnikin and I went through the GAIA qualification process together and I owe him a special debt, because apart from being one of the most skilled river fishers in England (particularly with upstream nymph technique), he has a very strong will. There were several times when I considered certain casting principles wrong or irrelevant in terms of coaching or guiding, but Stuart refused to let me get away with it and forced me to see the significance of what we were doing. Several times now he has brought me back on the right track. My great friend Barry Unwin, managing director of Fulling Mill, has also guided and supported me through thick and thin over many years. He taught me how the fishing tackle industry really worked, about business, and a lot about people.

Special thanks go to Chris Ogborne, a friend and team-mate of many years, who has provided a classic, tactically orientated contribution on salt-water fly fishing, one of the exciting frontiers of the sport.

Then my England team-mates who quite simply have changed the way I fish, my attitude and my passion: they have made me a tactician. Since I was a teenager, my grail was to achieve an England team place, and to this day, for me, the highest honour in this extraordinary sport is representing one's country. I have been in awe of so many of my team-mates and their incredible skills. I write about a lot of them here, but there is so much more I really should say to acknowledge what I have learnt from them and discovered on our shared journey.

These and other friends: so many that I cannot mention here, because the list would be too long and I might leave some out, which would be unforgivable, because I value you all so much.

1 DEFINITIONS AND AIMS

This book is a guide to the analytical, technical and tactical aspects of advanced and competitive fly fishing, with a single-handed fly rod. The time is so right for this book. The last forty years have been revolutionary in our sport, as with most others – perhaps all. Today we are more competitive in sport, involving more participants world-wide, than ever before. Fly fishing for trout and grayling has been the driving force of my own sporting life. It began as a passion, because in boyhood I struggled with inappropriate tackle on wild waters in the north and west of Britain, waters that were overwhelming, and way beyond the skills and abilities of one so young. And then there was Grafham Water, that legendary, magnificent, large, stillwater trout fishery. Grafham became the model for so much that was to follow: formative years for me – but then, incredibly, they still are.

The years of development since the late 1960s and 1970s have been tremendously exciting, and the advances that have been made in terms of tackle development, casting skills, watercraft and presentation skills, quite apart from the nature, diversity and multi-disciplined approach to the sport, are breathtaking, as I will demonstrate. Fly fishing remains a passion, of course, but it has become my lifestyle.

I like to think that I am a sporting aesthete, but my friends tell me that I am much more an analyst, intense and hugely competitive, which I cannot deny. I love watching any sport performed well, or a predator going about its hunt, but an angler with a fly rod represents a pinnacle for me, when the hunt is undertaken with skill, with perfection, with beauty. And it is beautiful, when it is performed properly.

The result of a perfect presentation with a Czech Nymph in technically demanding water: Paul Fear with a grayling on the San river.

The Primitive Hunting Instinct

These pages are concerned with instinctive fly-fishing abilities and needs, as well as skills. The former cannot be learned, though they can be accentuated and developed. Everyone who takes up fishing or hunting and sticks at it beyond the first few attempts will have some innate attraction to the sport, the primitive hunting instinct. It can remain as just this, and I think most of us leave it there: something deep, buried, only surfacing in brief snatches of our sporting lives, and never really developed. Then again, some of us extend beyond this, such that the instinctive approach becomes a wildly powerful influence, driving us to think and work with the fly rod and the watery environment around us, releasing the predator prowling within us. Without a doubt, the instinctive approach can be enhanced, often considerably, though most allow it just to be there, smouldering dimly in the background of their conscious fishing lives.

Developing Skills

Skills, however, are more tangible and can be taught and learned, and then developed to a very high standard. Casting, presentation, retrieve, reading the waters, and all the many and various aspects of the sport are all skills that can be learned, from first principles. Self-teaching, or learning from friends or relatives, are the typical ways in which most of us start the long process towards the fulfilment of fly-fishing skills. We also absorb lessons from observing others fishing, and learn from experiences on the water.

Many people, particularly in this current decade, seek professional help, to short-cut the route, via 'skills analysis', towards improved abilities with a fly rod. As never before, we comprehend that our time out there on river and lake, time spent fishing, is hugely valuable to us in this modern world, and in a lifetime so brief. We understand that we need to maximize the value of these special times, if only because of that brevity. Personal ego, of course, and that natural, selfish need to be good at something, and seen to be good at it, drive many still further. This enhances our skills, if properly controlled, beyond the average level of competence. We become 'driven' in our pursuit of the 'excellence' so often referred to in modern parlance. For all this, it is real and it is achievable.

Achieving Excellence

Combine the instinctive predator and the skills analyst, and we can achieve that heightened state, that excellence, and we understand the fundamental beauty of our sport. My aims in this work are several, and they include enhancing both the instinctive abilities and the learnable skills.

It should be clear at the outset that I am writing almost exclusively about the single-handed fly rod, with trout and grayling as the main target species – though much of this is applicable to double-handed fly rod, as well as other salmonid species. Non-salmonid and salt-water species are an ever more popular quarry, drastically increasing the scope and wealth of our sport, and these are considered where relevant. Indeed, my friend Chris Ogborne, one of the great English competitors of the 1980s and 1990s, has provided this book with a classic contribution on salt-water fly fishing.

Trout and (to a lesser extent) grayling historically represent the main target fish for fly anglers all over the world. They remain so, and in any case, concentrating on the approach to these salmonids has relevance throughout the spectrum of the sport, as you will appreciate. Trout and grayling very much make up the core of my own fly fishing, on river or lake: this is my domain, with single-handed fly rod. Some aspects of the sport possess skills that do not need to involve the fish directly. Casting and fly dressing are skills in their own right, and many pursue these independently and sometimes without any actual fishing whatsoever.

Wild trout on a copper bead head Pheasant Tail.

In my forty-plus years in fly fishing I have passed through several phases. From very primitive instinctive awareness and almost zero skills, based only on a reasonable ability to cast a bait with a centre-pin or fixed-spool reel, that passion was ignited, and I began the ascent of the steep learning slope. All these years later I find myself still very much on the gradient, and though satisfied with what has been personally achieved, am hugely hungry for more, and also mesmerized by the developments in fly fishing.

My Fundamental Approach

I have a standpoint that is, finally, my fundamental approach to a fishing session. Only in recent years have I qualified this, and rationalized the approach so that it gives me a stance which I can translate definitively for others. It consists of the *analytical, technical and tactical* requirements of any fly-fishing situation. It defines everything in the skills-based approach, and utilizes quite a lot from the instinctive

requirements of fly anglers. I refer to these components of approach throughout this book, and while we can reduce them and consider them independently, in practical fishing situations we must combine them. As such, they represent the ethos, the substance, of contemporary *tactical* fly fishing.

Let me be clearer. Many experienced fly fishers will approach a water and employ their learned watercraft skills to analyse the situation and conditions of the moment. They will read the waters to varying levels of expertise, and how this analysis affects their actual fishing will vary enormously. Sometimes it might even be largely ignored, as either instinct, or past experience of the water, drives them to react conversely to the prevalent signs. Frequently there will be little regard for the technical and tactical requirements of the situation. Indeed, the technical requirements are almost always reduced to the simplest levels, with tackle and rigs that are standard for the practitioner, common to his or her previous excursions to any particular location. Only the flies might vary

Grayling on a Pheasant Tail.

to any real extent. The tactical issues, which are probably the most important, even crucial, given reasonable coverage of analysis and technical requirements, are absolutely the most ignored aspects of approach and practice by the vast majority of fly anglers.

The Influence of Competitive Fly Fishing

You will see that competitive fly fishing is also central to this book, and again I make no apology for this. I stress that even if you have absolutely no interest in formally competing in the sport, knowledge of the nature of competitive fly fishing will enhance anyone's own fishing abilities. I claim that the majority of significant developments in trout fly fishing have come from competition, particularly international competition. It has been a key driver in our sport, delivering to the fly-fishing public at large developments in tackle and skills that would not otherwise be with us today.

It has been in competition, especially during my England team campaigns, that I have learnt the most. Symbiotically working with my team-mates, I have endured what can only be described as the emotional ravages of the competition, to witness some of the greatest fly-fishing feats of the world's best performers. I savour these experiences above all others in my chosen sport. To be a part of all that, over two decades, has been both humbling and a deliverance of sorts. It has at times left me feeling bereft of skills, or at least wanting in terms of range of skills, and conversely it has also lifted me to heightened states of awareness and ability: despair and euphoria, in equal measure. I hope it does not sound too trite to say that some of us touch, at times, a Zen-like state, in which we simultaneously experience humbleness among the infinite wealth of the sport's pursuit, and some measurable and high level of practice.

For certain, it takes many years, during which much else that is important in one's life must take second place. The worth and value of it can be judged only personally. What others think of your skills and achievements is lesser to this. No matter the number of trout you catch, or their size, or the competitions you win, only the inner man knows the truth of what you have achieved and learned. Deep down, your ability is only as much as you know it to be.

I was once staring at a podium place in a European Fly Fishing Championships. Lying in fifth place overall I went into my last session with a real chance of scraping at least the individual bronze medal. It was in Slovenia, but when I arrived at my sector my heart sank as I stared at a 250m race of turbulent flow. There were very few holding areas for the large trout and grayling populations of this famous river; the Sava Bohinka trophy water. I thought I had analysed every metre, picking out the areas worthy of the most attention during the three hours of the session. Technically, I reasoned that I had the measure of the situation, juxtaposing dry fly and single nymph on leader constructions that the team, in practice, had optimized. Tactically, I expended what I thought was every last gram of experience and energy I had in this regard; I even later told our team manager, Paul Page, that there was no way I could have fished it better.

I salvaged two fish from that session, a rainbow trout and a grayling, from water that others had blanked on (been fishless), and yet the England team came away out of the medals. And I had been wrong: I could have fished it better, though it took me months to admit it, even to myself. My analysis had been a little faulty, my technical ability reasonable, but it was the shortcomings in tactical strategy – for two of the three hours – that destroyed me. I now know that I should have come off that session with four, possibly five fish, and this would have kept England in contention. Tactical: finally it really does come down to this, and there is nothing to compare with international competitive fly fishing to enhance this component of skill.

Raising the Standard

The general standard of fly-fishing competence out there is not high. This might seem a sweeping statement, but, like it or not, the skills possessed by most practitioners are rather limited. This is inevitably the case for people who are only occasional fly fishers, and the same could be said for any sport. Each and every one of the skills and requirements of our sport requires practice to become natural, developed and honed. No one can pick up a fly rod and place a nice, accurate, 20m cast with perfect turnover and touch-down presentation without

Technically demanding on Sava Bohinka, Slovenia.

John Tyzack in a Master Class with the England team on the River Wear.

considerable practice, and most of us simply do not spend sufficient time on the water for this naturalization process to develop beyond the basics, so we really cannot expect to get very far.

To advance beyond just the fundamentals of the analysis component, and to achieve anything of a handle on technical requirements, is demanding on time and practice, and unless one fishes regularly, on a range of waters, over a long period of time, the tactical demands will invariably be crude at best. In my experience of observation they will be almost non-existent unless the practitioner has an enhanced instinctive ability, which is very rare. We should realize, however, that individual and general standards can be raised. Fly fishing can be enormously frustrating, but much more so if the practitioner has severe problems with casting, say, or presentation and control.

Achieving a High Level of Skill

Another aim I have here, and with all my guiding and coaching work, is to help develop fly fishers' skills and abilities towards the advanced level of competence. Almost all the people who come to me want to improve their skills on the water; they also want to catch fish, and learn something of the nature of the rivers and lakes we visit, but the driving force is a desire to improve. I believe that most of them yearn to achieve a high level of skill, at least in some specific areas, commonly, for example, with dry fly presentation on running water, or an ability to read better the water of their local lake fishery. Many nowadays declare this at an early stage in our guide/guest relationship, and we work together on a programme or course, with specific aims tailored to the fly-fishing goals and aspirations of the individual. It is particularly exciting for us, because beyond all the frustrations and mistakes, there is the achievement, in part or whole, of the goals. Along the journey, which of course is never-ending, we have distinct waypoints, and reaching one of these is an experience to be treasured. It is, after all, exceptional, as well as difficult and time-consuming to achieve.

The guide or coach can provide short-cuts. The advanced level of ability is the grail, and along with professional help, its achievement

13

Stuart Crofts on the Rio Gandara, the European Championships 2008.

requires considerable practice. It also needs a certain level of specialization. While one can achieve a generally high standard in fly fishing *per se*, a truly advanced level can be acquired only in specific areas by any individual. You would not expect, say, a medal-winning Olympic skeet shooter, say, to be able to achieve the same standing in the 10m air-pistol discipline. It is comparatively rare for a fly fisher to be a really top-flight loch-style drift fisher and to be able to win the same level of excellence with upstream nymph presentation. The top all-rounders are, after all, the national team members. Similarly, and more simply considering purely technical casting skills, it is unusual to find an exponent who is capable of consistently breaking the forty metre distance barrier with single-handed fly rod and achieving consistent performance in the variable-range accuracy pool, while also being able to demonstrate excellence with the double-handed fly rod. All of us need to concentrate on one area of development at a time. Specific disciplines within fly fishing provide good, clear waypoints, and practice, on the journey, is the means by which we arrive at each marker. But it can all be learnt,

and a truly advanced level is there for all of us for the taking. It is a wonderful aim in this consummately beautiful sport.

My Competitive Drive

Returning to the competitive theme, you will notice time and again how much emphasis I put on this area of our sport. This is only because it has consumed me and made me into the fly fisher I am today. Realistically there are not many more years that I will be able to compete at the highest level (I already perceive a few chinks in the armour – ageing, corrosion and fatigue are inevitable), and I will either have the sense to walk away from competition, finally to retire, or will simply be buried by better competitors out there. Right now that time scares me, frankly, because while still a qualified England team member and so engaged and excited by this, revelling in the prospect of another international campaign, the alternative seems like a wilderness into which I will be cast.

I was there once before, for many years, and some of my closest friends would wish that I might return there again, and sooner rather than later. They want me to retire from competing now because they say that it consumes me like a predator, haunts me, and sucks up other aspects of my personality that are probably kinder and gentler. Absolutely, they feel, I am much too intense on the water. But then, as my ex team-mate John Pawson told me on the eve of my first World Championships in Canada: 'You will never feel so alive as during the next few days.' I know that the bulk of fly-fishing existence is outside the competitive arena, and even that there is probably a place for me out there where I can happily exist while others carry on at the competitive frontier. It is just that I have yet to find the courage to seek it. My dear friend Stuart Crofts, 'Skippy', has recently retired from England team selection and made this part of his inevitable fly-fishing journey, and I know that he and others will be there to help me in my own transition. But not just yet...

2 ADVANCED FLY FISHING: RECENT HISTORY AND DEVELOPMENT

The last forty years of fly fishing have seen more advances than we could ever possibly have dreamt at the outset. All aspects have developed at a staggering rate. Large and small, the changes have been far-reaching and have extended throughout the spectrum of the sport.

When I think back to boyhood and my early, heady attempts at fly fishing with the limited tackle available, I recognize only the fundamentals: the to-and-fro cast of a silk fly line and heavy bamboo rod, traditional wet flies, and the crudest of presentations on a stream that had probably never, ever been fished other than with bait or spinner. And beautiful places, undamaged by agriculture: I remember them, in England. Fly fishing then, as now, was an esoteric pursuit, but it was still very much in the domain of the wealthier members of the community, with time on their hands for country pursuits, at least in Britain. In Europe, too, fly fishing did not have the meaning that it now has to millions. Fishing was not so much a sport then: it was rather a means of placing food on the tables of post-war Europe, and fishing with bait, for any edible species, was the norm.

Fly Fishing for the Masses

Europe has always had an element of extreme cultural advancement, and there was a period in the 1960s, during which so much was being challenged, that fly fishing became more of a cultural pursuit than it had been. It began to open up to larger, broader groups of people. It became accessible. It seemed very fresh and exciting, and captured the imagination of more of us than ever before.

There were the classical foundations, largely British-based, the forefathers of the modern sport and historically famous waters: Halford and Skues, the Fly Fishing Club, the pristine, perfect Test valley. There were the forays of wealthy country sportsmen to the salmon and sea-trout fisheries of the north of Scotland – to legendary Loch Maree, and even to Norway and the north-west United States. Many of the pristine rivers and lakes of the New World had been stocked with brown trout emanating from the famous Loch Leven fish. Fly fishing had the image of tweeds and heavy split-cane rods, strongly associated with shotguns, hunting dogs and travel to the most beautiful places on the planet. This is not irrelevant: it is very much at the cultural foundation of fly fishing, and it is from here that all has developed since.

Frank Sawyer

A river keeper, Frank Sawyer was a handsome, slim-built, weathered man who spent countless hours through his job and his passion observing the stream and the creatures within it. He learnt to 'read' waters, and he was able to communicate lucidly his wondrous findings to the fly-fishing public. *Nymphs and the Trout* was his hugely influential masterpiece. It was radical, it was revolutionary, and it became one of the most important milestones throughout fly-fishing culture.

Then there was Sawyer, river keeper and author, and the first real spark in the brave new world of the sport. Sawyer's impact was vast, and it coincided with the beginnings of other developments that were to define the whole sport of fly fishing with the single-handed fly rod all over the world. It happened in Britain during the 1950s and 1960s, where several lakes and reservoirs of various sizes began to open up as trout fisheries. Fish farm owners who had the water space for sporting use were opening small put-and-take facilities, while some of the more enterprising water authorities were buying in brown trout, and even rainbows, to stock the new experimental fisheries. Ravensthorpe in the English Midlands and Blagdon in the South West set the trend and were the catalyst for the proliferation of stillwater trout fisheries. Landowners keen to make more money than by farming converted their ponds and lakes into trout fisheries, even removing the coarse fish stocks by netting and selling these off to fisheries in need of them, particularly the cyprinid species.

Fly fishing for trout therefore opened up to the masses, and was not, as hitherto, strictly the province of the wealthy or those fortunate enough to live close to wild waters where the fishing was free. Sawyer knew Blagdon, and even extended his influence on the discipline of nymph fishing to still waters. But if it was Blagdon and the smaller reservoirs that ignited the fuse, it was Grafham Water that exploded on to the scene in 1966.

Grafham Water

On a hot July day in that historic year, Grafham Water was opened to a naïve British fly-fishing public. Hugely experimental, nothing on the scale of this East Anglian reservoir had ever been attempted in Europe. The clay-bottomed fenland valley, formerly grossly overworked by agriculture, had been dammed and flooded through 1965 and early 1966, and stocked during that period with many thousand Loch Leven strain, farm-reared brown trout and the only rainbow trout that were available then to the Water Authority, the progeny of British Columbian steelhead rainbows. The effect and the repercussions were staggering.

To a young boy fairly new to the wonders of trout and fly, the effect was monumental. I am quite sure that Grafham defined the fisherman that I was later to become, more even than Loch

Grafham, with competition under way, and with fish feeding on buzzers close to the shore. (Courtesy John White)

The perfection of a naturalized (overwintered) stillwater rainbow.

Maree and the wild lochs of northern Scotland, or the great European trout and grayling rivers. It really did have this much influence, as it did on so many of us. I wonder now what Sawyer would have made of Grafham, but then there was another giant figure in our sport, Arthur Cove, who was to lead the way to development from a tentative fly-fishing public full of hope, aspiration and excitement towards advanced techniques and an approach that would also be definitive.

The Rainbow Trout

The moment, the man, the following: it all came together at Grafham, and this was also the time of the rainbow trout. A New World species, indigenous to the western expanse of the North American continent, farm-reared rainbows were introduced primarily as food fish to Europe, and secondly, experimentally, to sport fisheries. While, during the Victorian age, Old World brown trout had been successfully introduced to places where they were not native as far flung as South America and the Antipodes, so the rain-

bows completed the exchange during the mid- to late twentieth century, and were stocked into all manner of European fisheries such as Grafham.

Most of us believe now that were it not for the rainbow trout, the sport of fly fishing would not have developed at anything like the rate it has in Britain or elsewhere in Europe. Wild waters would not have been able to sustain the needs of a sporting public, and development would have been stifling. Fly fishing would have been segregated in this sense, divided into the American school, based on rainbow and brook trout species (apart from salmon and non-salmonid species), and the European brown trout and grayling-orientated sport. Without a doubt, far fewer people would fly fish in Britain and Europe than is the case today. The stillwater boom, fuelled by fast-growing, easily reared rainbows, and brown trout that were aesthetically in demand, provided very high quality fly fishing accessible to almost anyone who wanted it. And Grafham was central to all this: it was the European model fishery.

Fly-Fishing Tackle

Fly-fishing tackle in the 1960s was still rudimentary in terms of both materials and performance. Design was also very traditional, and ensnared by the limitations of the available materials. We were still using cane rods and silk fly lines, with nylon monofilament leader material that had only quite recently (twenty-five years) been improved sufficiently to be able to replace cat gut and horse hair! Glass-fibre rods were revolutionary, and by the time Grafham opened, most of us were using these, though it was unusual not to see a few cane rods about. For all of 1966 and 1967 I used only a split-cane rod that was lent to me by a relative.

Synthetic fly lines were also just beginning to oust silk, but they were extremely poor quality in those days. They were essentially a core of braided polyester coated with drawn PVC, which provided the weight and the taper. Invariably they had terrible 'memory' and coiling, and their surfaces cracked early in their lives.

Floaters tended to partially sink, while sinkers sank at inconsistent rates.

Fly design, too, was crude, based as it was either on traditional wet and dry flies, albeit with the imitation-based influence of historic figures such as Skues, Halford and particularly Sawyer. Except for the latter, the fly patterns available to us were not generally appropriate for reservoir trout, particularly rainbows. We 'borrowed' styles of fly and lure from sea-trout and salmon-fishing disciplines, and also from the Americans who, after all, had much more experience of fly fishing for rainbows and steelhead than we did in Europe. We got by, of course, because such was the thrill of the new sport, particularly with rainbow trout, that it caught the imagination of the fishing public, and this in turn drove tackle design and development.

The sport actually developed in Britain along divergent paths for two decades. There were those who fished exclusively on the new man-made reservoir and lake fisheries, while others pursued wild fish in rivers and lakes. Essentially it was a geographical split: those who lived close to the wilder places in Britain fished there, while in a world that was less mobile than it is today, those living in the Midlands or south of England tended to be reservoir fishers. We saw distinct fly-fishing disciplines evolve (quite apart from salmon and trout, or double-handed and single-handed disciplines), and crossing over from one to another occurred to greater and lesser extents, based on an individual's needs and prejudices.

Among those involved in the stillwater boom, their fly fishing was largely based on the reservoirs, with perhaps holiday ventures to the wild waters in the north and west of Britain, or further afield. To some extent this situation still exists, though with greater mobility and the enormous wealth of variety in fly fisheries everywhere, more people sample a broader range of fly-fishing disciplines and locations than ever before. And this, too, has been a driver towards the development of high performance tackle and techniques.

*Mark Rooney,
England loch-style
team member at
Grafham, 2005.*

The Influence of Coarse Fishing

Coarse fishing also strongly influenced the trout fly-fishing disciplines. This was, and continues to be, essentially a one-way process because it seems that fly fishing has a lot more to learn from coarse (bait) fishing than the other way around. Much of this stems from presentation techniques. Coarse fishing, particularly competitive or match fishing, has historically had a huge following throughout Western Europe, very much including Britain. The development of bait presentations for specific water types and species was already a fine art back in the days of the rapid proliferation of trout stillwater fishing, and today, many fly fishers have developed a strong notion of the need for fly presentation as subtle as the coarse fisherman's bait presentation, along with commensurate sensitivity of bite or take detection.

Fly-fishing rigs for trout and grayling, and for coarse fish, can today be super-sensitive, and afford precise and controlled presentation. They are, moreover, significantly more versatile in usage than the coarse-fishing presentations (thinking here of fine, shock-absorbed pole set-ups, or hair and bolt rigs), though they certainly owe their existence largely to bait-fishing techniques, which were advanced while their related fly-fishing presentations simply were not.

Back in the exciting years of the sixties and seventies, glass fibre ruled in rod construction, while polymer lines were ousting silk. The fly rods available then were, not surprisingly, hardly more advanced than the traditional cane rods they were replacing. They were almost as heavy, though tubular, and similarly through- or slow-actioned. It did not take long, however, for the engineers to extend the potential of glass fibre and produce lighter, thinner-walled (to an extent) and longer fly-rod blanks from this material. Again, bait-fishing rods led the way, with the production of stiffer, longer match-fishing float rods.

The Grafham Ghost

It was from one of these that the brilliant Don Neish made his greatest ever contribution to the fly-fishing world. Don is an engineer and a

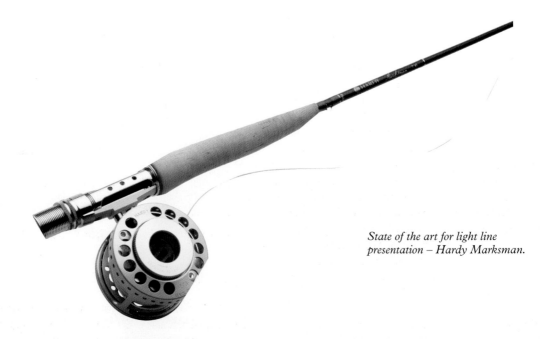

State of the art for light line presentation – Hardy Marksman.

hugely skilled tackle designer. He was in those years a tournament caster, and actually held world bait-class casting records. He was also an outstanding single-handed fly-rod caster. A great friend of Arthur Cove who was then pioneering the stillwater nymph revolution (on Grafham, of course), Don was able to combine his own tournament casting skills with the needs of the contemporary reservoir fly fisher (*a propos* Arthur Cove), and also with the materials and design capability of the times. He borrowed the technology and materials from coarse match fishing, and produced the radical Grafham Ghost fly rod.

While a university student I actually worked part-time for Don in his tackle shop in North London, and was, fortuitously, able to acquire a Ghost and also to use it standing at the shoulder of Arthur Cove on Grafham itself. I wonder if I knew at the time the impact and value of this (I think I did, actually): the mentorship of the great man, on the great lake, with the world's most advanced weapon for the purpose. Make no mistake, this was advanced fly fishing. We were able, then, to lay out thirty yards of line across the wind, to drift and swing teams of

appropriate nymphs, at controlled depths, with good take detection capability. We just about had the tackle to match our rapidly developing knowledge of the needs of the fisheries and the target species. We had taken the first steps right at the foot of the exponential of the learning curve.

The Grafham Ghost was actually a customized small range of rods based on the tip sections of a match-fishing blank. Don produced these in lengths of between 9ft and 9ft 9in, designed to take lines of between #5 and #7 on the AFTM (American Fishing Tackle Manufacturers) rating, commonly a six-weight. I no longer have that rod, remembering that I passed it on when carbon fibre developed to the extent that it made glass fibre obsolete. I wish I had kept it, though; not because I had caught several thousand trout with it, as well as sea trout and salmon from rivers and lakes all over Britain, but because now, many years later, I realize just what a significant tool the Ghost was at the time of such rapid development in the sport.

I had one of the longer rods in Don's range, and it was as viable a tool for loch-style drifting as it was for long-distance casting from the bank of the large reservoirs. It was a rod designed for a purpose, and it was certainly the first fly rod with which I felt completely comfortable. I used it so much, in a whole range of circumstances, that it felt like a living extension of my arms. It was a fast-actioned (for those days), aesthetically pleasing weapon, in its unusual buff/yellow blank colour, with dark brown American snake-guide whippings. Don fitted a down-sliding nickel silver reel seat for me, which pushed the reel to the extremity of the handle base and effectively gave the rod an extra 2in (5cm) of length, which was so useful for controlling a top dropper, particularly while drift fishing. I can still see it, can still picture loading it with a five-weight AirCel Supreme double taper, and casting off the north bank of Grafham.

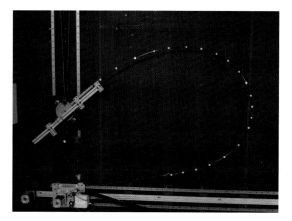

Achieving the best with materials and design – Hardy test facility, Alnwick.

The Hardy Superlite

Others saw the utilitarian beauty of the Ghost. Richard Walker, all-round freshwater fisherman – and then the long-term holder of the British carp record of 44lb (20kg) – turned to fly fishing in the latter part of his career and brought the same innovative approach to trout fishing as he had to coarse fishing. I only met him on two or three occasions, but remember how well he regarded the Ghost. Indeed, rumour had it that he was responsible for taking it along to Hardy Brothers for them to copy (fly-rod actions cannot be patented). The result was the excellent Richard Walker Superlite, a mass-produced reservoir rod that became a best-seller for Hardy within a year of its introduction.

Actually, the Superlite was not really as similar as it might have been to the Ghost, because the blank-making technology of those days was primitive; but it was a fine tool, fit for the purpose for which it was intended, and it became top of the list for the burgeoning converts to reservoir fly fishing. I had some friends who owned two Superlites, rather like pairs of top-class shotguns or Palakona split-cane fly rods. They were, after all, that good, while also being something of a fly-fishing fashion statement. It was unusual on the reservoir

trout fisheries in those years not to see fishermen sporting Hardy Superlites – while a few of us were loyal to the Grafham Ghost.

A New Generation of Fly Fishing

This was a time of rapid growth in terms of technique and tackle. The stillwater boom in Britain was having an influence elsewhere in Western Europe, and small lake trout fisheries began springing up in Belgium and France. Many of the new fly fishers were coarse fishermen who wanted to fill fishing time during the coarse fish close season, which, between mid-March and mid-June, coincided with one of the loveliest times to be out by the water during the European spring. While this brought new converts to an exciting new dimension of fishing, it also introduced new techniques to a sport that had been in comparative stasis for many decades – in fact really since Sawyer's work on nymph fishing, and Oliver Kite's charismatic approach to popularizing river fly-fishing skills. We were at the beginning of an exciting new generation of fly fishing.

We had the new waters, virtually a new target salmonid species (the rainbow trout, *salmo gairdneri*), as well as the established wild waters

Feral rainbow trout on Diawl Bach nymph.

with their brown trout and grayling populations. The salmon and sea-trout fishery was experiencing mixed fortunes, though this was well before the widespread destruction of the sea trout in European waters. We had the product to tackle the new direction our sport had taken, and we had the new emerging luminaries, some of them to become giants in the sport.

Fly fishing with the single-handed fly rod now had such a following of devotees that there was considerable differentiation into types. There was the upstream dry fly, old-school fishing derived from the chalk streams of southern England. There were the travelling sportsmen whose years revolved around sojourns on the great trout and salmon waters of northern and western Britain, and who were driven by the desire to catch the king of fish fresh from the sea, but in inclement conditions might settle for brown trout on the lochs. There were a few river *aficionados*, continuing in the theme set by Sawyer, and exploring beyond, on wilder, less agriculturally damaged waters than existed then in the south. There were even those who explored into Europe and the northern United States. Indeed, the North American influence was marked in this period, because while the average American fisherman was (and remains)

possessed of fairly basic skills, the best of the Americans were at that time probably the best in the world, at least in the river craft. And then, led by the British, there was the avalanche in stillwater fly fishing, largely for stocked rainbow and brown trout. We were realizing fly-fishing specialists, and sensed that we were moving into a new level in the sport as a whole. For the first time we were heading, *en masse*, towards the potential for advanced fly fishing, in terms of skills, differentiation of specialization and tackle design.

The advanced fly fishing skills dealt with in this book are essentially the sport undertaken for trout species, including to an extent the migratory forms (sea trout, steelhead and sea-run cut-throats) and grayling, but also with relevance to char and to non-salmonid species. This is the sport undertaken on still or running water, of all sizes, with single-handed fly rod. This is enormous in scope, of course, and no one man, one lifetime, even devoted to the single-handed sport, can sample all of this, in all its variety, and this is one of its many charms.

Considering the trout species, even here we have differentiation. In many ways, brown and rainbow trout differ, and then again the fish in rivers have different behaviours and characteristics to those in lakes. Migratory forms of these species – sea-trout and steelhead – are distinctly different to their non-anadromous relatives. Fly-fishing requirements and techniques for all of these, while sharing common ground, differ in many ways, as we will consider. And in all these ways we have made huge advances over the years.

The Benefits of Specialization

Progression through the sport inevitably leads to degrees of specialization, and for many people this remains the area in which they were introduced to fly fishing. In Britain the largest sector of the whole sport is without a doubt the stillwater community. Indeed, there remains a very strong following of large reservoir devotees, especially if their formative years were on fisheries such as Grafham or Rutland. Big waters have a way of 'getting into one's system'. I know a lot of experienced fly fishers who tell me that small lakes and pools, with stocked or even wild trout, simply do not excite them or fulfil their fishing needs; for such *aficionados*, only the massive lakes and reservoirs will do. There are echoes of this in many of us. No matter where one travels with a fly rod, perhaps out to the wild, glacier-fed waters of Scandinavia or the lovely rivers of Eastern Europe, there is a warm feeling within when on Grafham again…

With specialization, of course, comes increased and improved skills. Standards are inevitably raised. Watch the fly fishers of today on the banks of Grafham, and recall their efforts back in the 1970s: though the same sport and the same target species, the tackle is so far refined, and the dextrousness of use so much improved, that we should share a pride in just how far the sport has developed. Loch-style drift fishing is stunning in its diversity and effectiveness. Gone are the days when we drifted with such limited control and basic style. Today, we set and control drifts with far higher precision, exploring the three-dimensional water space with a continuous range of fly-line densities and leader constructions, with rods that can deal with them adequately, and fly patterns that

Arrival of the Europeans – the England team in Poland, 2005.

are generations of development beyond the traditional wet flies and crude lures of the past.

As for the river craft, this seems almost a different sport. Apart from a very few giant figures, the standards of river fly fishing in Britain were low, because relatively few people had access to sufficient fishing of this type, certainly compared with the stillwater proliferation of the seventies and eighties. The great southern chalk streams were very expensive, while some of them required more than just money to be able to access. In the north and west, however, the wild brown trout and grayling rivers have always been accessible. There was a long period of stasis in Britain with regard to river sport (at least compared with the fantastic rate of development in stillwater skills) until the 1990s and the influence of the Europeans ignited a whole new era of sporting evolution.

International Influences

Up until this period, the rivers of Britain had seemed comparatively devoid of fly fishers, while the lakes and reservoirs throughout the country were so popular. In Europe and the United States, however, the river sport was dominant, as it continues to be. Finally, partly because of overseas travel and partly because of

Arrival of the Europeans – the Polish national team in Spain, 2008.

a recoil effect with stillwater anglers suddenly finding a whole wealth of fly-fishing experience, our attention turned more to the rivers, actually as never before.

Throughout Europe, and particularly Eastern Europe, fly fishing was wildly different in approach to its practice in Britain. Fishing for trout and any other edible species was undertaken primarily for the table, and secondarily as a sport. The whole meaning of angling was different: a different history, a different development, and a different philosophy. Trout and grayling were the main target species, while 'catch and release' made as much sense to the Europeans as bulimia. This 'culture' of fishing, however, produced skills that were breathtaking to us in Britain, and finally the exchange process began, inevitably of our stillwater influence, and the wonderful river talents and experiences of the Europeans, merging and cross-fertilizing to lift the sport to much higher levels.

International travel and international competitive fly fishing were both responsible for the contemporary rapid evolution of the sport. Through the nineties and continuing today, the stillwater and the river scenes develop side by side. In both these major groups of disciplines the advances have been spectacular, as we will explore here, in depth. The benchmarks are so high today, while inevitably the general standards of the fly-fishing community at large are rather lower. Advanced fly-fishing skills are here for the taking now. We have the tackle, the precedents, the experience and a wealth of enthusiasm as never before. The state of the art, or craft, at its higher levels is sublimely situated, but it is reachable. Time on the water is hugely important in achieving this, of course, but we can accelerate the process by 'skills analysis', communicating the technical and tactical approaches to the sport. We are not so much short-cutting the route towards expertise, in any of the disciplines, as removing the superfluous, the failed experiments and experiences, or the less important, and streamlining the way towards the grail of advanced fly fishing. It is just a matter of going for it.

A Great Sporting Fish

One thing I would like to dismiss at this stage. Many will argue that fly fishing for rainbow trout is a poor substitute for real fishing, but this simply is not the case. Even stocked rainbow trout are an incredibly valuable resource, in the sport as a whole and in the water in which they are introduced. In brown trout and grayling fisheries where rainbows are introduced the objective may be questionable, but in other cases we just have to respect this sporting fish. I am not talking about fresh-stocked fish here, which, like immature brown trout or small shoaled grayling, should be left well alone. I am talking about the naturalized, acclimatized rainbow. This is very much one of the world's great sporting fish to be targeted with fly. Anyone who runs it down is speaking from a standpoint of ignorance, or the fortunate position of being able to fish for wild trout or other wild fly-targeted species. Anyone approaching the level of 'advanced' in our sport will recognize both the wild and naturalized rainbow (and the brown trout) as being great challenges, worthy of the demands of our discipline.

3 MODERN COMPETITIVE FLY FISHING

History and Development

If advanced fly-fishing techniques with a single-handed fly rod have come a long way in forty years, competitive fly fishing has been in no small way responsible for this, at least in terms of development of tackle and skills – that is, the technical and tactical aspects of the sport. This has almost all happened within the last two decades, during which competitive fly fishing has avalanched on to the scene. It has now become part of the landscape of fly fishing, or at least a very significant feature of it. I have often been convinced that just about every really noticeable development in terms of our effectiveness in catching trout and grayling has come about as a result of competition.

In my book *Fly-Fisher* (Cape, 1986), I was a little derisive about competition in fly fishing, even sceptical. I had perceived the negative aspects of this sector of the sport, which certainly existed, and still exist today, and I had considered these destructive. I had not, at that time, entered any competition, and I misunderstood it; neither did I realize any of the positive benefits that it could offer fly fishing at large. Though an experienced fisherman even then, I was inexperienced in the ways of competition, and I was wrong to judge it while lacking such experience.

The Influence of International Competition

That all changed in 1987 when I was invited by the British godfather of competitive fly fishing, Tony Pawson, an ex-World Champion, to enter the first ever European Open Championship, to be fished on Bewl Water in Kent. Tony and the Fédération Internationale de Pêche Sportive,

Mouche (FIPS-Mouche) were using this event in order to test whether it would be viable for a European Fly Fishing Championship event to run alongside the established World Championships. Bewl, in the extreme south of England, was the perfect venue for this, being close to the Continent and thus offering good access for the European teams as well as the British.

As well as its accessibility, Bewl was also one of the best of the new generation of large reservoir trout fisheries, superbly managed, with a resident stock of brown trout (some of them wild) and over-wintered rainbow trout (some of them huge), supplemented by regular stocking, mostly with rainbows grown on site. Following on very much from the Grafham model, Bewl was established as one of the top four large reservoir fisheries in Britain, the others being Grafham, Rutland and Chew Valley.

Over the few years previous to 1987, I had fished Bewl Water (Bewl Bridge, as it was known then) a great deal – more at that time even than Grafham, because I lived nearby and worked in London when not travelling. I knew it very well and had made some huge catches there, including several of the very large 'naturalized' rainbow trout and big browns. Also at that time, the pressure of my work, and the passion for my precious sport, were niggling away and leaving me feeling that there was something missing. Even then I was nudging myself towards a fly-fishing lifestyle. Then, just a month before the European Open, I met Tony at Bewl, and he suggested I enter as an individual, telling me that he thought the experience would be interesting for me.

Czechs, French and Belgian national team members collected together, along with World

Bewl Water. (Courtesy John White)

Champion Brian Leadbetter and the rest of the England squad, on a bright, warm day in late May. There had been buzzer activity earlier in the morning, but now the surface was almost fishless: nothing rose, and all the competitors suspected that catches would be low. In competition, however, you take it as it comes and simply make the best of whatever faces you. It is nearly always difficult. There are so many variables, many of which are out of our control, or over which we have limited control, that absolutely no one can lock them all down and derive the perfect solution. You do your utmost to find the best solution you can, in each of the many and different (*all* different) situations that

face you, and over time, the best competitors have the most consistent results.

The European Open turned out to be a milestone event in the development of competitive fly fishing in Europe, and I will write about this in due course. Up to this period, however, competitive fly fishing had been very quiet in Britain and elsewhere. The FIPS-Mouche World Championships had existed only since 1981, while the only other major international competition (involving a structured selection process for the competitors achieving national team status) was the four-cornered Home International between England, Ireland, Scotland and Wales, fished 'loch-style' from drifting boats under the rules of the International Fly Fishing Association (IFFA). This was already a key event in the history of our sport since the late 1920s, missed only in the war years. At first once a year, then twice (since 1971) in spring and early autumn, the four nations fielded teams on the largest, most famous lakes in each country.

Loch Leven was Scotland's historically important venue, the water from which the seed of brown trout had been taken and introduced to places where they had never existed, all over the world, during the Victorian age of exploration. Finally, following tragic years of nitrate pollution, the venue was switched to Lake of Menteith. Lough Conn, and other wild brown trout loughs in the Irish midlands and west coast, hosted Ireland's internationals. From 1971 Grafham Water became England's premier competition lake, though Bewl, Chew and Rutland were used in later years, and even Draycote and other less grand venues, mostly as one-off experiments. By this time Wales was hosting internationals on Trawsfynid, and later on the lovely Llyn Brenig in the remote uplands of the north of the country.

Until the 1980s there was very little structure to international events, and selection criteria for all the nations were vague, and certainly not understood by the fly-fishing public at large. Unless one lived in the right part of England, for example, or knew people who were involved in competition, the most one ever noticed was a brief write-up in *Trout and Salmon* or *Angling* magazines. While historic, it was very low key; yet it gathered a lot of interest from the growing numbers of stillwater fishermen in Britain. It was certainly a dream of many of that generation of fly fishers that they might aspire to representing their country in their chosen sport.

At this juncture I refer readers to Tony Pawson's outstanding book *Competitive Fly Fishing* (Pelham Books, 1982), which effectively maps the history of this sector of the sport right up to 1982, including the early World Championship events and the inauguration of FIPS-Mouche, as well as the results of all the IFFA Home Internationals from 1928 to 1981. Tony's book represents the state of the art up to the 1980s, and I take up the development from that point, when so much happened in the sport and a new generation of fly fishers set such high standards in the competitive arena and in advanced fly-fishing techniques.

Start of a loch-style international: Lake of Menteith, 2005.

Milestones in the 1980s

So what happened, what were the events and milestones that changed the course of competitive fly fishing? We can identify when it happened, because we left the 1980s decade with a completely different ethos in the sport than when we entered it. Understanding the personalities, the places and the competition in that period is key to appreciating how the sport has advanced. Almost all of us stand on the shoulders of giants who came before us. In the same way that a generation of river fishermen was so strongly influenced by Frank Sawyer, so the great competition fly fishers of the 1980s set the seed for what we have become today.

The stillwater boom in Britain fuelled an accompanying interest in loch-style drift fishing, which was the basis of the IFFA structure for fishing the biannual internationals. In a single decade the number of stillwater trout fishers had escalated, while the numbers of river specialists had remained fairly static. By the early 1980s the front line of fly fishing in Britain was very much the set of stillwater disciplines, broadly covered by bank and boat practices, the latter split into the very different approaches of drifting and anchored boats.

Gradually the ratio of anchored to drifting boats was shifting. As on wild waters, where the target species were brown trout and sea trout, so on the reservoirs and large lakes it became much more usual to see free-drifting boats, or boats with controlled drifts. There was even the somewhat unfair attitude that fishing at anchor was a crude form of fly fishing from a boat. What is not arguable, however, is that controlled drift fishing – loch-style – was developing at an incredible rate, quite unprecedented in any discipline in fly fishing, or fishing more generally.

Also in this decade, master practitioners emerged. There were many, but as with any sport, only a handful who wrote their names indelibly in history. Brian Leadbetter was one, an English Midlander who was to become a double World Champion, an exponent with an utterly instinctive approach, so natural, and actually so simple. I remember fishing on Bewl with 'Leady' one time and marvelling at the way he so quickly assessed the drift and adapted (to a water he did not know well) to make an impressive catch. He paid me a great compliment after that day when he told interested fishermen in the bar that evening: 'Jeremy doesn't catch a trout out of a shoal, he takes the whole bloody shoal!' From Leady that was a supreme accolade (because actually, on a lake I knew far better, I caught little more than he did). I bought him another lager, which was his favourite tipple.

Contemporary Competition on Stillwaters

Today we have a great many competitions in Britain and Europe based on stillwaters. At the top of the tree in England remain the loch-style qualifiers and national final, organized by the Confederation of English Fly Fishers (CEFF), which lead to qualification to the national teams that fish the Home Internationals in spring and early autumn. Many fishermen take hardly any interest in competitions other than these, preparing themselves each year for the one-off chance to qualify from the heats to the national final, and the possibility of going through from there to the national loch-style team itself.

Quite simply, this is the supreme achievement for many stillwater fly fishers, and it is often very difficult to attain. While some have reached this state of excellence in their sport at the first attempt, in their first year of going through the competition qualification process, others may have many years of fruitless attempts – a gruelling learning process – and some have never actually achieved their goal.

The CEFF is one of the home member organizations that make up the International Fly Fishers Association (IFFA), which organizes and administers the Home Internationals. Ireland, Scotland and Wales have their member organizations, and through the auspices of IFFA they conduct the internationals in turn on the great competition lakes of the member countries. There is the Irish Trout Fly Fishing Association, the Scottish Anglers National Association and the Welsh Salmon and Trout Association. The qualification systems organized by all these nations differ to some extent, though all involve qualifying heats and national finals in both river and loch-style disciplines. The bank-fishing still-water discipline is currently being developed towards full international status.

In one year the spring international (loch-style) is nowadays fished on one of the 'big four' in England (Grafham, Rutland, Bewl or Chew), followed by an autumn international on Llyn Brenig in Wales. In the following year the spring international in Ireland is held on one of the huge loughs in the Midlands or west coast, then the autumn international moves to Scotland on the Lake of Menteith. In two years, therefore, the cycle of competition venues includes all four host countries.

The Process of Qualification

The qualification process is similar for each of the home nations. In England at the senior level a competitor must enter a regional qualifier or (dauntingly named) eliminator, where he or she becomes a member of a federation. Each federation is awarded pro-rata places in the national final, which generally works out at about one place for every five or six entrants to the qualifier. Historically, a competitor must only enter one federation qualifier in any year, though this does not have to be in the competitor's home region. Several federations organize 'open' events for CEFF members coming from other regions.

Most federations fish a single one-day qualifier, known as a 'sudden death' event. A few, such as the South East or East Anglia, fish a series followed by a regional final, again gaining the same pro-rata places to the final. Because of the inconsistency and regional differences, it might seem confusing at first, but competitors soon understand the system and usually settle for the qualification process undertaken through their own regional federation. It is fair in all, and to all; but some competitors prefer competition within federations that organize a

Stuart Minnikin, in practice session for a qualifier on Stocks Reservoir.

series of qualifiers followed by a regional final. Not so long ago there were federations with the reputation of being easier routes to qualification to the national final, perhaps because of a less committed, or competitive, membership. Some of the more ruthless, out-of-region competitors would target these and rely on an 'easier' route to the national. These days are all but over, however, because the standard of competition is very high throughout.

The Ladies and Disabled Federations also hold similar qualification events leading to distinct Ladies and Disabled Home Internationals, though members of both these federations are also at liberty to enter the qualification process leading to a senior team place, which is open to all, other than those under nineteen years of age. The Youth Federation, enormously active nowadays, organizes the youth qualifiers and final which selects the youth home team to

The author returning rainbow in practice session the day before winning the Brown Bowl in the Home International on Llyn Brenig, 2004.

contest the Youth Home Internationals that mirror the senior events. The effectiveness of the Youth Federation in developing world-class fly fishers of the future should be stressed.

As we move into an era when competitive fly fishing is climbing much higher up the recognition ladder, sharing space at least with other sports not blessed with the media attention of others, we have seen, and will continue to see, great names coming through to senior level and achieving the highest competitive excellence possible. Scott Nellins, now a production assistant at Hardy/Greys, is one such, having achieved an exemplary record in the youth team at World Championship and Home Interna-

tional levels. The current manager of the youth national team, Phil Dixon, is another, while the simply outstanding Simon Robinson, one of the most capped of England's internationals, is poised as a future World or European Champion. All of the home nations can boast this success with their youth contingent in fly fishing, most notably perhaps being Wales with a very committed programme of developing potential at this level.

Today, as never before, the route is open and clear for an individual of any age to embark on the qualification process leading to a national team place, the grail of an ever-increasing number of fly fishers. Similar may be said about other European countries, though there are significant differences, not least being the comparative lack of loch-style competition discipline. Most of the Europeans are much more river-based in their competitions than the British have been traditionally; here the history of international competition is the oldest, and has therefore been much longer established, stemming from that first Home International between England and Scotland on Loch Leven in 1928.

Analysing the process of qualification statistically, we see that it is not too daunting. In England we enter a federation loch-style qualifier and have approximately a one-in-five chance of qualifying to the national final, which

nowadays hosts 100 finalists, usually in September, and by default held on one of the large reservoirs capable of having fifty boats (two competitors per boat), plus officials and safety boats (a minimum of fifty-five boats). From the final, twenty competitors will be successful in making it through to one of the two national loch-style teams, for either the spring or autumn Home Internationals. This also provides, therefore, a one-in-five chance of qualification.

Effectively, it is possible to fish just two matches, a regional qualifier and a national final, and actually qualify to the national team. Some manage it on their first attempt, far more make several attempts, while others struggle on for years, even at the eliminator stage, and never reach the national final. It is good to be aware of the statistics, however, because it gives you a basis on which to measure your performance. If,

The boats leave at the start of an international.

for example, one does not achieve that top one-in-five place at eliminator level after two or three attempts (a single attempt gives relatively little information), then it should provide good feedback as to the levels and types of improvement required. A competitor will, after all, absorb a huge amount of information by watching others out on the water and by listening to people at the results and debriefing afterwards. It often tells you not so much how others won, but where you went wrong, and it always holds you in good stead for future competitions.

Other Loch-Style Competitions

In stillwater sport, particularly in Britain, there are nowadays many other loch-style competitions, ranging from charity events for noble causes, such as the annual Alex Booth Heart Foundation event on Draycote water, to massive sponsored national and international events such as the Lexus European Open, an exhaustive series of qualifiers and distinct team and individual finals. For several years this latter championship has been the fastest growing competition of all in Britain. Organized by the renowned John Horsey, the most capped of England internationals ever (to date), the Lexus has even extended to capture the interest of competitors on mainland Europe.

For many years since the 1980s, until the ban on tobacco advertising, Benson & Hedges sponsored the biggest team event in loch-style competition, an international (in home nations terms). It was enormously popular, attracting even more contestants, via teams, than the CEFF national qualifiers. The B&H – later to be taken over by Hardy sponsorship, and then Fulling Mill – was also fished on a regional basis at heat level in the early stages, and was instrumental in increasing participation in loch-style competition.

Many tackle manufacturers sponsored loch-style events in this period, such was the popularity of the discipline. Partridge and Shakespeare both had competitions that involved three- or four-man teams, as well as the individual competition, whereas the B&H was very much a six-man (or woman) team event.

The Development of Club Teams

This was also the time when the Association of Major Fly Fishing Clubs was inaugurated by Peter Firth, a landmark development in the sport in England, because it was the first to hint at a league structure. With the growth in interest in stillwater trout fishing, and loch-style in particular, some large clubs had formed by the end of the 1980s. Invicta in the Grafham/Rutland area, Grafham Water Fly Fishers, Bewl Bridge Fly Fishers and the Bristol Reservoirs were all very large clubs, and there were several clubs throughout England with the minimum of fifty members that qualified for membership of the AMFFC.

The matches were, and continue to be, fished by rotation on major stillwater venues, exclusively loch-style, to international rules (established by the IFFA). Teams of six from each of the member clubs participate at each round. At the end of the season the positions of each club are worked out for all the year's matches, giving an overall position. Very soon, in fact after only a few seasons, the AMFFC was divided into leagues, such that clubs could participate with other clubs at similar level, and could also be promoted or relegated to other divisions. The AMFFC has also been unique in another way, in that it is exclusively a team event, with no individual prizes or medals being awarded.

The European Open Championships had still not developed into the official Fly Fishing Championships that were recognized and organized by FIPS-Mouche, and they continued for several years as one-off events, usually involving loch-style, to IFFA rules (as the Home Internationals), but with any size of fly allowed rather than the IFFA limitation of ⅝in hook size and just under 1in total dressing length for the fly. Again, this reflected the popularity, now extending into mainland Europe, of the loch-style discipline.

By 1990 it was clear that the British teams

Vince Brooks in harsh conditions in a European Championship bank-fishing session, Norway 2007.

completely dominated in loch-style events, and were strong in other stillwater disciplines. A very strong boat-orientated England team travelled to the 1993 World Championships in British Columbia, Canada, where the fishing was entirely on lakes, and returned home as team gold medallists, having led from the very first session. Even so, with the Czechs and several other European teams performing surprisingly well (it seemed at the time), many of us noted that this happy time for England in fly-fishing championships would not last.

Bank Fishing on Stillwaters

Through the late 1980s and 1990s the European Opens developed into three annual matches split over three stillwater venues, in Belgium, England and France, finally becoming the Grand Slam events which persist to this day (though completely differentiated from the official, FIPS-Mouche European Fly Fishing Championship). Several teams of three from all the European countries were invited to fish in the Grand Slam events, which developed an emphasis on bank fishing, rather than loch-style. These were not official internationals, however, and have never had that status in any of the participating countries. However, they have been a very good practice or training arena for budding or even experienced internationals. The main participating countries remain Belgium, England and France.

Competitive fly fishing from the banks of large and small stillwaters has thus far not had anything like the impact or following that loch-style has had, though it has developed. From small, annual bank-fishing competitions on the major stillwaters, several larger competitions developed, such as the novel Trout Masters. Anglers who caught a large trout from one of the numerous stillwaters that participated in the Trout Masters were invited to participate in a one-off final on that particular water in order to win a place in a national final on one of the major stillwaters.

It was not until 2004 that the CEFF, sponsored by the Airflo Company, started a dedicated bank-fishing competition, primarily fished on small stillwaters in all the home nations. Anglers could fish as many qualifying heats as they wished, on any participating water, which gave multiple chances to competitors to qualify for the final, always so far fished on Elinor Fishery in Northamptonshire in October. The CEFF/Airflo competition is for both teams and individuals. The top teams from each of the home nations in the final are usually invited to fish in the European Grand Slam events, though unfortunately there is currently no official national team status, or 'cap', the event not having been adopted under the IFFA range of internationals.

It seems a logical progression that the latter situation will change, and if and when it does, the CEFF bank-fishing championship is bound to develop because of the vastly increased participation it will enjoy if there is the potential of achieving official national team status. All the home nations need this development if they are to continue competing at the highest level, in European and World Championships, when many of the session venues are fished from the bank of various-sized stillwaters. Currently, in spite of having a huge number of specialist stillwater anglers dedicated to bank fishing (more than any other European country), England is only one of at least half-a-dozen countries that consistently perform well, in international competition, in this discipline.

Competition on Rivers

While British anglers have developed a justified reputation, worldwide, for stillwater competitive fly-fishing skills, we have traditionally been far weaker on rivers. Even at the height of our international prowess in the 1990s there were several other nations, all European, that were more competitive on river venues. The French and Italians climbed rapidly to the top, while the Czechs and Poles were also seemingly always in contention. On rivers, England seemed to adopt a natural sixth place in European or World Championships, markedly different to our traditional top placings in stillwater events. The Irish, Scots and Welsh fared worse.

While the influence of the British stillwater model had pervaded far from our shores, particularly the nature of loch-style competition, so the European, river-based influence was immense in return, and a new fly-fishing revolution ensued. The Antipodean fly fishers, along with the Americans and even the Japanese, all extended their influence, as well as their participation in World Championships, but it was the great European teams that made the difference, sparking the revolution.

In 1991, as so many World and European Championships were becoming more rivers-orientated, the IFFA member countries started the Home Rivers Internationals, based on the traditional loch-style structure. Federations or regions organized local qualifying heats for an annual national final, from which the top anglers were selected for the national team. The English National Rivers final was limited to thirty-two qualifiers and was fished in four one-and-a-half hour sessions to select the five-man team, plus one reserve (which is the same team structure as World and European Championship teams).

This began to give British fly fishers much broader experience on rivers, particularly as the Home Internationals were undertaken on some of the best (or variable in nature) rivers in each of the home nations by annual rotation. Very quickly, this formal national team-selection structure, and subsequent exposure in internationals, drastically improved the performance of the British teams in river-based competition.

We were back on a steep learning curve, in a discipline removed from our stillwater techniques, and we reacted well to it.

The Irish found particular benefit from the four-cornered Home Rivers Internationals, because it gave them exposure to grayling fishing (there are no grayling in Ireland), which is very much a part of most European venues. And for all the home nations, it pulled us away from what had been the dominant form of major competition fishing in Britain, which was essentially and mostly for rainbow trout on large reservoirs.

Range of Disciplines

The range covered in the following chapters of this book may be broadly categorized into the stillwater approaches of loch-style, anchored boat and bank fishing, on both artificial fisheries and wild waters of all sizes, and the river disciplines on all river types appropriate for single-handed fly-rod fishing. Tubing is also covered, but not in terms of competitive fly fishing as this is not a major recognized discipline in this sector of the sport.

All of these are differentiated further, both for clarity and because sub-divided they explore the individual needs and sub-set skills of each method or approach. I will highlight the sub-divisions in the relevant places.

We are considering primarily trout and grayling as the main target competition species, on both wild and managed fisheries. So far as trout are concerned, the emphasis is, therefore, on rainbow trout and brown trout, because these are the species most commonly available to fly fishers the world over, and particularly to competitive fly fishers. FIPS-Mouche has always thus far limited World and European Championships to salmonid target species, to include the various *coregonus* 'whitefish' salmonids and brook trout and char, but precluding migratory salmonids as well as non-salmonids such as chub, dace and barbel (fine, sporting fly-rod species though these

Czech national team – European runners-up, Spain 2008.

happen to be). The latter species, as well as other freshwater and some salt-water species, are however considered where relevant to non-competitive advanced fly fishing in tactical terms. To an extent I am also covering specimen hunting, a valid branch of the sport in which we seek to catch particularly large specimens of various species, on fly, often in clear waters where the fish can be observed and stalked.

Really, the emphasis throughout is on the tactical approach as developed largely through the practices of major competitive fly fishing throughout the world, particularly in Europe, where we are converging on formats of competitive fly fishing, largely via the IFFA and FIPS-Mouche.

Journeying through the skills base, and with mounting experience of a range of waters and disciplines, we arrive at the trained, competitive or tactical mind. It is a natural hunter's mind, honed in the analytical and technical ways of an esoteric and thoroughly elegant sport. Finally, our abilities at the advanced level of fly fishing, and in competitive fly fishing, come down to a state of mind.

4 EQUIPMENT FOR PURPOSE

I have already commented on the fact that today we have outstanding tackle and products within our sport, and very much more advanced than even twenty years ago. No matter what sort of fly fishing we are engaged in, there is tackle for generic use and also for specific purpose. Production methods, market demands, technology, materials and design have all compounded to lift tackle to levels of performance up to and often beyond the capabilities of even the most expert users.

Throughout the range of disciplines covered in this book there is tackle adequate for the task, to cover all scenarios. Even as a former research scientist I am astonished by the materials available nowadays and the design brilliance that goes into exploiting the qualities of these materials – the end product is so close to perfection, one wonders how improvements can possibly be made. They will, however, because no matter how tuned to the marketplace or the function a piece of tackle may be, the mood and the fashion will change, and product design will be driven in another direction. New materials and technologies will be developed, and inventive new minds will exploit them. As in any sport, fly fishers will always be pushing the boundaries, and so there will always be the demand for improvements in skills and the tackle used to perfect those skills.

In this chapter – indeed in this whole book – I do not endorse the tackle of any one company or manufacturer. Of course I have preferences, based mostly on years of experience with tackle from just about every large manufacturer worldwide, and quite a few of the small ones. In any case, no single manufacturer produces everything that a fly fisher requires; even in fly tying,

for example, we cannot cover everything one needs, from even half-a-dozen producers of fly-tying materials and tools. If one looks at the hugely competitive fly-rod marketplace, even the best fly casters in the world will not honestly be able to say that the casting tool of one manufacturer is significantly better than another.

I will, however, be highlighting some items of tackle from individual manufacturers, because experience has shown me that these have been the best, or among the best, that I have discovered during my intense fly-fishing career. I might suggest that these items have been the best for me, but I am not didactic enough to suggest that they are the best that exist *per se*, or that comparable tackle from other manufacturers might actually be better for other practitioners. At all levels, aesthetics and emotive issues are, in many cases, at least as significant as function in how one perceives an item of tackle. And this is important, because no one likes to fish with a fly rod (or any item of tackle) that they do not like the look of, even if it is a brilliant piece of design for its function.

There are still many practitioners who almost exclusively use split-cane fly rods. Few of them would suggest that these rods can compare particularly favourably with modern carbon-fibre equivalents (except for a very few purposes, such as hook setting on a tight line); these *aficionados* simply prefer the materials and the craftsmanship that goes into the building and finish of these beautiful rods to the high performance, contemporary, synthetic fibre tools.

A year ago I used one of American rod builder Jeff Wagner's wonderful built cane rods on the San river in south-east Poland. I was intoxicated, launched back to my early days in

Tackle for purpose: the author in the European Championship in Norway, 2007.

fly fishing when I was loaned a Hardy Palakona rod for all my fishing. I loved using this rod for short-range (6m/20ft) single nymph and dry fly presentation, even adapting my approach to accommodate the heaviness of touch and the sheer weight as the rod loaded the #5 line. Of course I caught trout and grayling, and was thrilled by the experience – split cane on the San – but it was miles away from (or years behind) the performance possibilities of a modern fly rod designed for purpose.

My point is that while I would not entertain the idea of using a cane rod in, say, a European championship, I might well choose one for the sheer aesthetic indulgence of 'jungle' fishing the lower reaches of an overgrown Pennine beck for wild trout. In all tackle and tackle products, aesthetics and fashion are as important as function and purpose, and it would be foolish for us to think otherwise. Anyway, advanced and tactical fly fishing is not only about competitive fly fishing: it is a lot else besides.

One of Jeff Wagner's masterpieces, designed for travel with a light line.

Split cane on San – another example of Jeff Wagner's outstanding craftsmanship, where technical excellence with traditional materials yields tackle fit for contemporary sport.

The state of the art in tackle nowadays leads us all to make almost impossible decisions. It is simply so good, and so extensive. We each need to switch off from the marketing and the hype as much as possible and take a considered, objective look at our own personal needs and skill level, and then analyse exactly what we require. Almost all of us specialize to a certain extent, once we realize we are in the 'intermediate' phase of our fishing development. We change, naturally, exploring other disciplines and perhaps seeking to become all-rounders; but for any particular specialization we need the right equipment for the purpose. In terms of tackle, however, there is much that is common to several disciplines, and it is possible to take a minimalist approach and employ all-round capability tackle to a broad range of the sub-disciplines. There is also a huge satisfaction in doing this.

Core Tackle

Many of my guests on river and lake ask me for advice about what tackle is right for them. I nearly always recommend a broad-range, compromise approach, going for the classic 9ft five-weight (mid-flex or through-action), of course in carbon fibre, loaded with a double-taper floating line in a mute colour. This 'core' tackle will enable most people to fish most

Perfect compromise outfit: a Hardy prototype test rod (later to become the stunning Angel 2), with a #5 Rio Selective Trout fly line, in olive, on a Redington GD mid-arbour reel; and wild Eden trout in high summer.

methods on both rivers and lakes, with some limitations in streamer fishing. Other tackle, in terms of rod length and line weight (and density), will be more suited to several methods, but this compromise outfit will do the job.

If my guest fishes mostly on lakes, I will often suggest a longer, more powerful rod, whereas if he or she spends more time on small rivers, a shorter three-weight becomes the compromise outfit. The reel is so relatively unimportant that I just recommend a lightweight, disc-drag, large arbour reel of a quality to match the rod and line, and whatever one is prepared to pay. There are certain subtleties in reel design that are very nice to have and can make a significant difference, as described later, but in the main a fly reel at the lower end of the cost spectrum will usually *almost* equal the performance of one costing five or even ten times as much. Again, the most significant differences are cosmetic.

Apart from the core tackle we can also find good compromises when it comes to peripheral and other gear. Advanced fly fishing does not absolutely need fluorocarbon leaders for deep nymph fishing, or copolymer for dry fly. Both can be accomplished well, if not perfectly, with conventional nylon monofilament (of high quality, such as the German Bayer Perlon). We will consider how specialized leader materials can certainly be made to provide the user with significant advantages in presentation, but these are not crucial. It depends on the specific needs of the individual in a whole range of circumstances, while leader constructions are almost as important as fly patterns and designs. Let us start, however, with the most highly developed core item of tackle, the fly rod.

Rods and Rod Furniture

From entry level to advanced, high performance tools in all disciplines, there are rods available throughout the price range. To confuse matters, some of the rods that are perceived as entry level because of their price points are actually suitable for expert use, and will certainly not prevent any angler achieving a very high standard. I am thinking of rods such as the outstanding Vision Intro or the Greys GRXi. Make no mistake, an expert could use rods within these ranges at the highest level of fly-fishing practice in any particular discipline for which they were designed, and actually over a range of disciplines for all-round use. I have used the Intro, for example, to achieve top section placings in European championships. I now use the Greys Streamflex range almost exclusively in my national qualifier and international fly fishing, and this is a rod sandwiched between the entry level and the high price tag Hardy, Sage and Loomis dream models.

Carbon fibre completely dominates the marketplace, with or without various other materials – apart from the resin matrix that binds the fibres together. Through the 1980s, the incredibly versatile carbon fibre swept glass fibre aside for fly-rod use, in tapered tubular form, largely because of its significantly lower weight. The Grafham Ghost, discussed earlier, represented just about the pinnacle of performance for a glass-fibre distance-casting rod for stillwater use – or even at the single-handed end of the grilse and sea-trout spectrum. But carbon-fibre rods made the Ghost and its copies or competitors obsolete at a stroke, and the top manufacturers in the world were quick to realize the new material's potential. Shakespeare and Normark started producing some good blanks, while Hardy introduced the outstanding Fibatube blanks. Other world leaders were Orvis and Sage, though naturally very much geared to the American market, which had significantly different needs to the British and Europeans in particular.

Today, all the above (along with many others, large and small) produce rods of the highest standards. Vision, Guide Line, Loop, Loomis, Daiwa, Scierra: the list is long, and all have something to offer. It is shifting sands at the top. I suggest, somewhat subjectively, that Hardy/

High value, high performance: Greys' Streamflex rig with wild river trout, a Streamflex 8ft 6in #4, with a platinum DT #4 on a Streamlite reel.

Greys is just about the world leader now, but with Loomis, Orvis (at least with the Helios) and Sage (incorporating Redington) not very far behind, and other notables certainly including Vision and Guide Line. Right at the top of the tree is the Hardy/Greys range, with outstanding tackle fit for the world stage (which is the reason, ultimately, that I became a Hardy/Greys Academy member).

What are the criteria for a top rod manufacturer? It is essential to realize that given a good blank, designed and produced for purpose, and access to the 'best' quality rod furniture, it is possible for anyone to produce the perfect rod for a particular function. The top manufacturers, however, cover all disciplines, focusing on each to produce the state-of-the-art tool for specialized use. They will also have several rods capable of more all-round capability, but to varying degrees within the discipline range spectrum. All the above-mentioned have this range, and beyond into double-handed disciplines, such that the contest for the best comes down to small aspects of materials, technology and design, as well as the aesthetic qualities.

And then there is the marketing, which we are largely escaping here for the sake of objectivity. There are rods within the Greys range that are actually at least as high specification (or fit-for-purpose tools) as those within the Hardy range. I am thinking principally of the simply outstanding Streamflex range and the technically advanced G-Tec series. Comparable ranges (currently) within the Hardy stable are the Marksman and the Angel 2. The latter are absolutely and uniformly delightful tools for specific purposes, but because they carry the Hardy reputation for excellence, and their trademark, they are double the price or more of the Greys equivalents.

Rod Guides

The emphasis on weight reduction has lasted a long time now. Initially seen as carbon fibre's greatest asset compared with glass or cane, the development of higher modulus, thinner walled blanks has extended to the search for lighter-weight rod furniture. Hard-wearing, stainless-steel and alloy rod guides have been developed, along with beautifully engineered tip and ceramic insert 'stripping' rings. Intermediate guides are generally of single leg or double leg 'snake' design. The advantage of the former is that there is only a single whipping required to fix each guide to the blank, whereas the double-foot snake requires two and thus adds slightly extra weight to the rod, changing its action (minutely). This is offset by the aesthetics, however, in that many of us simply prefer the look of the traditional snake guides, myself included.

The top-performing line guides are now so hard-wearing and light in weight that realistically any further development will be measured in micrograms. Modern line guides are so light in weight that we can accommodate the required number and spacing on a blank without adversely affecting the action of the finished rod, and can even incorporate the mass of the guides, whippings and sealant to achieve the required action.

Having a sufficient number of line guides is very important to casting performance in a fly rod. Too few, or with the wrong spacing, and the line is held too loosely between the guides with resultant loss of efficiency and energy due to line slap and friction during the hauling and shooting processes.

It is likely that line guides on rods will be developed along a different concept, possibly integral to the blank itself, and in harmony with a newly developed fly line technology.

Reel Seats

Reel seats are now technically excellent, and possessed of a very high standard of craftsmanship. While we recognize that a reel can be taped on to a cork seat below the grip and allow perfectly adequate performance, there are certain niceties that improve upon this. Hardwood inserts, because of their beauty, are still very popular, while woven carbon fibre or machined aluminium is also incorporated in novel ways. There remains a place for cork as

Greys' G-Tec reel seat and ergonomic grip.

the reel seat, with sliding aluminium (or polymer) ring and a fixed seat under the cork grip, aligning the reel with the guides. This very simple design has been with us since before carbon was used in blank manufacture.

The marriage of the reel to the rod is important in several ways. It must be fixed rigidly so there is no twisting or knocking, and it should be in alignment with the rod guides and in the right location with regard to the grip. Overlooked by almost everyone, it should also be fixed so that the wear in the fixing parts (reel foot and seat fixings) is minimal. No one likes to see excessive wear marks on a reel foot, particularly on a high cost reel. The problem is that metal parts moving or being clamped together will inevitably produce wear marks, which will eventually lead to movement between them, and increased wear. The issue can be resolved by introducing a synthetic or polymer insert between the metal mating parts, and some manufacturers are now working on this in high performance reel seats.

The reel should also be easily loaded and unloaded into its seat, with the minimum of movements. Alignment marks on the seat aid this process. The cutaway designs of the seats that have recently been introduced are beautiful and functional, in hard anodized or brushed matt alloy. The synthetic, compressible O-ring fitted between double-locking reel screw rings is a great innovation that prevents these over-binding together, which commonly happens with metal-to-metal fixings. All in all, a considerable amount of effort goes into the design of reel seats, and there remains scope for further improvement, including in the reel foot, or attachment point, itself.

Tweed grayling in March on a bead head PTN with the G-Tec system.

Handle Grips

Handle grips have not been developed very much since the days of split cane and glass fibre, but then, traditional turned cork is a lovely material and excellent for the purpose. The classic shapes persist: cigar for short, light-line rods; reversed half Wells for the mid-range; and full Wells, or scroll, for longer, more power-ful rods that often have a short butt extension (fixed permanently or detachable), so that the rod can be rested more comfortably under and against the forearm. Most of us are happy with these, though there is often an issue with the thickness of handles 'off the peg'.

For a tool you might hold and cast for long periods of time, perhaps up to eight hours with few breaks, it is essential that the grip is comfortable. Too thick or thin, and discomfort inevitably sets in. A fly rod is like a target pistol in this regard, and for perfect results the grip should really be perfect for the individual user. Some rod builders do pay a degree of attention to this, and will customize the thickness, if not the shape, of a handle to the user, but not a single mass-market rod is sold with grips to suit the individual purchaser, even at the top end of the price scale. Guide Line has made efforts in recent years in this direction by producing the Le Cie range of rods featuring ergonomic grips, but these are only ergonomic in a generic sense, and then only for a single type of grip (albeit the most common, thumb-up grip). Hardy/Greys produces the outstanding G-Tec series featuring a thumb grip in a dense foam material set into the cork handle, in the general position of a thumb-up grip.

The grip is one area that rod builders will have to pay more attention to in the future. The standard handles might be reasonable, largely because of the very comfortable feel and grip of cork in the hand (when dry), but they are not ideal. Many advanced-level anglers change not only the type of grip, but also the position of the grip on the handle so as to produce subtly different presentations and casting performance in various situations.

The grip is an underrated area in the techni-cal aspect of the sport, and it would be far better and more developmental for manufacturers to give this greater attention, than attempting to chase off a few micrograms from already suffi-ciently lightweight blanks. The increasing short-age of high-grade cork might well force the issue and lead to development; already Hardy/Greys is anticipating this and is researching new composite materials for handle grips, which may be shaped in ways other than in the tradi-tional lathe-turning process. This begs the development of more ergonomic, higher performance grips.

Rod Action

Seeking control over a rod's action is another crucial area of development. Here, manufactur-ers have it right, because casting action, and flexing action, should be suited to the type of casting and presentation for particular methods, more than for the user, and can therefore be produced in consistent batches that do not need to be customized to the individual. Also, all the major rod producers worldwide have utilized the expertise of top casters, fly fishers and fly-fishing instructors and guides as consultants, working with the designers and materials specialists.

For advanced tactical fly fishing, we need to understand rod actions. We need at least to recognize that for long-range casting we require a fast- or tip-actioned rod, while for short-range (6m/20ft) or medium-range (10m/30ft) fishing with nymph on the river, or traditional loch-style, we require a slower action, capable of absorbing shock and delivering roll and spey casts. We also should appreciate everything within these limits, the spectrum of actions which, combined with rod-length and line-weight loading, produce the fly rod suitable for whatever method or discipline we are pursuing at the advanced level.

We are very fortunate nowadays in that there are rods within most manufacturers' ranges that are suitable, in all matters of performance potential, for any particular discipline and water type. We may also find these at very good value,

Tackle perfectly matched to the target fish.

because the market is hugely competitive and modern production methods are highly efficient. Here we can refer to the marketing information, and probably be swayed by it, because so long as the rod is suitable in terms of length, line weight and action for your particular task, then it will probably be suitable. The only confusion is in deciding between the offerings of different manufacturers: aesthetics again, and the power of a brand name. With rod lengths and line weighting we can be more precise, though it is a fact that there has been a long-term trend for over-powered rods for stillwater use in Britain for the general size of our target fish. On our reservoir fisheries the average size of trout is around a kilogram (over 2lb), whereas on the wild fisheries it is less than half this (1lb). On some of the commercial fisheries, of course, we have to be capable of landing fish up to 5kg (11lb), and on wild waters we might encounter similar-sized migratory fish, and even very large brown trout. Nonetheless, there is a (minority) school of thought that is convinced that for the average size of our target species we are using rods that are significantly over-powered. In Continental Europe and the United States there is a trend in the opposite direction, though for a lot of the streamer-based fishing in the New World the tackle mirrors that among stillwater fly fishers in Britain, if not the presentations. In any case, rod length and line weighting should be geared to the type of casting and presentation that is practised, rather than the size of the target fish.

I have already described the rod lengths and line weightings for the general approach, with the benchmark standard set at 9ft for a #5-weight line, and if there was one rod I had to use for everything this would undoubtedly be it. However, at the limits of the single-handed disciplines this rod would struggle – for example, with streamer fishing with sunk line at 30m (100ft). Generally we can consider the 9ft to 10ft lengths for #5 through to #8 lines being the standard range for stillwaters, and for streamer or lure fishing, with some salt water demands up to #10-weight (though consider Chris Ogborne's contribution on this matter, *see* Chapter 5). For the more delicate presentations, principally involving nymph, spider and dry fly, the line-weight maximum tends to be a #6, though most commonly #4, with lengths of rod anything from a mere 6ft up to 11ft, again depending on presentation method and the nature of the water.

Put this into perspective: faced with a typical freestone river, with constantly changing niches over a few hundred metres, it would be reasonable to have three or even four rods set up with different rigs so as to give the best presentations in all the water types there. We do this in a major championship so that whatever type of water we are approaching, we have the optimized rig for the situation. It is, however, possible to take on all these water types adequately with a single rod, if not rig, and this would typically be the 9ft #5-weight. We need to compromise here and there, and will not have ideal control in several situations, but this is all part of a tactical approach.

Fly Lines

Lines are today generally of high performance, even though the technology has not moved on a great deal since the first PVC-coated lines of the 1960s, when we were converting from silk fly lines. The difference a good quality fly line makes to a fly caster of reasonable standard is at least as important as the fly rod itself. I have no hesitation in recommending that a practitioner in any method seeking the best performance should acquire top quality fly lines, designed for the particular methods practised.

The problem, as usual, is the choice among the very good lines on the market. You can still find silk lines, for example from the line maker Phoenix; these are truly exceptional, and actually much better than the now extinct Kingfisher silk lines that I used so much for sea trout and general loch-style fishing in the 1970s and early 1980s. Presentation is superb, and as neutral-density lines they match the modern stealth lines (clear intermediates) such as produced by Cortland, Hardy/Greys or Fulling Mill. They are very expensive, but considering the material used (Chinese silk) and the production process (long and skilled), and their final performance, they are probably unbeatable for the all-important just sub-surface region, for example with slow nymphing in the shallows on stillwaters. You can grease the running line section and leave the tip taper ungreased, thus producing variations in sink tip presentation.

The Floating Fly Line

The floater is by far and away the most important line in our armoury. Many anglers, particularly in river discipline, never use any other line – and this line is simply not worth any compromise whatsoever. Here I will make some specific recommendations, even though I recognize that in a few years' time the game will have moved on. First, the Greys' Platinum and Fulling Mill double tapers (DT) in heron grey and light olive are excellent; the former line is also a fine distance-casting line in a weight-forward (WF) format.

The Rio Selective Trout, which is a hybrid DT/WF format in a mid-olive, is probably the loveliest 'presentation' line I have ever used, and it is long lasting, too. I rarely achieve more than a season out of any floating line, but my DT #5 Rio has lasted four years with no sign of cracking at all. It is a beautifully supple line, reminding me of the lovely Cortland 444 that I used to employ on the drift while loch-styling.

The Snowbee XS has gained a very strong reputation in recent years, and is indeed a hard-wearing, excellent distance-casting line in WF format, with good presentation across the range, from 10m to 30m (30ft to 100ft) – most lines can be made to perform adequately at the crucial river 6m (20ft) range.

The Scientific Anglers AirCel Ultra 4, in the inconspicuous 'buckskin' colour, in WF #6 or DT #5, has been utterly reliable for me, and also something of a benchmark by which I have judged line performance (particularly on stillwater) for many years.

These main line profiles, double taper and weight forward, define the limits of a broad spectrum of taper profiles. The river fly fisher, and those stillwater *aficionados* concentrating on short to medium range, might be best advised to go for the DT profile. Presentation is so crucially important, and the DT profile is more consistent in this regard, married to the correct

The G-Tec system – state of the art for lake fishing from bank or boat.

a thick line grease such as Mucilin on the tip and line/leader braided connections.

Sinking Fly Lines

The range of sinking fly lines now available is staggering. The dedicated stillwater competition angler will need a lot of different line types, particularly in terms of density, possibly all the way to the very dense, tungsten-impregnated DI7 and DI8 (by Airflo). I have never actually found the need for the DI8, but have employed the DI7, as well as the Scientific Anglers HiD and the Rio fast sinkers, a great deal, particularly for accessing those fish lying at depths between two and eight metres (six and twenty-six feet). The DI range of lines is now advanced

leader. Also, a DT profile effectively gives you two lines in one, because if the taper on one end of the line begins to deteriorate (they all do after prolonged use – or abuse) then you can turn the line round. At longer range, because of the hauling and shooting requirements, and the necessity for a thin-diameter running line, the WF profile is ideal, most especially with sinking lines, in which a wide diameter in the running line portion of the fly line is a distinct disadvantage, destroying presentation and creating frictional drag during line shooting.

On the matter of floaters, even the most expensive and 'endurance' lines nowadays usually have a fault, in that water will seep up the core (by capillary action) and cause the line tip to become neutral density. The use of nymphs or wet flies, or even fluorocarbon tippet, will exaggerate this, effectively giving you a slowly sinking line tip. This can actually be a very useful aid to smooth presentation of the sunk fly, but it can also be detrimental to just sub-surface nymphs, and particularly to dry fly (causing drowning). Sealing the line tip with a touch of super glue (minimal) or a wader sealant such as Aquasure can reduce this effect, though nowadays I don't do this, even for prolonged dry fly fishing, but for preference use

Line Colour and Spooky Fish

The colour of fly lines is absolutely crucial to me. I have always hated brightly coloured lines, even floaters, and have absolutely no doubt that they spook fish, particularly during casting. The exception is a white, or off-white floater, though even here I would err towards mute or pastel colours such as ivory, buckskin or olive. Several of my team-mates over the last twenty years or so have disagreed with me on this point (though more have agreed); Iain Barr is convinced that it makes absolutely no difference whatsoever, while Brian Leadbetter used to say I was completely wasting my time by dying the bright 'Kelly Green' WetCel intermediate a darker green (because I liked the sink rate of this line so much, but hated the colour). I disagree with these two great competitive fly fishers. I have spooked too many fish, or seen boat partners spook them, with bright lines. On this point, never neglect side casting in your tactical approach to spooky fish, on stillwater, river or salt, even if you have a line that is apparently well camouflaged against the backdrop.

Howard Croston, brilliant all-round fly fisher and fly caster, central to Hardy/Greys' product development team. (Courtesy Hardy/Greys Limited)

and hard-wearing, and provides a very good all-round collection of tactical lines for sub-surface presentations. The forty-plus variants of these lines give astonishing long-range capability, like casting dense-shooting heads – though I would offer a word of caution about the complete lack of control one has at these ranges.

Where the ultra-long range is most useful is to enable presentation at an appropriate depth, for a sufficiently long period to be worthwhile, drifting fast in strong winds. There are also low-stretch versions of these lines and other makes, such as the so-called 'Sixth Sense' lines, which can be useful for fishing at the sort of range common among modern, competitive, stillwater fly fishers. It is perhaps worth noting that silk fly lines are also very low stretch.

Do not think that low stretch is crucially important. While it certainly does improve tactile sensitivity, it has its disadvantages at times, such as 'bouncing' fish on the take. Furthermore, many people find low stretch lines very uncomfortable to the fingers during prolonged use, preferring supple, more 'spongy' lines, which also absorb the shock of takes much better (rather than relying on the raised rod alone).

Lines for Stillwater Fishing

In practical stillwater fishing, even at an advanced level, one can get away with compromising the range of lines taken out there on the water. Absolutely vital is the standard floater, of course, but I would feel vulnerable without a stealth line, a DI5 and, for much of the year during harsher conditions, a DI7. Another line that has given great service in the last decade has been the midge tip or stealth tip line, such as the exceptional (other than its vile colour) Rio Midge Tip. These lines afford superb presentation for slow nymphing, straight-line nymphing or washing-line technique.

It is worth suggesting that the aforementioned silk lines can be used to replace both the stealth and the stealth tip lines (thus reducing the number of lines an all-round competitor will need). I know top rate stillwater competitors who nearly always go out with only three lines – a floater, a stealth (or other intermediate), and a sink rate #5 line such as the DI5 – while there are others who go out with up to twenty! I lean towards the former, but add the DI7. With so many variables at work out there, I try to reduce the options as much as possible.

Leaders and Tippets

Here we are down to the terminal tackle, and the enormous subject of tactical leaders. Forgive me if I labour this, but it is just so important in advanced fly fishing: if I were to single out one technical aspect of my own fly fishing, in all methods, that made the biggest difference to success, it would be leader construction (though I would add the flies themselves, as part of the leader rig, because these have a dynamic influence on the presentation). I am covering some leader rigs in relevant places in this book, but list here some fundamental constructions.

One should also appreciate that the range of materials – from conventional nylon monofilament, through pre-stretched nylon and copolymer, to fluorocarbon, as well as woven and braided synthetic and natural materials – all have a role in the construction of tactical leaders, so suitable quality in all of these is required. There is no need to compromise, as these materials are not expensive. Also, leaders are frequently constructed such that only the tippet

section is regularly replaced, while the main length of the leader has a prolonged use.

Fundamental Leader Rigs

Finesse leaders for dry fly presentation: In recent years the furled leader has replaced the braided nylon or tapered nylon leader as the butt section for very gentle presentation with dry fly. Properly treated – usually with Mucilin – they float high without absorbing water, so do not produce spray in false casting, and touch down very gently on the surface. They do not translate energy to the tippet and fly as well as tapered or braided nylon, but at close range or for downwind presentation this is not a concern. *See* diagram.

Standard short-range or upstream dry fly leader: This leader rig is ideal for windy conditions. *See* diagram.

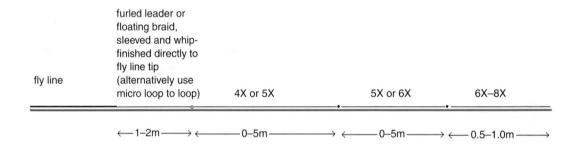

Finesse leader for dry fly presentation in calm conditions.

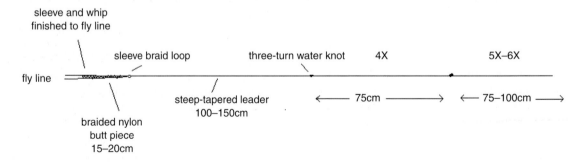

Standard short-range or upstream dry fly leader, ideal for windy conditions.

Medium- to long-range (10–25m/30–80ft), stillwater dry fly leader: *See* diagram.

Hybrid dry fly/nymph (short-range duo) rig: This is the 'compromise' or all-purpose leader rig that I have written about several times in the past. It is very easy to adapt in terms of dropper spacing for differing river conditions. It is level leader material throughout (beyond the tapered butt piece), relying on the weight of the appropriately chosen flies for good turn-over and presentation. *See* diagram.

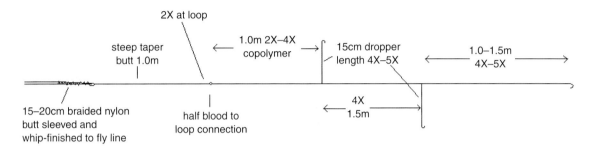

Medium- to long-range stillwater dry fly leader.

Hybrid dry fly/nymph (duo) rig for short range (up to 10m/30ft).
(Used throughout Europe since the early 1990s, but popularised only after the development of the New Zealand-style attachment rigs, post 2000. Comparatively low sensitivity, but less compromised presentation of dry fly.)

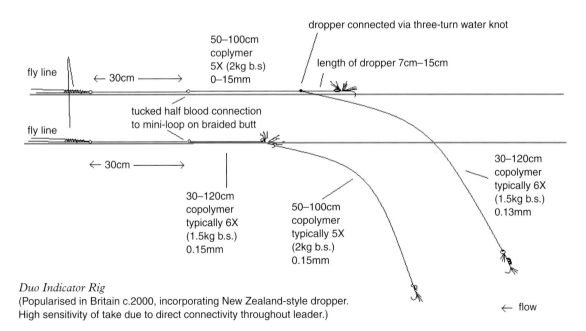

Duo Indicator Rig
(Popularised in Britain c.2000, incorporating New Zealand-style dropper. High sensitivity of take due to direct connectivity throughout leader.)

Longer-range hybrid (duo and trio) rig: *See* diagram.

Standard nymph rig (and nymph/spider hybrid) for short to medium range: This rig can also be used for the Czech nymph and semi bolt-rig style, for which line is tight and short between flies and rod tip, and takes are usually felt rather than visually observed. *See* diagram.

Nymph rig for longer range – stillwater, 'straight lining': *See* diagram.

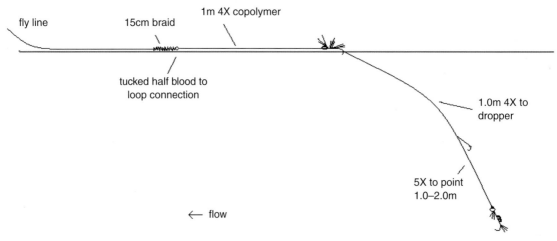

Medium-range hybrid rig (duo/trio).

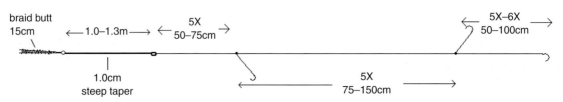

Standard nymph rig (nymph/spider) for short to medium range.

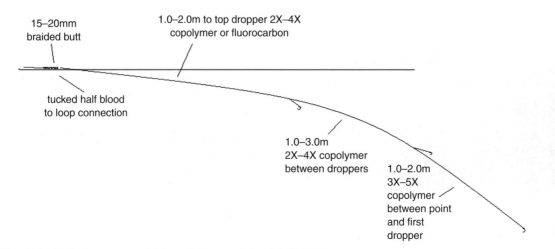

Nymph leader for longer range (stillwater), for nymph 'straight lining'.

Standard finesse (French) nymph indicator rig: *See* diagram.

Braid bolt rig: This rig is for river use, when 'straight lining'. *See* diagram.

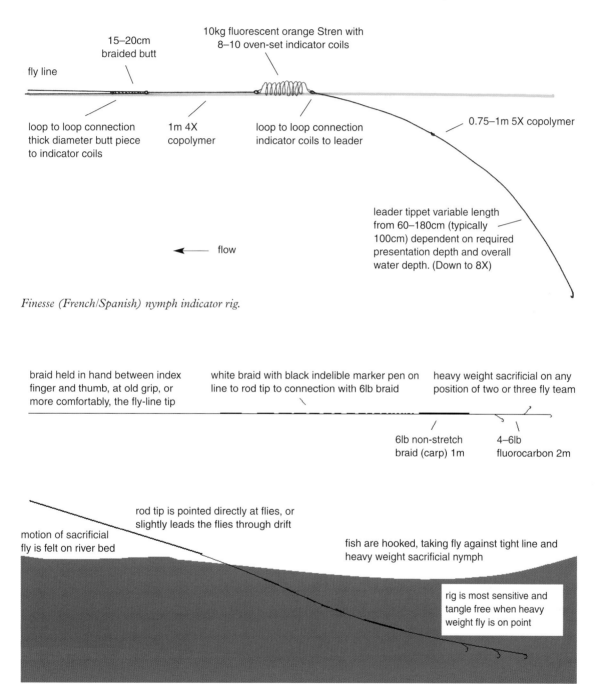

15–20cm braided butt

10kg fluorescent orange Stren with 8–10 oven-set indicator coils

fly line

loop to loop connection thick diameter butt piece to indicator coils

1m 4X copolymer

loop to loop connection indicator coils to leader

0.75–1m 5X copolymer

leader tippet variable length from 60–180cm (typically 100cm) dependent on required presentation depth and overall water depth. (Down to 8X)

flow

Finesse (French/Spanish) nymph indicator rig.

braid held in hand between index finger and thumb, at old grip, or more comfortably, the fly-line tip

white braid with black indelible marker pen on line to rod tip to connection with 6lb braid

heavy weight sacrificial on any position of two or three fly team

6lb non-stretch braid (carp) 1m

4–6lb fluorocarbon 2m

rod tip is pointed directly at flies, or slightly leads the flies through drift

motion of sacrificial fly is felt on river bed

fish are hooked, taking fly against tight line and heavy weight sacrificial nymph

rig is most sensitive and tangle free when heavy weight fly is on point

Braid bolt rig for river use, when 'straight lining'.

51

Single nymph/streamer leader: *See* diagram.

Washing-line rigs: *See* diagram.

Standard loch-style (three/four fly) leader: This is a compromise rig which is easily adaptable to the conditions and specific situation requirements. *See* diagram.

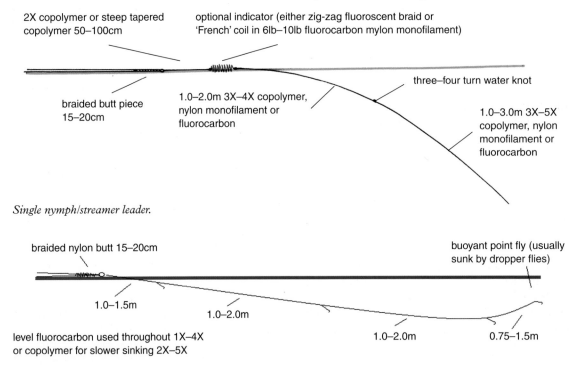

2X copolymer or steep tapered copolymer 50–100cm

optional indicator (either zig-zag fluoroscent braid or 'French' coil in 6lb–10lb fluorocarbon mylon monofilament)

braided butt piece 15–20cm

1.0–2.0m 3X–4X copolymer, nylon monofilament or fluorocarbon

three–four turn water knot

1.0–3.0m 3X–5X copolymer, nylon monofilament or fluorocarbon

Single nymph/streamer leader.

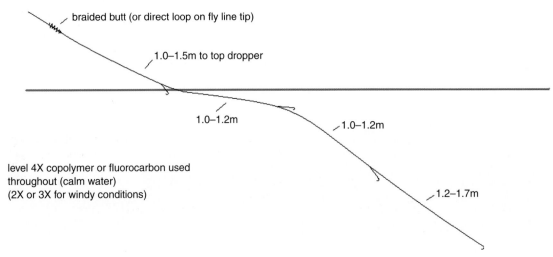

braided nylon butt 15–20cm

buoyant point fly (usually sunk by dropper flies)

1.0–1.5m

1.0–2.0m

1.0–2.0m

0.75–1.5m

level fluorocarbon used throughout 1X–4X or copolymer for slower sinking 2X–5X

Standard washing-line rig (four flies).

braided butt (or direct loop on fly line tip)

1.0–1.5m to top dropper

1.0–1.2m

1.0–1.2m

1.2–1.7m

level 4X copolymer or fluorocarbon used throughout (calm water)
(2X or 3X for windy conditions)

Standard loch-style leader for three flies.

Knots and Connections

Part of the whole subject of fly lines and leaders, and consequently presentation, concerns the knots and the marriage of the various materials to produce the holistic rig that is smooth and technically suited to the method employed. At best the rig is only as good as the weakest, or faulty link: there is bound to be a weakest connection, and this should in all cases be either the knot between the main leader and tippet, or the tippet to the fly. This is partly because if a break occurs when a fish is hooked, we need to leave as little as possible attached to the fish. One of the worst things we can do as anglers is to leave a team of flies attached to a live fish. It must be, and it can be, avoided completely. What probably cannot be completely avoided is breaking on a fish, from time to time leaving it with the hook in its mouth. Barbless hooks usually fall out in moments, and in most cases even barbed hooks will work loose very quickly.

One of the things I absolutely loathe in our sport is breaking on a fish at all, and I make every effort to minimize this eventuality.

Advanced fly fishing includes the ability to tie consistent and appropriate knots, and prepare other connections, to a very high standard; there are not many of them. As regards line connection devices, I have found that the polymer connectors, used mainly between fly line and leader, are poor for presentation and can easily jam in the rod guides, particularly the tip ring, and can cause a break in the leader. Attempting to pull these sharply through the top section guides can also cause a break in this section of the rod. Nevertheless, the tiny metal rings (1.5 to 2.0mm), while not quite so smooth as a knot, can be very useful for adding tippet sections or droppers to a leader, and can even help in sinking the leader for surface presentations in calm weather. Having said this, I very rarely use leader rings any more, much preferring knot connections in all cases.

The following list includes all the more important, or most used, knots and connections.

Tucked half blood knot: Used mostly for attaching a fly to tippet material.

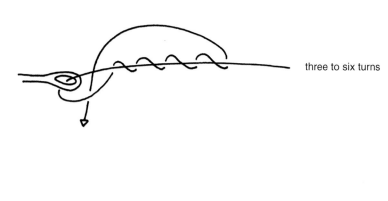

three to six turns

final tuck

Tucked half blood knot.

Turle knot: Used for attaching a fly to the tippet, or as a slip knot for attaching the tippet to a fly hook for duo and trio methods (a New Zealand-style attachment).

Three-turn water knot: Used for joining two pieces of similar or identical leader materials and for forming droppers.

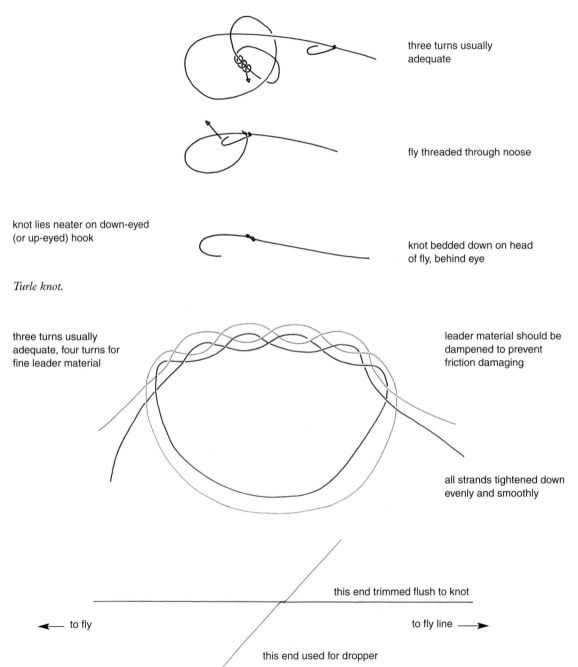

three turns usually adequate

fly threaded through noose

knot lies neater on down-eyed (or up-eyed) hook

knot bedded down on head of fly, behind eye

Turle knot.

three turns usually adequate, four turns for fine leader material

leader material should be dampened to prevent friction damaging

all strands tightened down evenly and smoothly

this end trimmed flush to knot

← to fly

to fly line ⟶

this end used for dropper

Three-turn water knot.

Whip finish: Used variously on fly lines and line connections, and for forming ultra-smooth loops without knots.

Braided loops: A method of forming loops by 'sleeving' and locking in braided material, and also sleeving fly line into braid for ultra-smooth connections; it can also incorporate a whip finish, and can seal floating fly-line tips from water ingress.

Loop-to-loop connections: These provide connectivity in various places, such as a tapered leader to fly-line connection loop.

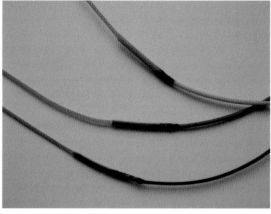

Whip finish.

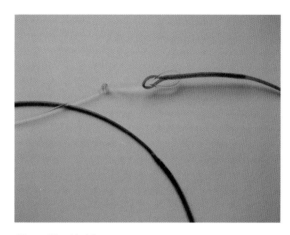

Sleeved braided loop.

loop formed with single overhand for thick diameter leader material or double overhand with finer material

forming the loop with an overhand

Loop-to-loop connection.

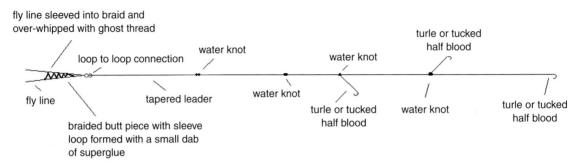

fly line sleeved into braid and
over-whipped with ghost thread

loop to loop connection

water knot

turle or tucked
half blood

water knot

fly line

tapered leader

water knot

braided butt piece with sleeve
loop formed with a small dab
of superglue

turle or tucked
half blood

water knot

turle or tucked
half blood

Compromise, all-purpose leader showing all connections.

Compromise rig: The diagram shows a fly line to leader connection, together with a hypothetical leader rig incorporating all the highlighted connections. It is effectively a 'compromise' or all-purpose leader rig which can be adapted for specific situations to form a tactical leader rig.

There are other knots and connection methods, of course, but the above provide a concise base on which we can be assured of high level connectivity throughout our fly line and leader system.

The Fly Reel

Some people collect them, while some expert fly fishers make do with battered and scratched old faithfuls that were not great pieces of engineering even when they were new. Fly reels are highly personal parts of our fly-fishing equipment, more even than fly rods. In fact, because in order of magnitude they are less important than all other items of the core tackle (including leaders and flies), there is oddly more scope for emotive choice. They are extraordinarily beautiful items of equipment, and hugely desirable. At the more fundamental level they are a means of line storage that will not bind up or overrun when stripping off line. For the latter purpose, it doesn't matter whether the tool is machined from high grade aluminium or moulded from

thermoset plastic; but it matters to many individuals. There are, moreover, several characteristics, or features, that a reel should have beyond the fundamentals in order for it to serve its function perfectly.

While being a line store – and sometimes a reel must store line for long periods of time – the reel should allow the line to be stripped off so there is limited coiling. The modern mid- and large arbour reels allow the line to be wound with comparatively open turns, thereby reducing coiling and semi-permanent deformation so that lines seldom have to be stretched before the fishing session. This does not mean that the classical narrow arbour is obsolete, but users of these need to build up the spool diameter substantially with backing to avoid the semi-permanent coiling effect, and then line capacity is reduced. Large arbours are not merely fashion features.

A high performance reel will also avoid the infuriating overrun that occurs with poor or incorrectly adjusted drag systems. Anyone who has hurriedly stripped off line – which is almost all of us – in order to cast at a rising fish, only for the fly line to spill and tumble into a mess that needs several minutes of attention to untangle it, will appreciate that an anti-overrun system is a huge benefit in a fly reel. This 'bird's nest' catastrophe has happened to me twice in internationals as I have stripped off the old Scientific Anglers' Hi-speed Hi-D lines, and I lost more than ten minutes on both occasions while sort-

Hardy Demon 5000, with feral rainbow.

ing out the mess, cursing the inadequacies of the reel (a Leeda LC 80 – actually a great reel of the early 1990s, being a precursor to the large arbour, wide spool design, and what I term a tactical reel, having a rapid-change cartridge system).

Fly reels are developed, and new models appear from major manufacturers on virtually an annual basis, so one hesitates in making any specific recommendations – tomorrow an opinion might be dated. Right now, however, I would suggest you could do no better than go for a Hardy Demon 5000 (for 5- to 7-weight lines) as a 'tactical' reel. It is indeed tactical, because this reel comes with three spools that are rapidly interchanged, so that you can alternate between fly lines very quickly. Certainly there are more attractive reels out there, and possibly some of even more tactical utility, such as the very high value Greys GRXi or the aesthetically lovely and ever-popular Vision Koma (more beautiful than the Greys, but not so tactically versatile), but the Demon is a most

attractive item of tackle, with its very hard-wearing, brushed aluminium looks and utilitarian design.

One also hesitates to mention specific reels (or any item of tackle) in the fear that it offends someone else's choice. There are countless anglers who have Orvis Battenkill (original and large arbour), or the British Fly Reels' Dragonfly, for instance (I have owned and enjoyed both), or even the old-fashioned Hardy Marquis (which I still own and enjoy), which many say should have been shelved, or sold to collectors with a passion for antiquities, more than a decade ago. The fact is that in this area of highly emotional choice there is considerable scope for personal taste above and beyond utilitarian function.

Equipment for Wading

As a result of development in materials, and because essentially river-based anglers are constantly seeking better performance, wader design has been driven to quite a high standard, although there is obvious scope for further advancement. The breathable materials now dominating the marketplace essentially replace neoprene, other than for some cold weather/ cold water applications, and have allowed the construction of lightweight, reasonably long-lasting waders.

Footwear has also developed, with foot- and ankle-protecting designs, with reasonable grip being afforded on a variety of substrates from gravel to weed-covered rock to lightly silted, firm mud. Felt soles definitely have the edge on hard or soft substrate, while studs give more grip on slippery surfaces, although these

do produce a lot of fish-scaring noise and vibration. Hard, 'tread-formed' soles seem to be falling out of favour. Sole designs and materials all offer a compromise between safety and stealth, and there will be further advance towards achieving a better compromise, as well as improving the longevity of waders. With current wader designs, I would go for the stocking-foot models, every time; there are several reasons, but importantly, these pack more easily and also allow the versatility of boot choice.

Other safety features can also be built in, such as intrinsic buoyancy aids, or belt systems to prevent waders filling with water in the event of an immersion – although the safety integrity of

The importance of organization and control in a river: Andy Smith in Hardy EWS waders, fifty metres off the bank on the River San.

the latter is actually questionable, in that it might be better for leggings to fill with water and thus have neutral buoyancy, rather than trap air and have positive buoyancy and the prospect of the feet up/head down position of an angler in the water.

I will be discussing wading technique in some detail under tactical wading (*see* Chapter 9), but I should stress that wading is a dangerous activity, even with good grip (or as good as is possible) in any circumstances. As a professional guide I am increasingly careful with my guests: I have had many mishaps myself while wading, with numerous total immersions. If you are intent on tactically wading and really attacking a river in order to get the best out of the fishing possibilities, you are bound to fall in from time to time, no matter how good the equipment. So I would definitely go for the best available, such as Hardy, Simms or Snowbee breathable designs, with compatible micro tungsten-studded, felt sole boots.

I also strongly advise safety devices to go with these. A buoyancy jacket is essential, and a wading stick readily to hand is to be recommended. For many years I have used neither, but I have been very lucky, and I would not wish it on any one of you to take similar risks because you might not be so lucky. Of course, the best safety device is your brain. Always remember that if it looks fast and deep, it is. If it looks like an unstable river bed, it is. If it looks as if there is no easy escape (remembering that the easy way in may not be the same as the way out), there probably is not.

On the subject of wading, you are exposed out there, both in and on the water, but contemporary clothing is so good that there is no reason nowadays for you to be unduly cold or damp. Layer structures are best, and remember that a large amount of heat is lost from the head, so wear a hood or hat in cold weather, and you will be a lot more comfortable if you cover up your ears as well. The modern tube scarves are wonderful innovations for cold weather anglers, and in hot weather I use one of the lightweight versions of these to keep the sun off my neck; I sometimes even soak it in the water and wring it out before wearing it – it has a lovely cooling effect as the residual water slowly evaporates in the sun.

In hot weather or in warm water, wet wading should be considered: this 'flats-style' wading is an underrated means of exploring shallow water in river, lake or sea shore, giving a wonderful sense of freedom in that you are fishing unrestricted, or unburdened by layers of unnecessary clothing and waders. If there are sharp rocks, just beware and protect your ankles and lower legs; although I usually wear open rubber sandals for wet wading, 'flats' shoes are better, or even your wading boots with sockets or pairs of socks to pad them out.

Boat and Float Tube Considerations

Even more exposure is suffered while in a fishing boat for any period of time. Most anglers will take a boat out for a whole day, or at least for several hours at a time, and loch-style international competitions are fished over eight-hour periods.

I have dealt with tactical drift-fishing requirements elsewhere (*see* page 164), and it should be clear that a drogue is essential. This should be one of the modern designs of semi-adjustable drogues with two attachment points, because this allows a degree of flexibility in presenting the deployed drogue, such that the boat can drift slightly off axis, angled to the wind. A drogue with a single attachment point will cause the boat to swing and drift with an unstable pattern with very little control, particularly in strong winds.

Other drift-controlling devices exist, not the least important being the oars, but only a drogue will appreciably slow the rate of a drift, which is usually desirable. Battery-powered electric outboards are quite popular; these are very good for precise drift control, though again they do not significantly slow the rate of drift, and the sophistication and power demand give their own type of frustration and limitation.

The importance of organization and control in a boat; Robbie Bell on Menteith.

Even nowadays I prefer the use of oars to adjust the angle of drift and presentation. The oars must be fixed – roped in to the rowlock or preferably set on oar pins – and require just an occasional trimming 'touch' by either the angler in the boat, or the boatman. It is a great skill in actual practice, and makes a huge difference to the effectiveness of fly fishers on the drift, particularly in drifts that are close to shore.

One great innovation to the sport that has stemmed from the United States and Canada is float tube fishing, now ever more popular in Britain, Europe and elsewhere. In the UK we are very much at entry level in this area of pursuit of freshwater species with fly, and yet the possibilities are enormous. We are restricted only in so far as it is difficult to access remote stillwaters because of having to hump in the float tube, quite apart from the other fly-fishing tackle.

Where access is easy, float tubing significantly increases the possibilities of presenting the fly to fish, in ways that would be difficult from the bank. It is extraordinary just how close we can approach even spooky trout from the vantage point of a tube. We are comparatively low in the water; the bulk of the lower body, and the legs and flippers in the water itself seem not to trouble most fish. It feels rather like a diver would feel, in among shoals of fish, a beautifully unperturbing means of being close to nature.

Nowadays, tubes are safe and very well designed for the exploratory fly fisher on stillwaters, tailwaters, or lower river systems where there is sufficient depth and a slow water-flow rate. An understanding of manoeuvrability is essential, as well as the use of flippers to control drift and repositioning. A few sessions on stillwater provide sufficient experience to give confidence, but extra care and much more experience is required on rivers, where a guide, or company, is essential. Rivers are dangerous to wade, and big rivers (those suitable for tubing) are much more dangerous than they seem for a tube fly fisher cast adrift on the flow. Many tube fishermen have been killed out there on big rivers, mostly on those with fast flows and rapids. The danger of fast, deep water, where there are obstructions and snags that can perhaps catch a foot or a leg, must never be underrated. Like the sea shore, it is a totally hostile environment, and the float tuber is vulnerable out there.

I am not going to recommend any particular float tube. I have used several and all of them have been up to the task, though I would certainly recommend that you go for the mute-coloured models, and as with most things, I would lean towards simplicity, as well as ease and speed of inflation and preparation. The nature of this section of the sport is all about a close approach to feeding fish – getting right in among them – in a way that is impossible from the bank because of range, or from a conventional drifting or anchored boat because of the way these perturb the water space.

The Advantages of Boat and Tube

Both boat and tube allow the fly fisher to approach fish that are unreachable to the bank angler, and the tactical fly fisher uses them as manoeuvrable floating platforms with varying vantage points to access fish. They both lack the simplicity and freedom of the roaming shore-bound angler, but they allow us to get to otherwise unreachable fish, thereby providing us with an enormous extension to our sport and a whole range of subset disciplines.

Fly fishing within all these disciplines involves the ideas of closing the range to our target as much as is possible, and ideally making the best angle on that target. The ways that we achieve this with the drifting or anchored boat, or the wading position, differ. The analytical, technical and tactical requirements of boat fishing, be it from anchor or drifting, float tubing, approach from the shore or wading, are all subtly different. While the fly fisher wading in the water needs good wading technique and then line control, so the boat or tube angler requires good control over the drift, or positioning for the anchored boat.

There are parallels here. If the wading fly fisher gets his wading approach wrong, then the game is blown; so too if we set a drift at the wrong angle to the wind or, say, positioned too far off a shoreline, then we can totally miss the opportunities of the situation. Wading technique, boat control and line control all amount to tactical fly fishing.

Float Tube Fishing with Mike Roden

The following notes on float tube fishing are provided by Mike Roden, who is something of a champion for this approach to stillwater fly fishing. Mike is an APGAI instructor endorsed by the Hardy/Greys Academy, and has a special way of delivering a beginner to the advanced level of expertise in this sport.

Float tubing is great fun, but may not be for everyone. If you are comfortable in water it will help, and if you are confident in water then it will help even more. Contrary to what you may imagine, it is a very safe activity, but you need to use a bit of common sense and follow the rules.

Equipment

Originally float tubes were doughnut-shaped, having been made from a tractor or lorry inner tube with a cover on it. Then came the first open-sided tubes that were horse-shoe shaped, which have been superseded by the V-shaped hulls. These are the better option, being much more manoeuvrable and better for getting up-wind. In addition there are pontoon-type tubes which have two main bladders with a seat suspended in the middle, almost like a small catamaran. These pontoon tubes have the advantage of sitting you up higher so there is less of you actually in the water (though this might have a disadvantage in terms of visibility to the fish).

Float tube meeting. (Courtesy Mike Roden)

Most modern tubes are covered in strong Cordura and will have three main air bladders, and normally two more in the backrest. So you would really have to have a lot of bad luck for one of these actually to sink! The valves are an important feature, and I prefer the ones that you blow up by mouth, just like the valves on an airplane life jacket. It is easy to blow up all five bladders by mouth, and can be done quite quickly.

Fishing Techniques
There is no point at all in getting out in a tube and then fishing as if you were on the bank! You can obviously fish areas that are not normally accessible even by boat, but try to use the uniqueness of the tube to your advantage. Imagine fishing from an embankment on a reservoir, where you cast out and retrieve the flies 'up' the slope of the embankment. Now think of being in a tube and facing an embankment, casting to the bank itself, finning slowly backwards and letting line out as you do so, and allowing the flies to sink down the slope. This presentation is the complete opposite to what the fish are used to seeing, and is a 'killer' method!

Also you need to realize that you are propelling yourself backwards, always facing where you are fishing. So use the wind to good effect and let the flies drift across to the side, or fin yourself sideways in a calm. Finning backwards is another way of imparting movement to your flies, with or without retrieving – and I'll let you decide if this is trolling or not.

The Float Tubers' Checklist
- Always inflate the tube to the recommended levels, and no more. There is always the temptation to add a few more breaths, or to over-inflate using a foot pump.
- Always wear a lifejacket – manual, not auto – and make sure it has a whistle.
- Try to launch and exit from the windward shore or bank.
- Never overdo it, especially on your first few sessions. Finning is like pedalling a bike backwards: you will find muscles you didn't know you had, and cramp a few hundred yards from shore is not fun! Nothing should be done in a hurry. If you want to go fast, get a powerboat, not a float tube!
- It's always a good idea to fasten your fins to your legs so you can't lose one. The novelty of going around in a circle will soon wear off!
- Choose very high-backed waders and then sit up straight in the tube; most beginners get wet

because they slouch down too much and water gets in the back of the waders.

- Dress for the conditions. Getting cold should not be an option.
- A 10ft-long rod gives you more versatility; AFTM #5 to #7 is ideal.

Summary

Introducing the idea of tackle for purpose is the intention of this chapter, and you will have read how I have leaned towards tackle and approach that is general, with some specific application. I hesitate every time to make any firm recommendations for proprietary tackle items. Finally, times change, fashion changes, needs change, and even as I write this I find myself compromised to a certain extent. I am a Hardy/Greys Academy member and I know that the reader will expect me, therefore, to recommend this tackle; but I am a member of the Academy because I am completely convinced that this company leads the way in most aspects of tackle in the sport as I experience it, precisely for my requirements: for trout and grayling, with single-handed fly rod disciplines. I see the developments by other tackle companies, and am constantly impressed by many of them. But then I am more or less immune, cocooned from the fashion, the glitz and the marketing hype, because what interests me in this area of our sport is tackle that is fit for purpose.

Greys' Streamflex/Streamlite with feral rainbow.

5 METHOD

Including 'Fly Fishing to Range in Salt Water'
by Chris Ogborne

The Fundamental Approach

For many years my England team-mates and I were going through a fishing process that was largely subconscious. It was only international competition that really made me work out what we were doing before and during a session in terms of applying our skills and knowledge to make the best of the water in front of us. We had reasoned that it was enough to know that we were going through some sort of process involving watercraft and technical skills, but during the intense team briefings and debriefings we began to realize the importance of reducing the whole procedure to more specific elements, so as to maximize the effectiveness of each one, and consequently the entire fishing experience.

Over the years we came to realize that there were three essential components to the process: these may broadly be termed *analytical, technical* and *tactical*. Given experience, and attention to each, the combination produces a formidable fly fisher. Someone relatively new to the sport, or of more limited experience, can also benefit hugely by addressing these aspects. Most of us do it in any case in a haphazard, defocused way, but breaking the process down into its components and working systematically on them, at least at the beginning of a session, drastically improves performance.

Experience enhances all the above, of course, because with experience comes mastery of all the methods at our disposal. The range of methods is very broad, and increasing. Methods also overlap, and it is the tactical aspects of our approach that fine tune these so that we optimize for particular circumstances. It is the tech-nical approach that determines the method(s) employed, however, and following the analysis of the fishing situation we need to choose how we are going to tackle the situation. This includes the selection of tackle, flies and leader rig, all of which are so intimately married to the method.

It is almost impossible *not* to differentiate between methods for stillwater, and those for rivers. In several ways, however, we limit ourselves with our approach to any fishing situation by differentiating in this way, particularly by limiting the range of our approach; but there are not necessarily methods for stillwater, and methods for river, and the two are not necessarily so different. Beyond a certain point we can start putting it all back together for a more holistic approach, although at the outset, for clarity, we have to reduce the variables.

Also, we need to differentiate between fishing for wild fish and fishing for stocked fish: there are numerous approaches that work very efficiently for the latter (often even better than the more traditional or imitative methods), but which are both nearly useless and counterproductive for wild trout. Finally, for river, lake or saltwater, for whatever species, we hybridize or optimize our approach from all the methods in the spectrum of fly fishing, and sometimes borrow from non-fly techniques. This chapter is a tour through those methods.

Methods on Stillwater

Fishing from the bank of a stillwater, of any size, provides our most fundamental approach (not saying that this is necessarily the easiest form of fly fishing). We cast from the bank or a wading position, and search the water up to perhaps forty metres off shore, usually much nearer, within walking and wading range. We can exploit all the methods that we use from a boat, or even that we use on moving waters, but there are subtle differences, mostly related to the control of fly line and flies. As with fly fishing from boats or on rivers, we also need to be cognizant of the features and conditions, and these have a bearing on the method chosen.

The Floating Line Approach

The floating line gives us a foundation from which to work. Many advanced-level fly fishers use nothing else, even in the cold waters of spring when nymph and lure presentations will be the likely approach utilized. From a stable standing or kneeling position we have the greatest control over the line and flies.

Nymphs can be cast at various ranges and allowed to fall to the target depth. We control this by appropriate ballast in the fly itself, and the length of the leader, even the leader material and diameter; fluorocarbon, especially in thick diameters, sinks a little faster than conventional nylon monofilament or copolymer, for example. A long leader also considerably increases the scope for exploring at depth, allowing the fly to fall comparatively unhindered, whereas a short leader will tend to hold up lightly ballasted flies close to the surface – when presented with a floating fly line.

We use all these variations in leader material, length and taper, as well as structure and

Vince Brooks letting fly off the bank in the European Championship in Norway, 2007.

weighting of the flies themselves, in order to control the depth and presentation of the flies. Takes may come 'on the drop', as the flies, particularly nymphs, fall through the water column; or 'on the swing', as the wind catching the fly line bellies it around on the surface, dragging the nymphs in an inducing arc towards the shallows. Takes are frequently induced during the active retrieve phase (as opposed to the wind-created movement and swing) as the angler draws in the line at varying speeds.

The retrieve may be anything from a very slow figure-of-eight, bunching in the line hand, to a full-bore, arm-stretching 'strip'. Even wild trout can respond to the stripped retrieve with nymphs, traditional wet flies or contemporary lure patterns. It is a constantly surprising experience that you simply cannot outstrip a trout, either rainbow or brown, that really means to take the fly. The same can be said for migratory salmonids, and just about any fly-targeted salt-water species. This is not to say that you should always strip in line among hungry fish; there are only limited occasions when they need, or will react positively to, a fast-moving fly like this. It is much more common, indeed, that wild fish will take on the drop, or with a slow, 'nymphed' retrieve.

Static Presentation

The static presentation is also viable for dry fly, nymph and lure, though most commonly the former, and for the presentation of imitations of slow-moving invertebrates such as chironomid pupae, or buzzers. Indeed, dry flies are nearly always most effective when fished static (or nearly so), left out on the flat calm, or the waves, perhaps for several minutes between casts, incorporating such a slow retrieve that it causes the fly to make absolutely no surface disturbance whatsoever. As in river dry fly fishing, the wake or drag of an imitative dry fly is often counterproductive and will alarm fish.

There are exceptions, however, and more so than on rivers, when a moved or retrieved dry fly will detonate far more of a response than a static presentation. Rainbow trout will often give chase to a waked dry fly, or a stripped buoyant lure. Brown trout on lakes also do this, taking a waked top dropper fly, for example, in the waves – the very substance of the beautiful loch-style approach. This can be a far more difficult presentation than it appears, because fish frequently require inducing before they will commit to a take, even if they are seen to follow the fly over several metres. A straightforward stripped retrieve, while hoping for the lock-up, is rarely completely satisfactory.

'Make them have it!' I can hear some of my team-mates and fishing companions say, because this is often what we have to do, and only experience teaches us how to do this. Sometimes just stopping the fly and hanging it induces the commitment, and the fish takes as we are poised with the rod tip high. The visible take is a lovely moment in our sport, while the rod is tapped upwards to set the hook.

Slow Intermediate and Stealth Lines

The development of slow intermediate and stealth lines (very slow, transparent sinkers) has improved our presentation and control of nymphs, particularly from the bank in an appreciable side wind. With a floater, the speed of drift of the line belly can be much too fast, calling for frequent up-wind mending, and consequently moving the nymphs too quickly in their upward sweep. Stealth lines sink very slowly, almost immediately below the surface and away from the worst effects of drag, and allow much slower and smoother presentation of the nymphs, even at reasonable depth (up to two metres).

Note that there is something of a renaissance involving silk lines, which act as low stretch (highly sensitive), thin diameter, intermediate lines that are perfect for loch-style presentation and near-surface nymph fishing.

The Hang Technique

In the early 1990s the hang technique was popularized. Firstly, with floating lines, following a long, nymphed retrieve, we would hang the flies, again with the rod held high, and

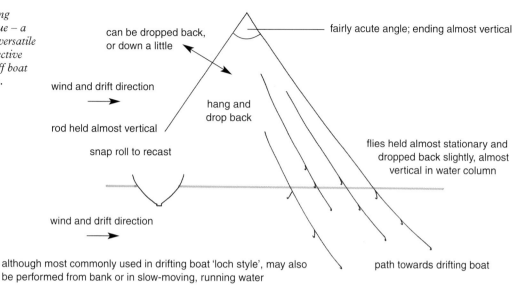

The hang technique – a hugely versatile and effective tactic off boat or bank.

can be dropped back, or down a little

fairly acute angle; ending almost vertical

wind and drift direction

rod held almost vertical

hang and drop back

snap roll to recast

flies held almost stationary and dropped back slightly, almost vertical in water column

wind and drift direction

although most commonly used in drifting boat 'loch style', may also be performed from bank or in slow-moving, running water

path towards drifting boat

sometimes for up to thirty seconds. Usually, if a take came, it would be within a few seconds of the commencement of the hang. The line would twitch, or you would become aware of a weight on the line; perhaps it would simply draw away. Often we would just sense a take and not really be able to explain it.

The method is particularly lethal while nymph fishing. Fish will follow a retrieved fly a long way, never committing to a take until the moment it stops, or perhaps accelerates. Loch-style fishermen have often referred to fish 'coming short', swirling at the fly as it is lifted off at the beginning of a new cast. If the flies are left where they are, even for a few seconds, the difference this makes is extraordinary. A mere moment, it seems, after the point in which you would be tempted to lift off and cast again, the fish strikes.

It helps to have a deeply sunk point fly, with the droppers held between the point fly and the tip of the fly line which is close to the surface, above or below by a metre or so. The hang developed further with the use of sinking lines, particularly from a drifting boat presentation. After the full retrieve, again the flies are held near-motionless. With the use of high density lines and a long cast, the flies can be fished and hung at depth, easily down to six metres, but commonly around three metres, where daphnia and chironomid pupae feeders hunt, especially in bright weather.

Combined with a stripped retrieve, the hang also gave us a novel presentation, radically altering our approach for rainbow trout, both wild and stocked. The idea and practice is to have a bright attractor pattern on the top dropper, and nymphs on the middle dropper and point. A line of suitable sink rate is chosen to suit the conditions and the depth at which the fish are feeding or holding. The line is cast and counted down (roughly timed) to the desired depth. Fish often take on the drop, or they might be attracted to follow the bright top dropper pattern, particularly with a stripped retrieve. Commitment usually comes during the hang phase of the retrieve, and most commonly to one of the trailing nymphs. Think of a rainbow chasing behind an attractor, unwilling to take, though excited by this alien object stripped through the feeding depth. At the end of the retrieve the fish turns away, only to find the nymphs in the water trailing behind the attractor; this results in many of the takes we experience on the hang.

Even after a slow retrieve or a constant 'figure-of-eight' or bunched retrieve, it is worth

Figure-of-eight bunching; with practice one can collect up to 20m (65ft) to hand, shooting all during hauling. This is very useful in keeping the retrieved line off the water, the bottom of a boat or the ground.

hanging the flies even for a few seconds. Perhaps the single most useful retrieve, however, particularly with nymphs, is the slow, constant retrieve. This is most easily achieved by bunching line in the hand, perhaps dropping it in stages (without breaking the constancy of the retrieve), or simply shooting all of it from the hand during casting. It takes a lot of practice to do this repeatedly through a day's fishing, particularly at pace, but once the technique is mastered the stamina needed for long sessions of bunching develops quickly, and the process becomes natural. The classical 'nymphed' retrieve, referred to a great deal here, is the result of the bunched retrieve style. You can retrieve quite quickly in this way, though the method is best suited to the very slow, constant draw of nymphs through the water at even depth.

Fast Constant Retrieves

Fast, constant retrieves can only be achieved by line stripping, either by using the hand-over-hand or the 'roly poly' retrieve, with the rod handle and reel tucked under the rod arm, or by employing a fast strip accompanied by a see-saw rod motion to build in the constancy. The latter involves pushing the rod forwards as the line is stripped with the other hand, then clamping down on the line with the rod hand and pulling the rod backwards while the line hand reaches forwards to grasp the line for the next strip. Again, it needs practice to perfect it, but it doesn't take long and it's worth the effort.

It takes a lot of stamina, however, and most anglers can manage less than an hour of hand-over-hand fast stripping. It can be a useful retrieve for rainbows in particular. We are tending here towards what used to be referred to as 'shock' tactics. With fish either not feeding, or preoccupied on a particular food form – typically a small, difficult-to-imitate invertebrate, such as daphnia – we have for a long time depended on startling them out of their preoccupation, inducing them into a momentary lapse of normal behaviour by giving chase and snatching at a lure or nymph rushing across their field of vision.

The approach developed from fly fishing for salmon in Europe and steelhead rainbow trout in the western United States. These fish barely feed once they have run from the sea into freshwater on their spawning runs, yet they can be induced into taking a fly, or lure, often fished fast or with an inducing retrieve close to or on the surface. In Britain, and consequently the rest of Europe, it was Grafham that brought about the first radical developments of flies, presentations and retrieves, such as the fast stripping of lures and attractor patterns. The rainbows that were stocked (and quickly naturalized) in the big Midland reservoirs brought fresh challenges, ones that are very well met by today's reservoir trout angler.

Disturbance Patterns and Methods

A natural progression has been the use of 'disturbance' patterns and methods. The Muddler Minnow and variants were among the first lures to be used with regularity on British waters as a means of getting trout to give chase at the surface. Again the floating line and a long cast were called into play, and the buoyant lure was stripped – even ripped – back across the surface and through the waves. The sight of a big rainbow giving chase is spectacular, and we remain to this day amazed at just how fast a trout can swim when in pursuit of prey.

Flies soon evolved that made a disturbance on the surface, or even at depth. The ubiquitous Booby in its myriad variations is now in every serious reservoir fisherman's armoury. The late John Hatherell, of Bewl Water, designed a superb fly called the Fidget back in the 1980s. The Fidget is a fry pattern employing a (then) novel ethafoam structure in the head to give it buoyancy and to make it fuss and pop on the surface during a retrieve. John always used to put a Fidget on the point position of a team of flies at fry time, but I preferred it on the top dropper of a loch-style team, favouring the idea that trout would be attracted to it, but if not committed enough to take it, would gulp at the nymphs or small traditional wet patterns on the middle dropper or point, especially when hung

John Hatherell's Fidget fly, precursor to surface 'disturbance' patterns.

at the end of a retrieve. The Fidget worked for us in either of these positions in a team of flies.

Disturbance or attractor patterns are today essential components among teams of flies for stillwater use, and combined with retrieve styles and leader rigs they considerably increase the range of methods we employ. Attractors have come a long way from the bright traditional wet flies such as the Dunkeld or the Soldier Palmer, and even the steelhead streamers from the US. The British stillwater fishing boom has accelerated the evolution of these patterns, along with the methods used to deploy them.

Coupled particularly with the disturbance or attractor patterns, we often fish nymphs or more imitative patterns on middle dropper(s) and point, especially when using the deadly hang and 'drop back' techniques at the end of the retrieve. I have written a lot here about the hang for both stillwater and river use, but the drop back is less frequently discussed. At the end of the retrieve – and I am concentrating here on the moments before the roll cast on stillwater, or the new cast on the river, when the flies are trailing downstream of the angler – the flies are poised. Very often a fish will have followed the flies to this point, and unless the angler takes appropriate action, even by pausing, these fish will usually go unnoticed. Hanging, and even dropping the rod tip and line such that the flies sink a little deeper, or further downstream in a river, will often induce a confident take.

The 'Washing Line' Presentation

The discovery and perfection of the 'washing line' presentation has also been a great breakthrough, partly because it is not only applicable to stocked rainbows, but can often work on wild brown trout in lakes. This latter quality makes it a thoroughly worthwhile method; one is always suspicious about methods that seem to work only on stocked fish, particularly 'fresh' stockies.

The basic washing line rig incorporates a buoyant pattern, often a Booby, on the point of a leader that has two or three nymphs on droppers, all presented on a floating line. The nymphs, you understand, are like washing hung out to dry between supports (the floating line and the buoyant point fly). With this rig it is very easy to control the depth at which the nymphs are presented, and at a life-like, slow retrieve rate. If lightly ballasted nymphs are used on droppers, the point fly does not have to be over-buoyant. Suitable Crane Fly or Grafham Hopper-style patterns can be superb on the point of a washing line rig, often more successful than the ubiquitous Booby.

Adaptations of the basic rig include using a buoyant pattern on the top dropper as well as point, with one or two nymphs hanging between. Sinking and sink-tip lines are also incorporated to give altogether different, very controlled presentations at depth.

The washing line method offers a remarkably adaptable range of presentations. It is an evolved state of the traditional loch-style approach: the beautiful method.

The Importance of Fly-Line Choice

I will illustrate the importance of fly-line choice. It was the 2008 FIPS-Mouche European Championships on Lago de Alsa in Cantabria, Spain, and I was ill. Stuart Crofts and I had suffered with a virus over there, and I had become dehydrated and was suffering from low blood sugar, a condition that was to land me in Santander Hospital as an emergency admission. I had fished a morning river session and managed to save the blank, catching a single, sizeable trout to keep the team alive in the Championship. After the terrible (for me), drawn-out journey to Alsa, I stepped off the coach to meet my team captain, Paul Page, and Vince, who had waited for me there, following on from Iain Barr's morning session. I had a migraine and was beginning to shake. There was no way I could focus enough to make decisions about a lake I had never fished, in a competition in which Team England simply relied on me to catch just one trout.

This would have been enough: just a single, wild rainbow trout, from a lake where most competitors of all nationalities were blanking, and where it was marginal whether or not I could even step into the boat, let alone make choices and decisions. Iain Barr had caught three fish in his morning session, which was enough for second place. Paul and Vince briefed me, so I did not need to make any decisions. The location of a rainbow trout shoal close to an island was pointed out, and the line for the occasion, which Iain had used, was selected: a DI 3 Forty Plus. Vince set up the rod for me, even the leader and the necessary flies, but it was the DI 3 that made the difference, because more than anything it was line choice (as almost always) that was the most significant variable. Get the line choice wrong, and it's all over.

Paul and Vince helped me into the boat where my Slovenian boat partner for the session and our Spanish boatman waited. Paul had

Lago de Alsa, northern Spain.

convinced my boat partner that I knew where the fish were, following Iain Barr's experience of the morning session, so between us we managed to persuade our boatman to row out to the distant island. It was a long haul, the first of many that afternoon as the wind picked up and we repeatedly had to regain the top of the drift. I tried to shut out the pain, relying on physical rather than mental actions, while Vince's words echoed in my pounding head: 'Just cast thirty metres, count down five and then long, medium-pace pulls until the flies are close to the boat; and then hang them, you must hang them. All three of Barny's fish came on the hang on the DI 3.'

And I did this, methodically, unthinkingly relying on 'method' fishing, with that crucial DI 3. After the session, Paul and Vince helped me from the boat. I was near collapse, but I had caught two of those wild rainbows and had not let down the team. More than anything else, the DI 3 and the hang had made it possible.

Championship sector on Lago de Alsa, 2008.

Indicator Rigs

Indicator rigs developed in part from the washing line, in that they incorporate a buoyant pattern that suspends a team of nymphs hanging below at fixed depths. At its crudest, the infamous 'bung' consists of a highly buoyant fly, or no-nonsense float or indicator, close to the tip of the floating fly line, with a string of nymphs, attractors, or a mixture of both, hanging beneath. The method has been refined by the use of dry flies and other buoyant patterns such as fry imitations, capable of both catching fish and acting as an indication of takes to the nymphs. Rigs are further refined particularly in terms of the depth at which the nymphs are hung below the dry pattern. These rigs give control over depth as well as good indication of a take.

The Loch-Style Approach

Loch-style fishing has fascinated many of us for a long time, and it will continue to do so. It embraces actually a range of presentation methods, especially from a drifting boat, which are almost infinitely adaptable and include everything from static dry fly, through the washing line, to the strip and hang with high density lines (though some people argue that the 'bung' has no place in what they consider to be the sacrosanct loch-style approach).

This is contemporary loch-style, while traditional loch-style employs the floating line (originally a greased silk line) with a team of three or four traditional wet flies, cast at short range in front of a drifting boat, or one controlled by drogue or oars. The traditional approach still works today, no question, it has merely been refined and developed as contemporary fly fishers adapt it to suit specific requirements. It is part of its beauty that it can be adapted so readily.

Fly-Line Selection

The modern range of fly-line types is sophisticated, while the sheer scale of the range is so complex and varied that choice can be confusing. Continuing our exploration of stillwater methods, it is not simply a matter of choosing a floater if fish are seen rising, or known to be close to the surface, and progressively increasing the density of the line choice for fish-holding in deeper water. Actual depth of the fish is a major factor, of course, but the presentation and control features of modern lines are at least as important, and introduce further variables into our choice.

I have already described the use of a stealth line, or slow intermediate, for the presentation of nymphs close to the surface in order to minimize the effects of surface drag, particularly in side winds. Many top class loch-style competitors possess upwards of twenty fly lines, which they will have with them for a serious practice session or major competition. My European Championship team-mate, Vince Brooks, is currently one of the best lake specialists in Britain, and Vince would not think of going out on an important qualifier without the full complement of lines. Of course, he has the experience and expertise to be able to choose the right line for the prevailing conditions and circumstances, and fish-holding depth is only one of the factors he considers.

Line choice, leader rigs and flies, in that order: get them all right, and with a suitable retrieve in a suitable area of the lake where there are catchable fish, you will have a combination and method that will work. The illustrations in Chapter 4 show the fundamental constructions that we adapt to produce leaders suitable for specific methods, tuned to particular circumstances. The variables here are many, and just by altering the dimensions by a few centimetres, or the diameter or structure of the leader materials, can bring about subtle, or even profound, differences in presentation.

We can choose, even at an advanced level, not to go down this route, just as an imitative fly fisher need not necessarily have more than a passing knowledge of aquatic entomology. We can remain with simple, compromise leader constructions, ones that have proven reliability for specific methods, or ranges of methods. I know top guides and international competitors who adopt this stance, even relying on basic, conventional nylon monofilament – for example, the German-made Bayer Perlon – for the construction of standard, time-tested leaders. Then again, I know many of the same who go to painstaking lengths to produce highly tuned leader constructions for specific methods and situations.

Methods on Running Water

The flowing water of rivers produces a further variable that we have to consider and account for in our choice of method. Many believe that river fishing is more difficult in some way than fly fishing on lakes. This is not the case, but neither is it generally easier. It has *different* requirements associated mostly with presentation, so fly fishers unaccustomed to the needs of appropriate casting and delivery in running water will inevitably find rivers more demanding than lakes, or vice versa.

In the same way, the time-honoured, sacrosanct upstream dry fly method is often considered the ultimate in fly fishing. This has been exacerbated through the history of our sport by the Halford/Skues – dry versus nymph – debate, and the fact that on some rivers, particularly in

southern England and the north-western United States, dry fly has been seen as the only 'sporting' approach to fly fishing. The truth of the matter to an experienced rod is that the upstream nymph is actually considerably more demanding than the upstream dry, as is nymph fishing in general compared with dry fly.

The pleasure derived from the highly visual aspects of dry fly fishing, as well as the more abstract idea of beauty in the sport, are quite different matters. Few will argue that the aesthetics of watching a wild brown trout sip down a size 20 Pale Watery from glide water can be beaten by a similar fish invisibly snatching at an olive nymph deep in the stream. For that matter, on stillwaters the sight of a surface-cruising rainbow engulfing a Ginger Hopper is surely not beaten (for most of us) by the stab of a deep-lying rainbow hitting a Minkie on a DI 7. However, almost all of us will gratefully accept the latter types of fish when they are simply not feeding from the surface, and, as such, advanced fly fishing encompasses all presentations, on lake or river.

The Upstream Dry Fly
So most of us feel that while loch-style is the beautiful method on stillwaters, so the upstream dry fly is the beautiful approach on the stream.

Lawrence Greasley stalking with an upstream dry on the River Eamont.

Wild brown trout caught from Yorkshire's River Cover.

Beautiful, and simple. Fish in a river will always face the current, which facilitates the flow of water through their mouths and across their gills. They have a field of vision, a 'window', of roughly 300 degrees, in front and on either side. Only in that 60 degrees or so – the cone lying behind them – is their vision reduced. We approach whenever possible from behind, therefore, so that we can be as close as possible to our target, affording us the greatest control. A cast up and across the stream is the ideal, currents and obstructions allowing, with the fly alighting a metre or two upstream of the fish's station, and drifting down without drag.

The Dead Drift

In dry and nymph (including spider) presentations, the dead drift is crucial. Drag, particularly with dry flies, is usually counterproductive. We are aware, of course, of exceptions; that in the dark, or in the evening in summer, a dragged dry fly will entice aggressive sedge feeders to strike, and that the low sun angles of arctic and sub-arctic latitudes often produce conditions that will have both trout and grayling careering after a skated dry fly. Generally, however, a dry

fly needs to be dead-drifted, drag-free, just as a static dry fly on a stillwater is usually a better option than a moved fly. Sub-surface nymphs and spiders are also usually best presented with a period of dead drift, to allow them to sink before the 'inducing' period of the retrieve, the lift and swing, or the 'drop back'.

We have to understand the current, and then we have to allow for it; only then can we use it, and it becomes our ally. It is no good, for instance, to cast a fly at the rings of a rising fish. We have to allow a period of drift, so that the fly falls on the current to where the fish rose, above or close to its station. This is even more important when we appreciate that the deeper a fish is lying, the further it might drop downstream (or across), tracking the fly, finally 'taking' up to several metres downstream of its station. Moreover, drag a dry fly at any point in its drift, and the game will very likely be all over; wild brown trout and big grayling are particularly unforgiving in this regard.

Beating drag, therefore, is probably our prime concern when presenting dry fly on rivers. This stems from the analytical component of our approach, which should have identified actual fish rising, or likely fish-holding areas within range, and how the currents between fish and angler will affect the fly line, leader and fly. Now the river fly fisher goes tactical, utilizing his knowledge of currents and fish behaviour so as to be able to present that fly, drag-free, in exactly the desired place. At least with dry fly there is only the two-dimensional river's surface to concern us. Dead drift is also important for nymph presentations, and then we have to think in the third dimension of water depth and sub-surface currents: the river column space.

Downstream Presentation

The downstream presentation of a dry fly is also a tactical approach that becomes of immense use when there is a downstream wind. Casting upstream with a dry fly into anything of a wind becomes limiting in that, without precise timing, the dry fly will be blown back over the leader or, worse, the tip of the fly line. You can sometimes steal a bit of angle by casting across the wind a little, but presentation is always compromised in strong downstream winds. We can eliminate this, however, by actually using the wind rather than fighting it, and reverting to a downstream presentation, which keeps the wind essentially from behind. It is all about making the right angles.

Of course, the potential for drag is higher with downstream presentations, because the dry fly is drifting away from the angler from the moment it alights on the surface. We reduce this problem by pulling back on the forward delivery (as in an adapted parachute cast – *see* Chapter 6, 'Casting') in order to 'dump' the dry fly on the surface while the rod tip is held high. This places a lot of slack line on the surface and allows quite a long, downstream, drag-free drift while the rod tip is slowly lowered. Also, with the use of a very long leader, up to 8m (26ft), comparatively little fly line need be cast, so that only leader is laid on the surface, slack and snaked, for the downstream drift. This is important for keeping a maximum distance between the fish (which have good visibility upstream) and the angler.

Wading

I have lost count of the times when I have suggested that it is far better to wade towards a fish than cast a long line at it. Get close to it, as close as you dare (as long as you are down-stream – or across the stream – of the fish). Remember that the longer the line you cast, the more out of control you will be, and the more your fly will be affected by the fly line interact-ing with the currents. With dry fly in particular, 10m (30ft) is quite a long cast in anything other than the smoothest of flow, and 6m (20ft) is better. If possible, take them on with no fly line on the water whatsoever.

Learn to wade aggressively, precisely and smoothly. Wade tactically. You can get amazingly close if you choose the right angle from down-stream of your target (remembering that 60-degree cone, and that a fish can also feel and hear disturbance). The closer you are to the fish, the fewer currents there are in-between to affect the fly line, and the less fly line we have on the water to be affected by those currents. This reduces drag and increases control.

It is a compromise, of course, always a compromise. You see a fish at 15m (50ft), rising fairly steadily at a nice angle up and across the stream from your position. You have a clear back cast. The temptation is to punch out the line so that the fly drifts down over the fish, but in so doing you have a lot of fly line and leader on the surface – so much, in fact, that any current immediately begins to have an effect, and drag sets in within seconds.

If you take the alternative, wade up on the fish, shortening the cast to lay out 6m (20ft) or so; like this there is much less line to be affected, and the period of drag-free drift is drastically lengthened. The flip side, however, is that you might disturb the fish by your wading: thus you compromise. With practice, you will learn to approach fish closely, optimizing the angle of attack, such that the presentation will be as good as it can be, and the chances of a success-ful hook-up are exponentially improved over what is possible with a long-range cast. It is largely down to wading technique.

Fishing Upstream Nymph and Spiders

The above applies just as much to fishing upstream nymph and spiders. The same element of control is needed, and this is facilitated by a short length of fly line on the water. After a period of dead drift, which allows the nymph to sink and be carried into the target area by the current, we can allow it to pass through this area while dead-drifting – often best – or impart a degree of movement which can induce a fish to take. This is what we refer to as 'sub-surface drag', or simply 'lift', which often has the opposite effect to the drag of a dry fly.

The idea is that the nymph, within the taking zone of the fish, abruptly lifts though the water column as if about to escape, bringing about the induced predatory response of the fish. Sawyer spoke a lot about the induced take, particularly with regard to grayling in clear, chalk-stream waters where their reaction to movements of the nymph can be seen. It applies just as much to waters in which the feeding fish cannot be seen.

Line-imparted movements of the fly are actually inevitable while nymph fishing, so we can build these into the actual drift of the fly. As soon as the fly line begins to 'bite', reacting to the current, there is a tightening and the flies will lift towards the surface. As the cast drifts down below the angler, even if line is fed out to an extent, there comes a point when the line tightens, lifting the flies again.

We can exaggerate this by clamping down with the line hand, or with movements of the rod, to set in a series of little induced lifts, interspersed with dead-drift periods, throughout the drift of the flies. At the limit, as the fly line and leader is well downstream of our position in the water, we can swing the flies, even pointing the rod tip in towards the bank behind us to exaggerate the swing. Brown trout are particularly susceptible to this movement because they will often follow a fly for an appreciable distance, only taking it right up in the shallows or close to the bank, a sort of commitment point: take it or lose it. In nymph and spider fishing on the stream, or any wet presentation, the fly fisher exploits highly primitive hunting behaviour.

The Drop Down or Drop Back

A further exaggeration of movement, and indeed a lengthening of the drift – the time during which the flies are working in the taking zone of the stream – is accomplished by the 'drop down' or 'drop back', described above in terms of stillwater presentation at the end of a retrieve. This is one of the least exploited, minor tactical approaches on the river. The flies are falling downstream away from the angler. A gentle induction is set as the fly line bites, and is then abruptly relaxed as a metre or more of fly line is released. Alternatively, we can drift the flies, tracking them with a high rod tip (a method referred to as 'high sticking') and then dropping the rod tip down towards the surface, downstream. The effect on the flies is that they effectively dead-drift again, dropping down through the water column until the next bite, and inducing lift.

Teams of flies are often used in nymph and/or spider methods (or hybrids of the two), rather than a singleton. It gives us a way of presenting different patterns at different positions in the water column. Often a spider (general imitations of mature nymphs on the point of eclosion) is placed on a dropper, and will fish closer to the surface, while a nymph is placed on point and will (given a dead-drift period) fish deeper. We commonly utilize three flies on a team, which provides a compromise, searching approach. In some countries the number of flies presented is limited by national or local rules. In Poland, for example, the national rule is for a maximum of two flies, while in Slovenia it is one, as is the case on some English and French chalk streams. In Spain there is no limit, and anglers sometimes employ teams of six or more wet flies on a team. We choose the number and type of wet flies on a team according to the rules of the water and also the specific needs of the situation.

Stuart Crofts: upstream lift, hang and hold technique, with single nymph, Sava Dolinka, Slovenia, 2006.

Stuart Minnikin: master of upstream nymph technique (without indicator) on Eden.

Sight and Indicator Fishing

A hugely controversial method (or group of presentations) employs the use of devices that help indicate that a fish has taken a sub-surface fly. They are controversial because many anglers suggest that they are tantamount to float fishing, and are not fly-fishing methods. I do not agree with this attitude, although I hope I have made clear that the upstream nymph and spider technique, *without indicator*, is probably the most difficult, and treasured, skill in the river fisher's array of methods; those die-hards who use no more indication than a floating fly line, aided by a greased line tip and leader butt, must be respected.

If fish can be seen, and especially if the fly can also be seen, then takes are reasonably obvious, but these circumstances are comparatively rare. Often there is no sight whatsoever of the fish, and the only way we can sense that it has intercepted the fly is either by feeling it, or by seeing

a movement on the greased fly-line tip or leader. This requires great eyesight and concentration, as well as supreme line control, and there are very few anglers who can do this at what might be regarded as a consistently advanced level. Most of us go through the stage of employing polypropylene wool or 'pimp'-style indicators, and I would suggest that most nymph fishers tend to become over-reliant on them, to the extent that they cannot see the disadvantages of using such devices.

It was inevitable, therefore, that various indicator methods crept into the river sport. Buoyant material attached to the fly-line tip or leader butt is the crudest approach, but reasonably effective. This is rather like the bait angler's stick-float method. It is also analogous to the stillwater bung method described above. Sufficient buoyant material, such as polymer putty or foam, is fixed on the line in order to support the weight of the nymphs and act as an indicator when a fish takes. In principle it is simple, but in practice, rather like the stick float, or 'trotting' technique, it requires a level of skill and control to elevate it away from a fundamentally crude presentation. That buoyant, often brightly coloured indicator can be the kiss of death in clear water or for spooky fish. It also drastically affects presentation, usually adversely by setting up drag and loss of control.

An innovative refinement of the above was to use one of the flies of a team as the indicator, for instance a dry fly on the top dropper with nymphs suspended below. This led to the 'trio' and 'duo' methods, trio involving a dry fly above two nymphs, while duo is a dry fly and single nymph combination. Most anglers see the dry fly as largely 'sacrificial', being primarily an indicator of a take to the nymphs. The greatest breakthrough in the methods, however, came with the use of dry flies that effectively take as many fish as the nymphs, while also acting as indicators. This is improved by very careful fly design (*see* Chapter 8, 'Tactical Flies'), as well as the presentation.

Duo has now been so much developed that it is one of the most effective of all the upstream presentation methods. There are actually more refined methods of presenting upstream nymph, but none with the extra benefit of having both a dry fly and a nymph in the target water simultaneously. Duo has a further advantage over 'pure' upstream dry fly presentation, in that in anything of a downstream wind, an upstream presentation becomes almost impossible, or at least seriously compromised by the wind blowing the dry fly back over leader and even fly line, necessitating, therefore, an across or downstream cast, which is not always desirable. The extra weight of the nymph, however, can allow a much cleaner turnover of a dry fly into the wind. Moreover, the sunk nymph then stabilizes the drift of the dry fly, often preventing it skating in gusty or cross-current conditions.

Indicator Leaders

There have been huge advances made by the major European national teams in the development of ultra-sensitive indicator leaders for

Stuart Minnikin again fishing upstream nymph on the River Cover, North Yorkshire.

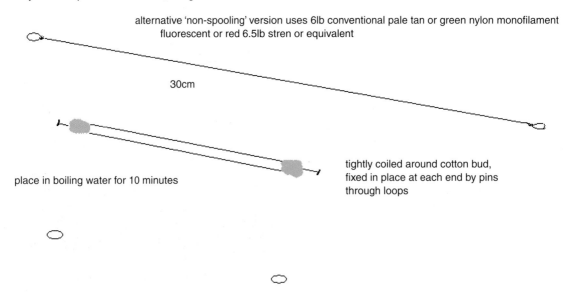

very small loops tied at each end, using double overhand knot

alternative 'non-spooling' version uses 6lb conventional pale tan or green nylon monofilament
fluorescent or red 6.5lb stren or equivalent

30cm

place in boiling water for 10 minutes

tightly coiled around cotton bud,
fixed in place at each end by pins
through loops

left in freezer overnight to set in permanent coils
thick application of silicon Mucilin or equivalent produces high floating indicator coils

Coiled indicator construction.

nymph fishing in rivers. In most cases these are actually more sensitive than the duo, or any method requiring a dry fly or a buoyant indicator device. They also produce reduced disturbance on the surface, vitally important for nymph presentation in difficult conditions or to wary fish. So-called Italian and French leaders have been documented, but I will refer to them generally as indicator leaders, partly because experts in various countries (most notably the Europeans) have had various levels of input to the design.

It is worth recognizing the circumstances in which such leaders are employed, in order to appreciate their design features. They are ideal, for example, for use with single, small nymphs, particularly on smooth water, and where fish are wary. Their use can be extended, of course, to double nymph presentations and to broken water with less spooky fish. It is the smooth, delicate presentation with supreme take detection, however, that led to their development.

Presentation with these indicator leaders is approaching the sensitivity of the ultra-tuned and balanced float rigs as used by contemporary pole anglers.

The fundamental design features of a generalized (all-purpose) indicator leader are shown in the diagram on page 51 (in Chapter 4, 'Equipment for Purpose'). Crucial aspects include the length of the various sections, as well as the overall length, which can be varied, particularly in the tippet section. Other considerations are the amount and position of taper, and the all-important indicator section(s). The coiled indicator section was a fantastic breakthrough.

Greased, the coil sits high and proud of the surface, with the nymph sinking only the tippet section of the leader. It is like watching the dry fly of a duo rig for indication of a take to the nymph, and calls for similar concentration. Sometimes the coil stretches and plunges away, but it might also merely twitch or just stop running down the stream. Occasionally the nymph has caught in weed or the river bed, or in an unsuspected cross current, but one soon learns to recognize these 'false' takes, or most of them. The take of a fish is qualitatively different and instantly recognizable, so that with experience you are left in no doubt nearly every time and you tap the rod tip to set the hook.

There are many variations on the theme of indicator leaders, but one of the major adaptations commonly adopted is the tippet length. Typically, we might be using 6X (0.13mm diameter) or 7X (0.10mm diameter) copolymer as tippet material. With lightly ballasted nymph in shallow water, we might use as little as a 1m (39in) length of tippet, while at greater depth and with a more heavily loaded fly we might typically extend the tippet to between 2m and 3m (6ft and 10ft). For presentation to ultrawary trout in very clear water, the tippet section might be as long as 4m (13ft).

Such long leaders require adaptation in casting style because energy has to be loaded into the rod, fly line and leader, with very long pauses while forming the (open) casting loop or

ABOVE: *Coiled indicator with a spool of Italian Asso fluorescent nylon monofilament.*

BELOW: *The ultimate in control: Louis Otano Perez, Spanish international, stalking with an indicator rig on the Rio Miera, northern Spain.*

back-cast. Long rods, such as the continental 11ft to 12ft, slow-actioned #2 and #3 weights, lend themselves to very long leaders, with or without indicator coils, and to the presentation of both dry flies and nymphs at the 6m to 10m (20ft to 33ft) range with a superb level of control, but it does take a lot of practice, particularly for those who have been used to shorter, faster-actioned rods, such as the British and Americans.

There is one special property of the indicator coil, however, that helps in fly presentation with long leaders: it effectively acts as an air brake, dragging through the air while catapulting the nymph ahead of it. The trick is to put enough energy into the cast (mostly by pausing long enough before tapping the rod forwards) and to aim the forward cast with quite a high trajectory (using a high, forward stop-point). The coil is fired upstream, and as it drags towards the end of its travel in the air, the nymph and tippet shoot ahead of it, giving good turnover.

Perhaps the most advances in the river sport have stemmed from these high-performance indicator rigs, and the expertise to use them, simply because they give better access to difficult fish. Visual indication of a take, however, is often not possible and we have to rely on tactile approaches, feeling for the take, or at least relying on various mixtures and permutations of visual and tactile indications.

The Tactile Detection of a Take

River anglers are very used to the tactile detection of a take, with the traditional across and down approach with teams of spiders or other wet flies. Often, feeling the take is the only sort of detection, and the problem, of course, is converting these felt takes into properly hooked fish. By the time the take is registered in the hand the fish is either already hooked or, more often, just pricked or alerted, and then bolts for cover. If one relies entirely on feeling for a take it results in very low conversion rates. Many are satisfied with this on prolific waters, where a conversion rate of one in five, or even one in ten, might still give a reasonable catch at the end of the day; however, it is highly inefficient, and on waters where takes are less frequent, such a low hook-up ratio will result in, at best, a poor catch and at worst, frustration and a blank.

There are various approaches to maximizing positive hook-ups while fishing wet fly across and down; these include increasing the visual component by, for example, keeping the rod tip reasonably high above the water's surface and tracking the flies downstream. This forms a belly of line hanging between rod tip and

John Tyzack high-sticking with nymph on the Rio Pas.

Paul Fear with Czech nymph on a seam on the San river.

surface, which acts like a swing-tip indicator. Often the takes are felt as the line straightens, giving us simultaneous indication (tactile and visual), and it certainly increases the hook-ups. It is a matter of control, and being able to register a take before the fish has dropped the fly. Another approach that has gained popularity in recent years is to go in the opposite direction and tighten everything up, maintaining almost direct line contact with the flies; this is known as contact fishing. Non-stretch fly lines are ideal, even non-stretch Kevlar or other polymer braid between fly line and short leader. A heavy fly is tied on the point position, with one or two droppers armed with imitative nymph patterns suspended between the non-stretch line and the semi-sacrificial point fly. The cast is made across the stream, and the rod tip lowered to the water's surface so that there is an almost straight line between the rod hand, with the fly line clamped against the grip and the flies.

The parallel in bait fishing is the bolt rig. A fish picks up one of the dropper nymphs, and with any movement away from the tight, non-stretch line, the hook is set. Many argue that this bolt-rig technique, sometimes referred to as 'braid nymphing', has no place in fly fishing; others are simply pragmatic about it, and see it as a means to improve hook-up ratio with the basic across and downstream method of presentation. Braid nymph is not a panacea method, however; it is best suited to fairly fast-flowing water where there are not too many obstructions (which would cause too much hook and line fouling), and reasonable depth, 1m (39in) or more. As such, it might be regarded as a minor method for specialist situations.

The Czech Nymph Method

The extraordinary Czech nymph method, however, is far from being a minor tactic. It also blends tactile and visual take detection, the latter by virtue of everything happening very close to the angler. Czech-style nymphing is ideally ultra short-range fishing, virtually under the rod tip. Typically, a short leader is used (2–2.5m/6–8ft), with two droppers close together, allowing three nymphs to be presented,

Paul Fear hooked into a big grayling; note the indicator section of the furled butt leader.

and the well-oxygenated faster flow. These creases are recognized as typical Czech nymph water.

Czech nymph is rapid cast-and-search fishing, and rather rhythmic. A switch cast (constant tension cast) lobs the three nymphs upstream – plop, plop, plop – and the rod tip holds up the fly line, often completely off the water, while it tracks the nymphs downstream. Takes come at any time in the drift, and betray the depth at which the fish are holding. Each cast and drift might last no longer than six or seven seconds, so a huge number of casts can be undertaken in a session. The line stops or dips, or kicks upstream – again we have that lovely 'swing tip' indicator – or the fish is felt with a strong take, jabbing down against the rod tip.

Polish Rolled Nymph

The Czechs, unsurprisingly, remain the grand masters of this technique and they have developed it to a high standard; other Eastern Europeans, most notably the Poles, have extended the method to include double nymphing and what is referred to as 'rolled nymph'. In many European countries the maximum allowed is 'one or two flies'. It is two in Poland, and partly for this reason the top Polish anglers essentially adapted the Czech nymph style to be applicable to two flies. Changing from three to two considerably affects the dynamics and presentation of nymphs at short range. Indeed, the Poles fish generally much longer lines, extending the range up to 10m (30ft), with a more pronounced track and swing during each drift. There is a potentially very long dead-drift period immediately following presentation of the flies up and across the stream, while line is gathered to keep a reasonable contact with the nymphs. A series of inductive lifts and pauses is introduced when the two nymphs are square to the angler's stance in the river, and then downstream, ending in a marked swing and hang.

This method searches more of the river, with the angler shifting position less frequently than with conventional Czech nymph. Common to the two styles, however, is appropriate presenta-

with about 50cm (20in) separating any two. Only a short length of fly line (less than 3m/10ft) extends beyond the rod tip while short casts are made up and across the stream. Again, long rods dominate among most Czech nymph specialists, but rods as short as 8ft can be used. The maximum range that the flies are presented from the wading angler is, therefore, 6m (20ft), and it is often as short as 3m (10ft). The nymphs are tracked down with the rod tip to just a little below the angler's position before being recast with a lob or switch cast. The angler must be highly mobile so as to cover new water rapidly, ideally almost every cast, at least until a shoal of grayling – for which the method is supremely suited – is found.

The nymphs themselves are sparse and weighted, most particularly the point, so they will sink rapidly to the grayling feeding depth. The method excels when fish are feeding close to the river bed, in streamy water that is not too fast or shallow (when spider/nymph hybrid rigs are more effective). We tend to look for 'crease' water, that interface between fast water and slightly held-up water, sometimes deep, closer to the bank or a mid-river feature. This is where grayling shoal, near the cover of dark, deep water, but on the edge of the nymph food lane

tion at the feeding depth, with excellent contact with the flies at all times. Both afford the mixture of tactile and visual aspects of the takes.

Presentation at Depth

Polish rolled nymph – often with the nymph on point rolling across or touching the gravel and stones of the river bed – has been adapted by some British anglers to incorporate non-stretch fly line and braid, such that contact is maintained between the point nymph and the rod hand (with the line clasped between the rod grip and the hand). The nymph can be felt tapping and bumping on the river stones, while the nymph on the dropper is drifting with the freedom afforded by the length of the dropper, wafting in the current. When a fish takes this nymph it is either felt almost immediately, as with the bolt rig mentioned above, or the tapping of the point fly stops, because it is no longer rolling along the river bed.

We have adapted these methods further by allowing presentation at significant depth, for example in plunge pools or during times of river flooding or heavy spate. One of the nymphs on a two- or three-fly team is essentially sacrificial

and very heavy, up to 6g (0.2oz); it might be placed on point or on the top dropper. The other flies are generally more imitative. The practice is for the heavy nymph to drag the imitative flies down to the quieter pockets of water, where the fish are seeking protection from the faster flows, and to keep them there for long enough to be taken.

It is a method akin to touch or rolled legering in coarse fishing with bait, and it is right on the boundary between fly fishing and bait fishing. While conventional fly casting is certainly not involved in that it is the weight of the sacrificial fly that allows the cast to take place (as with legering), artificial flies are still being presented to the fish. It is a highly pragmatic method to employ in appropriately hostile conditions to other styles of imitative fly fishing.

Streamer Fishing

We cannot really use high density fly lines to achieve the same end, because these are influenced by the current much more than the high density structure of sacrificial weighted nymphs (which are, moreover, only partially sacrificial in that it is surprising how often these large

Paul Davidson demonstrating braid nymph technique on the Tweed.

Polish national team member using the rolled nymph technique.

patterns are actually taken by even small fish). Sinking lines do have a role to play in river fishing, however, in that in fast, reasonably smooth-flowing water they allow the presentation of flies and streamers at the feeding or holding depth of the fish, with some degree of control, or contact with the flies. The general method is used a lot for migratory salmonids and on the larger European rivers for brown trout, particularly in cold water.

The method is most akin to Polish rolled nymphing described above, with a sinking or sink-tip line cast across the stream and swung downstream, usually stripped or worked during its track. Single streamer or lure patterns are used, often on short leaders so that the fly is dragged down deeper by the sinking line (if a long leader is used the fly tends to spend too long near the surface, unless it is heavily weighted). A dropper is frequently attached, or even two, producing the dynamic and multiple fly effects as utilized in traditional loch-style or fishing with teams of nymphs.

Streamers do not have to be fished across and down the flow, and upstream presentations are frequently superior, particularly at short range.

In coloured or floodwater, the sheltered pockets and eddies are searched – for example with a 'tadpole'-style stream (*see* Chapter 8, 'Tactical Flies') – irrespective of their relative orientation up- or downstream of the angler.

Streamer fishing can also encompass a highly imitative approach, more ideally suiting the needs of the predatory species in rivers. In many countries, including England, streamer fishing in rivers has been largely overlooked until recent years. The tradition of the historic southern chalk streams has been systemic and far-reaching, but a few radical thinkers, such as Oliver Edwards, have pioneered the method on northern British rivers and have enjoyed staggering success. More recently still, outstanding international river anglers, such as John Tyzack (five times England National River Champion), have evolved the approach to even higher levels of expertise, using minnow, crayfish and other prey-based imitations. John has told me on several occasions, when viewing a new stretch of river, that the streamer approach comes first to his mind – this from one of the finest upstream dry-fly fishers on the planet!

It is a consideration of streamer fishing that brings us full circle back to stillwaters, because it is on lakes that streamers, or lures, are most commonly used, as opposed to rivers, in most fly-fishing areas throughout the world. Almost everywhere, after all, when approaching a river, we are primarily thinking in terms of dry fly or nymph. On lakes, either from bank or boat, there is frequently the likelihood of streamer being the prime choice. On lakes we rarely have to consider grayling, but will have the more predatory species such as trout, perch and pike as our targets. Fry imitations are likely to feature strongly, and this means streamer fishing, or lure fishing with static or near-static fry patterns on or below the surface.

We are almost back to loch-style, coupled with that North American streamer school influence, in that we are enticing the predatory instincts of fish, utilizing bait fish imitations, or lures with various trigger features designed into them, rather like our traditional loch-style flies. The main differences between streamer

fishing and loch-style are actually just the general sizes of the flies used in each approach, and the length of the casts made in each sub-discipline. We tend to fish streamers and lures at much greater range (up to 40m/130ft) than the 10m (30ft) ideal range employed in traditional loch-style. Nonetheless, the two approaches are suitably merged and hybridized in order to meet the specific needs of the lake, or for that matter the river.

In Conclusion

There is nowadays a very broad range of possibilities open to fly fishers using the single-handed fly rod. The deft touch and attention to entomological detail of the North Americans, coupled with the essentially streamer approaches of the river rainbow and steelhead fly fishers from this continent, have been strongly influential on the sport as a whole. The brilliant Eastern European masters of nymph presenta-

Ideal streamer water: fast flow on the Sava, Slovenia.

tions in rivers have launched us to a level in our sport that is massively elevated from where we were even twenty years ago. The continental Western Europeans, and possibly the French above all, have certainly led the way with very precise and delicate nymph and dry-fly presentations on rivers, coupled with incredible attention paid to take detection, while the British and Irish have dominated the stillwater area of the sport, most notably with the beautiful loch-style approach. All in all, the wealth of opportunities now for method selection across the whole range of the single-handed fly-rod sport is overwhelming, and even the most experienced fly fishers have to specialize to a certain extent.

Fly Fishing to Range in Saltwater

The following contribution is from my long-time friend Chris Ogborne. Chris and I shared a few loch-style internationals and World Championships for the England team, and knew a time when attitudes in our sport were rather different. Chris is undoubtedly one of the all-time great fly-fishing competitors England has ever produced, and for many years captained the World Championship squad. He is known for his light line approach and imitative fly-fishing styles. In latter years, however, he has concentrated on saltwater fly fishing in his beloved Cornwall, and is undoubtedly the most appropriate person to give us advice on this area of the sport. Chris is also a consultant to the world-renowned Hardy/Greys company. I asked him to concentrate on the ideas of fishing to appropriate range in this contribution, knowing how important this idea is in freshwater fly fishing in all disciplines. The result is this classic piece, which just has me itching to take a six-weight out on to the southern beaches.

When giving advice about our sport I used to say that it was much better to present a fly properly at fifteen yards than to land it badly at twenty-five. But I also used to say that the farther the fly lands from the point of disturbance, namely the angler, the better. With saltwater flyfishing both these yardsticks remain true, but with a whole load of other considerations as well.

Until someone finds a way of stocking our shoreline, saltwater fly fishing is all about wild fish. Nowadays I spend all my time fishing for wild fish as I've had more than my fill of stockies. I hasten to add that there's nothing wrong with a stocked fish. Rather, it's just that after a lifetime of fishing, if it isn't wild and preferably straight out of the Atlantic then I don't really want to catch it! The only exception to this are the fabulous wild brownies in the moorland streams of Devon and Cornwall – but that's another story.

And the key word here is 'wild'. Anything you catch around the shores of Britain, or indeed anywhere else in the world, is going to be a wild fish. The principal sport fish for me is the sea bass, a truly great fish among fishes and one that takes a long time to grow. A bass of 2lb can take five years or more to reach that weight, and they don't get to five years old without learning a thing or two. All the natural predators (as well as the unnatural ones that are man-made) make for a fish that is wary in the extreme – arguably the ultimate challenge for the true fly fisher.

This rather lengthy preamble is meant to stress one thing: saltwater fly fishing demands very close attention to every aspect of the sport: watercraft, an understanding of the aquatic environment, stealth, attention to detail and ultimately presentation. If you don't get it right, and very particularly the bit about presentation, you can hear the fish laughing.

First Principles

For a variety of reasons you need to forget – or at least bury for a while – most of your river-fishing disciplines. With river fishing you normally have a fair degree of choice in determining the range at which you fish. You can wade with stealth, adjust your position on the bank, or vary the angles by moving above or below the fish's location. If you make a mess of things then you can wait half an hour for the fish to start rising again, as most game fish are conveniently territorial.

Chris Ogborne changing flies in a session on the beach. (Courtesy Hardy/Greys)

Not so in saltwater. Consider a typical scenario: you're on the beach and ideally out on the sandbars. The spring tide is running at around 3 to 4 knots and the fish are swimming in with the tide, probably doing another 3 to 4 knots on their own. This means that your target is swimming past you at around 8 to 10 miles per hour, give or take. At this speed you get one chance, or at most two. You need to cover the fish by laying an ambush several metres in front of its path, pull on the line to straighten the leader, and then get ready to give life to the fly at just the right moment. Crucially, you can't do this if you're overextending yourself and fishing at maximum range all the time.

So for me, the ideal mean range for saltwater is 20m (65ft). This puts you far enough away so as not to disturb the fish whilst casting, yet close enough for accuracy and good presentation.

John Wolstenholme double hauling with an eight-weight into the surf. (Courtesy Hardy/Greys)

Casting Range

One word sums up saltwater fly fishing – unpredictability. In a reservoir bank situation you can generally expect to be casting 20–30m (65–98ft), most of the time. On a big river you know that big casts will be needed, whilst on the little moorland streams of Cornwall I'm surprised if I ever need to go beyond 5m (16ft). It's all relatively predictable and you gear your tackle and approach accordingly.

But not on the beach: whilst a typical cast is metres, there are still times when you'll need to extend to maximum range for that solitary big bass, just as there will be occasions when you frantically strip back all the line to cover the mullet that suddenly appears at your feet. Exciting, yes, but totally unpredictable.

As ever it's compromise. I gear everything to twenty metres, but try to be flexible enough to cover the extremes as well. As we'll see later in the tackle section, the six-weight line is my first choice and probably the best all-rounder, but if the surf's up and the wind is keening in from the Atlantic then compromises have to be made.

Visuals

All over the world, the one element that makes saltwater fly fishing so exciting is that it's visual.

At its best, you get the chance to spot and cast to the individual fish.

Apart from times when sport is dour and you're prospecting with sinking lines off the rocks or the drop-offs, most of the best sport is on the beach. My absolute favourite scenario is to locate the sandbars at the bottom of the tide and fish the beach as the fish come in. The relatively shallow water means that you can see the shapes of the fish, and they are especially visible when they 'ride' the waves. Grey mullet seem to love doing this, and nothing gets the adrenalin pumping like seeing upwards of thirty mullet hurtling towards you like shadowy grey torpedoes in the building wave.

Bass are often just as easy to spot, although I have a distinct preference for a bright sunny day to make things easier. I've lost count of the number of times a client has said to me 'There's two fish over there', and I have to (tactfully) point out that actually it's one fish and his shadow on the sandy bottom!

The school bass are great for providing visual sport, but the real challenge comes from the larger fish, which tend to become solitary after they reach 3lb or so. Here you have the chance to do some good old-fashioned stalking, and it can be fascinating to watch them forage around the rocks, probing for shrimps or small fish.

My own 'home' estuary, the Camel, is ideal for these tactics, but in truth most decent estuaries will provide similar opportunity. In Devon and Cornwall alone there are literally dozens of such places: the Exe at Exmouth, Salcombe, Hayle, Bantham – to name but a few.

Food

It's worth registering here that saltwater fish tend to be far more catholic in their taste than freshwater – the bass, for instance, will eat almost anything that moves. I once took a three-pounder for the BBQ and found the following in its stomach: crab, a small sand eel, small flat-fish, prawns and a baby pollack. And all this was fresh, eaten within an hour of the fish being caught!

Most of the game fish that I target on my home estuary are the same. Mackerel, gar and pollack will chase anything. The only (infuriat-ing) exception is the grey mullet, a hugely worthy sporting fish but one that defies most anglers' efforts at the fly-tying bench. Mullet are primarily vegetarians and eat weed. They will often be seen 'skimming' the water surface, literally eating the film. There are a few good flies for mullet that work occasionally, but I've yet to meet an honest man who reckons he's found a panacea or even a fly that works with any genuine regularity.

Watercraft and Locations

These two topics need to go hand in hand because of the way that most sport fish feed. Out on the beach and sandbars the bass love to chase the small sand eels – we call them 'boot-lace' sand eel as they're about that diameter and overall size. Indeed, ask any regular or commer-

Spotting and hooking bass at 15m (50ft) in hollows between the rollers. (Courtesy Hardy/Greys)

Juan Del Carmen (former England team guide) into a bass in the surf. (Courtesy Hardy/Greys)

cial fisherman and they will all agree that sand eel (particularly lance, the giant sand eel) is the top bait for bass. Fortunately they are relatively easy to imitate and so there are plenty of good artificial patterns around.

Instantly though, the question of range applies. Any artificial pattern must, of necessity, imitate the size of the natural. Therefore we're talking about fishing a fly at least 3in (7.6cm) long and often with a little weight to take it down a foot or so. If you like fishing two or more flies, which I do, then the problems are magnified. This is why 20m is my optimum range: any longer and turnover will suffer. Much longer, and presentation is totally compromised.

Apart from the sand eels, most other food items are not generally found in open water. Crabs, small fish, prawns and shrimps all prefer some sort of cover, usually the kind of cover found around the rocky shoreline. One of my basic yardsticks is to look for rocks with plenty of weed on them, particularly the kelp banks that get exposed on the lower end of the tide. A rocky promontory higher up the beach with good drop-off may look enticing, but if there

isn't any weed on the rocks you're probably wasting your time.

Depth

The ethos of this book is about finding a way of improving presentation and thereby improving the catch rate. I firmly believe that depth is every bit as important as range in this respect.

Out on the beach and sandbars, I use a floating line for 90 per cent of my fishing. Even with a heavily weighted fly, I doubt that I'm ever fishing at a depth of more than 4ft (1.2m). The flow of the tide, the need for speed and constant casting and recasting to cover a fast-moving fish, all conspire to make for surface sport of the highest calibre.

It's also about belief. When you're standing in water barely a foot deep you simply have to convince yourself that this is a good depth. Bass will happily feed in this depth on an incoming tide, even if they tend to be a bit more wary on the ebb. The absolute ideal is to be standing in about 2ft (0.6m) of water with a reachable drop-off that lands the flies in 4ft – it doesn't get any better!

Free-swimming sea fish tend to look 'up' for their food. They also look 'up' because predators like gannets and seals come from this direction. It follows, then, that a floating line will achieve most of what we need in most situations.

The obvious exceptions are the faster drop-offs or when fishing over or around the rocks at slack water. Here you'll need a fast intermediate, preferably the clear variety.

Kit

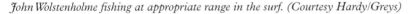

With such an enlightened angling public as we now have, you'd think there would be little room for myth and mystique any more, but you'd be wrong. It's a total myth that you need heavy gear and 9-weight lines for saltwater fly fishing, at least around the shores of Britain, and arguably in many of the more exotic destinations.

When clients talk to me about what gear they should bring to one of our beach days, they invariably assume that it will be 9-weight shooting heads, twenty-pound leader, and flies that carry half an ounce of lead in them. They also assume that sea fish are mysterious, hard to find and even harder to catch. Thankfully, the reality is somewhat different.

A long time ago I was responsible for pioneering what was then called 'the light line approach' on stillwaters. At a time when the whole reservoir world was using dog nobblers or some such, and shooting heads, I set out to prove that you could catch a lot more fish, win competitions and, most importantly, *have a lot more fun* by using light lines tactics. Respect for the quarry was the very real bonus that accrued from such an approach.

John Wolstenholme fishing at appropriate range in the surf. (Courtesy Hardy/Greys)

Exactly the same is now true on saltwater. My default choice for a day on boat or beach is a 9ft rod for 6-weight line. If the school bass are in and the ocean is quiet, then I'll happily drop to a 9ft 5-weight outfit, whereas if it's late evening, prospecting from rocks or drop-offs, or if there's a big surf and rougher weather, then I might upgrade to a 9ft 6in 7-weight, but rarely more. Even when we're out on the boat and using big flies for pollack, there is little that cannot be achieved with the latter.

Although there are many rods and reels made specifically for the salt, and undeniably they are triumphs of engineering if they can cope with the corrosive effects of long-term exposure to sea water, the reality is that *any* fly rod and reel is capable of doing the job. If, like me, you're sea fishing day in and day out, then I'd certainly recommend a dedicated saltwater outfit, particularly a reel that's able to sustain the treatment;

but for holiday use or occasional visits your normal stillwater gear is just fine. Rinse everything thoroughly in freshwater afterwards, and all will be well.

Leader choice is an area where it's possible to overcook things. Bass are very, very wary and there are many occasions when they will react negatively to heavy leaders, particularly on calm days in very shallow water. Equally, in big surf or heavy water, or simply when the fish are in a good mood, you can take liberties to the extent where you feel they wouldn't mind a metal trace! The middle ground is common sense: don't use tiny flies on heavy leaders because they won't 'swim'. The reverse is unnecessary as well, as a big fly on an overly light leader looks all wrong in the water. My own choice is for 2X or 3X fluorocarbon for probably 80 per cent of the time.

The power of bass among breaking waves. (Courtesy Hardy/Greys)

Extreme fly fishing. (Courtesy Hardy/Greys)

Boat or Beach?

Having the use of a boat is an undoubted bonus, not just for the fishing but for getting to your chosen spot. Many of the 'marks', as they are called – that is, known bass-catching places often passed down over generations – are not easily accessible, and whilst you may not actually fish from the boat, it's very useful to get into coves or hidden beaches that are inaccessible from the land.

I enjoy boat fishing on occasions, but by far my first choice is to fish the beach. Wet wading gives you an amazing sense of freedom, and of course you're right in there with the fish, right in the essence of the angling environment. Waders are OK in early season or if the water's really cold, but come May I'm always wet wading, for the sheer pleasure of it. No bags or clutter to weigh me down, as all the tackle I need is on my neck lanyard: spare leader on a dispenser, snips, forceps and a small fly box. This gives the free-

dom to roam at will, and rarely are the feet in the same place for two casts. My favourite beach is over two miles long, and that's a lot of fishing on a big spring tide.

Range is relative in saltwater, just as it is in fresh. When a novice arrives at Rutland Water it's easy to become daunted by the size of the place. Three thousand acres feel vast, and the tendency is to overcompensate by casting as far as you can out into the distance. It's very much the same on saltwater – you feel you're not really trying unless you're casting thirty metres. But that's the psychological hurdle that needs to be crossed. Just by analysing the environment you can cut down on the variables and turn a five-mile-wide estuary into a small intimate fishery just for yourself. The rules are surprisingly similar to stillwaters:

- Which way is the wind blowing? Where is all the food being pushed, and will you be able to cast into the teeth of it if necessary?

The author stalking on island water, Eden.

- What's the state of the tide? Is it a big spring one with all the latent power, or are we on the neap tides where everything is slower?
- Where are the rocks? Specifically, where are the rocks and weed banks that provide genuine cover for the food items? How much *time* will I have on the rocks, before the rising tide calls for a retreat?
- Where are the drop-offs? You can see the deep water 'blues' just by looking at the colour of the water.
- Where are the gulls feeding? Lots of screeching and diving means only one thing – bait fish in the water!
- Is anything moving? Sea fish can 'rise' as they feed on the surface, and some species (mullet for example) spend much of their time on top.

All of this brings an area of many thousands of acres of water down to a small, often compact little area. No longer is there a need to over-extend the casting arm – instead, that fifteen-metre range looks just right for the conditions!

You're fishing within your capabilities, relaxed and with more confidence. And because of that, you're fishing *properly*!

Chris has eloquently described here one of the fly-fishing frontiers for us, which brings me back to the methods that we have developed, and how they are developing further. Tactical fly fishing will always show us the frontier in our sport. We have described this evolutionary process through the development of methods in all single-handed fly-rod disciplines, and we should be comforted by the knowledge that it will never remain in stasis. In another decade we will have moved on, with tackle, with methods, and with tactical ability. We will further explore, for example, the ultra-sensitive long leader and indicator leader approaches with micro nymphs. I would be surprised if we did not probably develop novel new fly-fishing methods, though I suspect they will be extrapolations of the established methods described here. We will be more extreme, with destination, with method, with technique. This is what I mean when I describe fly fishing on the frontier.

6 CASTING

The purpose of this chapter is not to teach high level fly-casting ability, or any casting at all. This is not possible in text, at least beyond the basics. I should refer the reader, however, to the series of brilliant articles on the subject by my friend Charles Jardine in the magazine *Fly Fishing and Fly Tying*. This series, well worth digging out of the archive, uses text and diagrams to achieve its purpose, as well as this medium allows. Another very good source of casting information is the relevant section of *Fish & Fly*, the online journal, including the forum section. There are several good online resources for this area, and I would certainly include Paul Arden's *Sexyloops* site to those seeking a higher performance with any particular casting issue.

There is no substitute, however, for going to a qualified casting teacher, and I strongly recom-mend that anyone in Britain wishing to develop their casting could do no better than contact a Game Angling Instructors Association member in their area (it is a national network). Again, GAIA can be found online.

I intend here to identify the type of casting necessary in various situations, and to point out the common faults that prevent fly fishers from achieving their potential. While long-range cast-ing should often be used either for fulfilling sporting needs, or as a last resort in practical fishing situations, there is always a need for *tactical* casting presentation. To this end, I stress the need for tactical wading (or bankside stance) and for appropriate use of the floating platform (boat or tube), which is at least as important as the casting itself, mostly because of reducing the range to one's target.

The single greatest feature that defines an advanced fly fisher is his or her casting. Conversely, it is a lack of casting ability, more

John Tyzack, exhibition casting.

Stuart Minnikin, an APGAI level caster.

than any other single factor, which tends to hold people back from developing in this sport. In all guiding and general fishing situations, one always observes casting, and it is this that most frequently lets anglers down and significantly reduces their catch potential. A professional guide or instructor usually has a very tough job of it, particularly with more experienced anglers (and most especially older men). To fault someone's casting ability can easily be perceived as a personal attack. The 'hunter male', with all his instinctive skills, prowess and competitiveness, is only very slightly beneath the veneer of modern man. One has to be very tactful. It is always best to be able to start at the beginning, to work on the basics and to build casting with no faults, through a very long period of practice. The reality is that such a situation is extremely rare, and really means working with children, or adults completely new to the sport, or those who can be utterly honest about their abilities with themselves and with you.

Casting Qualifications and Coaching

It is not without very good reason that casting is such a crucial element of the courses of the Game Angling Instructors Association for the attainment of qualification for the certificate level (GAIAC), and even more so for the advanced level, APGAI. These have even been referred to as 'casting' qualifications. The certification awarded by the American-based Fly Fishing Federation, FFF, is presented categorically as a casting qualification. In practice, the GAIA and the FFF awards are standards indicating that one has been trained to these defined levels; in reality they are teaching or coaching qualifications, and casting is justifiably dominant within them.

I unhesitatingly point fly fishers, from beginner through to advanced level, towards an appropriate coach in order to help them with their specific needs, which we all have. The process of learning techniques, particularly in casting, is so much faster when taught by an expert in that category. Within the CEFF we are at the start of a coaching and training development initiative, a large part of which involves casting technique. In the England team we have for several years now concentrated on one-to-one and master-class sessions to improve individual performance with any particular approach. We have had Paul Davidson educate us in the finer points of the astonishing braid nymph method, which requires a rather novel casting technique more akin to bait casting than to conventional fly casting. John Tyzack has demonstrated the finest quality of upstream 6 to 10m (20 to 30ft) range presentation. Stuart Crofts has made us all much more aware of 'beat preparation', maximizing the potential of a particular beat, in part by incorporating suitable presentation throughout the various micro-niches of the water, and the use of short, furled leaders for super-delicate dry fly presentation. It has been a tremendous, shared experience for us and has drummed home to all of us the need for a highly attuned ability to read the water and to adapt one's casting and presentation accordingly. None of us could have done it alone: we needed each other. We need coaches to lift us to advanced level in any particular discipline in our chosen sport.

Choosing the Appropriate Tackle

Casting is our means of delivering the fly to the target. Discipline, accuracy, range finding, and adjusting accordingly to the prevalent conditions are all features that we must build into our casting for it to be of consistently high standard.

In this regard it is no different to hunting with any other type of weapon. A fly rod and fly line, married to our own physical abilities, provide us with a sublimely elegant skill, one worth the effort to master simply because of its aesthetics, and crucial if an advanced level of fly fishing is to be attained.

First, some important points that need to be appreciated: a good fly rod will not make a poor caster any better; it will, however, perform consistently well for a good caster. It will enable better general casting, and also for any particular purpose for which it might have been designed. A poor fly rod is hugely damaging to the development of casting skills, although a good caster will be able to get by with it, knowing how to compensate for its faults. Fly rods should not strictly be considered independently: what is important is the rod and line combination (including the leader) as a casting and presentation system.

Expensive, high performance rods are not necessarily the best for any particular individual or situation. Many expensive rods are very light, and have a very fast action (we are not here considering bamboo rods), particularly in the 7 to 10ft length range. These rods are invariably not suited to beginners, and nor are they suited

Wojtek Gibinski, a San river guide, double hauling with streamer.

in many instances to several advanced techniques. We are all, to varying extents, seduced by marketing, heavily biased towards 'label' and fashion. Armed with a Hardy or a Sage, an Orvis or a Loomis, we feel good with these beautiful, top label rods – but the harsh reality is, if we don't know how to use them, or if we have the wrong tool for the particular purpose intended, then their specific design functionality will destroy our fishing, and their wonderful aesthetics and labels will not save that. Think about being on a river, fishing upstream dry at 6 to 10m (20 to 30ft) with size 20 flies and 0.11mm tippet, but using a modern Sage (6-weight) designed for medium- to long-range distance casting. Only a very good caster and fisherman will make this work reasonably well, and quite apart from producing good presentation casting, avoiding a break on a taking fish would really test ability!

And think about the reverse case – taking a rod suitable for the dry fly fishing described above (probably an 8ft 6in 4-weight with mid-flex) on to the lake shore where you are going to have to punch 30m (100ft) across a side wind, and maintain control over a team of flies on the retrieve through the waves... Apart from the casting skills, we require the rod and line for any particular purpose. I labour this point because experience has shown me that guests arriving on the river or lake for the first time frequently come armed with inappropriate tackle, which only slows their development towards advanced level.

Casting Categories

We can loosely group fly casts into roll-based casts and overhead (or more descriptively, to and fro) casts. There is enormous variety and hybridization within these two groups, such as the so-called 'presentation' casts. I suggest, however, that every single cast requires, ideally, perfect presentation, so it is justifiable to consider all casting covered by these two groups alone. The fundamental casting principles are common to every type of cast in both groups, although there are a few exceptional casts that break the pattern and require a slightly different fundamental approach, as explained later.

The Roll-Based Casts

Every advanced-level fly fisher utilizes roll casting. On rivers, an ability to execute all the roll casts, including the Speys, is absolutely essential, while on stillwaters it is highly desirable. In all casting, successful execution relies on the same principles: the weight of the fly line must load the spring of the rod, in whichever direction the rod tip is aimed. This weight can take the form of a static D-loop of line behind the rod, with an anchor of the fly-line tip and leader in the water to provide surface tension or drag, which loads the rod during the process of delivery.

This is the classic roll cast, with D-loop and anchor in a straight line with the target (all in the same direction) and the rod held high, ready to tap forwards as the cast is delivered. It is a very simple process (all casting is a process), and yet while it is essential to get right, it is the most commonly abused of all the casts! Indeed, the importance of the roll cast is frequently completely overlooked by many fly fishers who consider themselves to be at intermediate or advanced level, or at least experienced. Perhaps it is the simplicity of the roll cast that produces this nonchalance, with anglers trying to improve on casts which look more technically demanding, such as the double haul distance cast. This is a shame, because the most important cast to be able to perform well every time, and with all its variations, is the roll cast.

With the principles outlined above, the only other factors that need to be appreciated are that the fly line will always follow the rod tip, which in turn follows the thumb (in a thumb-up grip). A small movement along a straight-line path of the thumb produces a large arc of movement (the casting arc or power stroke) on the rod tip and a very long distance (and fast-travelling) movement of the fly line – in exactly the same direction. Or view it like this: a 25cm (10in) movement of the casting hand (or thumb) can produce a 3m (10ft) movement of the rod tip and a 10m (30ft) travel of the fly line.

In a static roll cast in still or nearly still air, the rod is held with a high rod tip just past the vertical behind the angler's casting shoulder. The D-loop is hanging between rod tip and anchor until the casting hand is accelerated, smoothly, to the forward stop point. The D-loop lifts up and follows the trajectory of the rod tip.

The Snap Roll

A slight variation of the roll cast, used a great deal when fishing upstream on a river (wet or dry fly), is the snap roll. This involves incomplete formation of a D-loop, or formation of only a small loop, and not necessarily behind the angler. It is almost a dynamic roll, a precursor to the jump roll or Spey. There is no backward movement, however, only a snap or tap forwards from a near-vertical stop point to a similarly high (about 45 degrees from horizontal) forward stop point. It is very rapid in its execution, and also has the effect of knocking spray off a dry fly with no need for false casting.

As with a conventional roll cast, the snap roll can be developed into a Spey or a combination (with overhead) cast. The snap roll is only different from the basic roll cast in that the distance of travel of the rod tip during cast execution (the casting stroke) is shorter, and the speed of the rod tip faster.

Common Faults with the Roll Cast

I will outline the common faults with the roll that ruin good casting. During guiding and coaching I do this all the time, concentrating for long periods until the roll cast is at least reasonable. It is this important for good fishing.

- Not forming a big enough D-loop (not waiting long enough for it to form) or sufficient anchor, will in both instances require too much power, and will result in an inefficient,

John Tyzack, composing a roll cast in flat calm on San.

noisy cast; although note the snap roll above, where a very rapid movement between stop points is necessary.

- Not observing the stop points – just beyond vertical in the loop formation stage and just above horizontal at the forward delivery stage – will also spoil the cast.

More positively, if all these components are right, and the angler remembers that the anchor and loop should be in a straight line with the target (or nearly so), then the roll cast becomes the simple, elegant process which it always should be. Moreover, performed well, a roll cast is the only cast that is necessary for several methods of fishing, including traditional loch-style (working a top dropper in the surface) from a drifting boat, and spider or nymph fishing at 6 to 10m (20 to 30ft) range across the wind or stream.

The roll will also be used to bring a sunk line and fly to the surface, while extending line at the start of other types of cast, such as an overhead. It is frequently the case that a roll-based cast is the only one possible because of bankside obstructions reducing the possibility of a clear back cast.

Casting should be an efficient process. We achieve efficiency by observing stop points and by casting in straight lines – that is, our casting hand moves in a straight line, as does the rod tip and fly line. Also, in a roll-based cast, we ideally have our D-loop and anchor in a straight line with the target. As soon as we err from these straight lines we lose casting efficiency. When we change the direction or angle of the cast, we have to create these straight lines in order to maximize efficiency. Roll casting in a river, or across the wind in a stillwater, necessitates these angle changes. The line and leader ends a drift downstream or downwind of the angler. We need to replace the cast across the stream or wind, usually by about 90 degrees.

Consider the diagram below.

The Spey Cast

We accomplish this angle change in two fundamental ways, though they are related. In both cases we have to set the loop behind us, and the anchor as near as possible in a straight line to our target. This requires manipulating the loop and anchor into place before forward delivery of the cast. This is most easily done with a Spey cast, or fastest with a snake roll. These casts are essentially dynamic roll casts, with changes of direction by up to about 100 degrees. The static D-loop of the conventional roll cast is replaced by a dynamic (moving) roughly D-shaped loop, thrown in the opposite direction to the anchor and the target, so ideally loading the rod in the direction of the final delivery.

In a downstream wind we can perform a double Spey or a snake roll safely, the fly-line loop and fly always being downstream or downwind of the angler, and therefore safe. When the wind is upstream, it is safer to employ the single Spey, which keeps the moving fly line and fly well away from the caster. The single Spey is a jump roll (a dynamic roll cast) with an angle change up to 100 degrees. These are all supremely elegant casts, and highly efficient, ideal for placing the fly at a range of 10m (single-handed fly rod). Without being able to

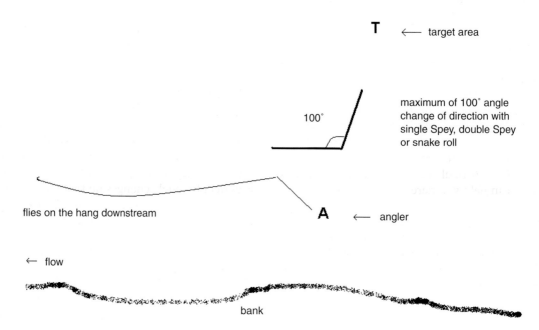

Changing the direction across the stream.

perform these casts, and hybrids of them to suit the various subtleties of conditions, situations and variety of angle changes, leaves the river fisher, in particular, wanting for presentation possibilities.

If there is one thing that defines advanced fly fishing in rivers, at least with nymph, spider and streamer, it is an ability to perform at the very least these casts. Streamer fishing in the surf (salt water), as well as fishing from the shores of lakes and reservoirs, also require ability with these dynamic roll casts, in combination with hauling techniques.

Hauling

All the roll-based casts can be improved by suitable 'haul' techniques with the line hand. Hauling increases line speed, which in turn increases line control (because of less time in the air for the wind to affect the fly line) and distance. Timing of the haul is crucial. It need only be a tap with the line hand, producing the acceleration required, though in strong winds it can be a sharp punch of the line in order to develop sufficient line speed. This is the so-called 'turbo-Spey', an accelerated Spey-style cast that is very useful in non-ideal wind or river conditions.

It can only be appreciated by demonstration and practice, but I urge every river fly fisher to develop, at least, an ability to haul on roll-based casts. One perceives the benefit of this only when faced with inclement winds, but imagine arriving at an expensive, or exclusive, river fly-fishing destination and not being able to present flies to the dream fish out there in the flow. Only an ability to haul, on both roll and overhead casts, can help you here.

The Snake Roll

The snake roll is a beautifully elegant cast that in most circumstances where it is applicable for angle changes supersedes the double Spey, mostly because it is much faster, taking less than half the time than an equivalent Spey. I do not suggest that the double Spey is obsolete, however, because for one thing it is a very good cast for teaching change of direction presenta-

Snake roll on San: John Tyzack.

tion casting, and its slow speed of execution also suits a lot of anglers better than the more demanding, rapid snake roll, an altogether more aggressive cast.

An adaptation of the snake roll, which I call an aerial snake roll, is very useful for dry fly fishing. It is identical to the 'conventional' snake but does not involve anchoring the line before the forward delivery. This keeps the dry fly in the air, and because it is moving so fast the fly is also dried in the process. Because there is no anchor, however, there is also a loss of efficiency and to a degree control, so it is best employed for short-range fishing; but for 6 to 10m range it is perfect for angle changes up to 90 degrees in a single, snaking motion: supreme for rapid-fire across-stream dry fly technique.

To-and-Fro Casting

Apart from the 'bread-and-butter' roll cast, the basic overhead cast is probably the most abused of all the casts. We load the rod by casting to and fro, or back and forth: very simple mechanics and highly efficient, provided the basics are observed. We require a clear back or forward cast, and if these do not exist we have to adjust the cast accordingly, often simply by adopting a roll-based cast, or by changing the casting plane from (near) vertical towards horizontal.

As above, I will describe the problems or faults that spoil good overhead casting, rather than attempt to teach good technique through text and pictures. I will, however, describe how we use overhead and any other type of casting as a part of our tactical approach. We will start with the idealized situation of using a floating line on a stillwater in windless conditions, and extrapolate from there to more tactically demanding techniques and situations.

Floating Line on a Stillwater

With the line extended 10m (30ft) over the surface, and using a dry fly, or lightweight nymph close to the surface, the situation is simple. Ten metres of fly line will (if the designation is correct) more or less suitably load the fly rod for a back cast to be made. We can lift off, accelerate to the stop point, pause for the line to straighten behind, and then tap forwards to deliver the perfect cast.

The faults that usually spoil this simple delivery, however, are many, and include starting with the rod tip held too high, which results in not building up that nice, smooth acceleration, and leads to consequent jerkiness; not observing the correct stop points; and not firing the fly line along the correct paths, or trajectories. There is an awful lot going on in a fly cast, of any type, and the whole must be brought together in a fluid, efficient set of motions. If any of the variables are wrong, such as starting with the rod tip too high, the fault will echo through the entire cast, and compromise presentation.

Fly casters frequently aim too low, behind and in front. Remember what was said above about high stop points, and the fly line always following the path of the rod tip. If we stop the rod tip too low, the fly line's path will be too low. In this situation – which is enormously common

– the fly line will be too low on the back cast and will clip the bankside vegetation (or slap the water behind if we are wading or out in a boat), or will not achieve good turnover, even crashing into the surface on the forward cast; either way this will ruin presentation.

We have to think more in terms of casting 'along a curtain rail', or like a paintbrush sweeping back and forth across a ceiling – either way along a nearly flat, horizontal plane. The stop points are on this plane, and as such, we can shift this plane to convert the overhead cast into a side cast. The principles are identical; all we have shifted is the plane of the cast, up to 90 degrees. We do this to avoid overhead obstruction, such as tree branches, or to keep the fly line low to the ground or water to avoid spooking fish. We can also shift the plane of the cast during the actual casting process, in the 'Belgian style', but this has limited, specialist application.

Incorporating Hauls

To-and-fro casting is always under more control if hauls are incorporated, as in roll-based casting. Hauls increase line speed, giving greater distance; but their prime function is to yield control over the line. This is accomplished by increasing line speed, which means that the line will spend less time in the air, where it can be affected by the wind. Energy dissipation is also more efficient in fast-moving fly lines. All fly casting is about line control and is strongly influenced by subtle aspects of hauling. In either distance casting or accuracy casting, I always remember Charles Ritz's dictum, 'High speed, high line'. In fact it is even better to think in terms of high speed, and high stop and aim points.

The Side Cast

Slipping away from the overhead cast, we continue with to-and-fro casting, but shift the plane of the cast over either shoulder towards the horizontal, and achieve the side cast, either fore- or back-hand. We do this in order to avoid any overhead obstruction, or to keep the line

High speed, high line; high stop points; the author on a fast tail water.

low to the water to avoid scaring fish. Also, in strong side winds it is much safer to side cast, downwind of the body, over either shoulder, keeping the line and fly downwind of face and body.

The principles of the side cast are identical to the overhead to-and-fro. It is a matter of shifting the plane from vertical to horizontal and preventing the fly-line tip or fly ticking the surface or bank-side foliage. Hauls are nearly always necessary to build up sufficient line speed. Also, side casting often requires an open stance, with one foot or the other (or knee in the kneeling position) leading and pointing towards the target.

Angle Changes

Angle changes are necessary no matter what discipline of fly fishing is being employed. At the end of a drift or retrieve, we need to lift the fly line and fly from one place and to present not only at a different range, but at a different angle, sometimes between each and every cast. The most significant points about this (with either roll-based or to-and-fro casts) are that ideally you must finish with a body stance more or less facing the target, and it is important that at the commencement of the forward delivery the rod tip moves in the direction of the target, in a straight-line trajectory.

To achieve this almost automatically, it is nearly always advisable to lift off in a straight line with the target (with a line up to 10m (30ft) out of the rod tip), which leaves the rod tip in the perfect place for the commencement of the forward power stroke. Extreme care, however, should be exercised when doing this if the back cast might bring the fly line and fly directly over or into the face. Always have a sense of the effect of the wind on the line in flight.

Considerations on Stance

I have introduced stance here, and this is something that is often not considered adequately. Classical casting teaching involved the use of the closed stance and very restricted body and leg movement. This is fine for short-range casting from a standing position in calm weather. Throw in a variable or two, such as a side wind into the rod arm, and altering or opening the stance becomes crucial for both safety and casting efficiency. Never hesitate to turn your back to the wind, and cast with the line downwind of your body. This will often require an open stance. Double hauling and the achievement of extreme distance absolutely necessitates open stance, as well as significant upper body movement.

Presentation Casts

The so-called presentation casts (notwithstanding what I wrote at the beginning of this chapter) involve delivering a cast such that compensation is built in to allow for surface drift or other specific conditions of the water and air space in front of the caster. The reach, mend and curve casts are all part of the same family, and all involve placing an upstream or downstream mend in a line on the forward delivery. This is accomplished by tapping the rod tip left or right during a line shoot; an early tap places the mend towards the fly, whereas a late tap places it towards the rod tip.

Multiple mends, as in the wiggle cast, can afford a long, drag-free drift in complicated currents or fairly strong side winds. The wiggle is also one of the slack-line casts which present a lot of slack line (not immediately influencing the fly as drift sets in). The parachute cast, involving a high stop point and a very late follow-through, is another example. These are most useful for downstream presentations, or in strong surface currents with floating lines on lakes, or with any line in a cross current on the beach.

The Stun Cast

A variation of these casts is one I call the stun cast, or drag back (because these terms describe it well). You cast as if for a parachute, stopping the rod high – typically at eleven on the clock face – but don't follow through. The line collapses on to the surface, and there is a long, sweeping arc of fly line between the line tip on the surface and the rod tip. The dry fly (or nymph) begins its drift downstream while the angler lowers the rod tip in pace with the flow rate, such that contact is just about maintained with the fly.

The distinct advantage of the stun cast over more conventional slack-line casts is that contact with the fly is maintained throughout, such that when a fish takes, a very small movement of the rod tip sets the hook, unlike the very large stroke necessary when absorbing a lot of slack line. When using very long leaders, as with a downstream presentation with micro dry flies

in clear water, it pays to use this stun cast, but drag the fly line and leader back a bit, with the rod tip reached back behind the angler, leaving it there until fly and leader begin their passage downstream. This significantly lengthens the drift distance of each cast, and is manifestly a very useful presentation when stealth fishing on shallow, broad freestone rivers, such as the Eastern European giants.

Constant Tension or Switch Cast

A hugely underrated cast for short-range fishing in rivers (up to 10m (30ft)) is what is referred to as a constant tension cast or switch cast. For the river nymph fisher it is probably the most useful change-of-direction cast of all, switching the position of the fly from downstream to upstream by up to 180 degrees and in a single fluid motion or casting stroke. The diagram shows this motion, and also the path of the flies during the drift. Important things to remember in the execution of this cast are to load the rod sufficiently at the beginning of the cast, as in a single Spey cast, by lifting gradually and bringing the flies to the surface, and then accelerating all the way to a high stop point upstream, towards a point in the air above your target.

Braid Nymphing

There has been some development in recent years with a technique generally known as braid nymphing, which involves the use of little or no fly line, and usually a section of non-stretch braid between the rod and the leader. Sometimes the braid is used all the way to the fly reel, though this is rather uncomfortable in the fingers. Because there is no fly line involved, the casts are highly unconventional and have little in common with other fly casts. They have much more in common with bait casting, because while we are using the spring of the rod (as with all casting), we are loading it not with fly line, but with the weight of the fly or flies. A heavy, semi-sacrificial nymph is used on point, or on a dropper, with imitative nymphs in other positions on the leader.

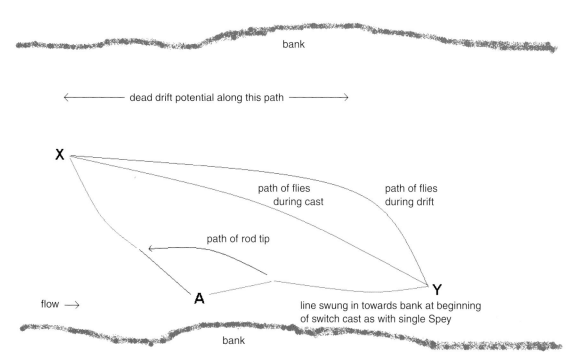

The constant tension, or switch cast.

The technique has closest parallels with touch legering (or rolled legering) with bait and is certainly very sensitive, with a line in very tight contact with the nymphs. The method has some application to smoothly bedded gravel or stony rivers, with few obstructions. There is a school of thought that claims the method has nothing to do with fly fishing. Whatever, we have to adapt our casting technique considerably in the reality of numerous situations in the course of a fishing session, perhaps more so on freestone rivers than anywhere else. Braid nymphing and the bait-fishing cast, with a sweeping change of direction, the rod loaded by the weight of the nymphs, is but an extreme example of such adaptation.

Tactical Awareness

All casts can be hybridized and adapted to varying degrees to suit particular situations. In prac-tice it is usual that we adapt to a certain extent from the ideal, because we are not always stand-ing on a nice gravel bed facing a nice even flow, or calm stillwater, with few obstructions within casting range. In reality there are rocks and rushing waters, weedbeds and interestingly placed trees, and fish on the edge of kick lanes or beneath the overhanging foliage on the far bank. We adapt, using whatever stance and cast is most appropriate in a tactical sense.

We are considering advanced presentation and advanced casting skills here, and in this con-text I just want to stress the need for minimum disturbance casting. Chris Ogborne always gave this advice concerning stillwater casting: 'It is always better to cast fifteen yards with good presentation than twenty-five which ends in a heap.' Good turnover and gentle presentation are always crucial, and, nearly always, this means the angler should relax more, and put less effort into the cast, relying more on timing and allowing the rod and line to do the work.

It also means selecting the appropriate cast, or hybrid cast, for the purpose. One should not, for example, choose a double Spey when repositioning a dry fly across and up the stream (from a downstream position); to do so would both drown the dry fly and splash the surface, thus disturbing fish within the target range during the anchoring phase of the process. Similarly, if one is nymphing across the stream, particularly with fairly heavy nymphs, and needing to reposition in an up and across direction, selection of the obvious single Spey (in an upstream wind)

would not only be potentially dangerous, but would certainly result in disturbance, again while planting that anchor.

In the first example an aerial snake roll would usually be the better cast, even combined into an overhead, while in the second situation a switch cast would almost certainly result in better repositioning as well as minimal disturbance.

Appropriate casting, presentation, minimal disturbance, fishing to range, choosing the angle: it is all a matter of tactical awareness.

Paul Davidson leaning into a big grayling on the Tweed. Note the soft-action Greys Missionary rod used for braid nymph technique, and for all tactile nymph fishing.

Casting master Charles Jardine with a Greys through-action rod, tactically using the reeds as cover on a stillwater.

7 READING WATERS

This chapter concerns what is always referred to as watercraft. Some think of it as witchcraft. Every fisherman, even the beginner, looks out over a stretch of water and searches for fish: it is impossible for a fisherman to walk over a bridge and not stop and peer into the waters, searching and hoping for a glimpse of fish, hovering in the flow. This is at the root of the fishing/hunting spirit. If we can see rising fish, or fish nymph-feeding in clear water, say, then our analysis is simple and fish location trivial.

Usually, however, we cannot see fish on a river or lake unless they are rising to surface food forms, so instead we look for features, imagining ourselves into the multi-dimensional depths, working out from any information we can glean where fish may lurk. This is where an ability to read the signs, read waters, comes in; this is the essence of the fly fisher's watercraft.

Analytical Considerations

Consideration of the local environment of river, lake or sea shore is always the first step towards successful fly fishing. It is such a common requirement of every fly-fishing situation that we usually undertake the process subliminally, constantly adjusting as the situation and conditions dictate, along with the behaviour of the target fish. Taking the time to analyse a stretch of water at the start of a session is always worthwhile and will never be wasted time, even on water well known to the fisherman. It is always tempting to get fishing as fast as possible, but when we realize that the analysis phase usually leads to a much improved tactical approach to a

session, and to far better results, it tempers the urgency of making the first casts.

A river, with its complex array of non-laminar flows set up by every bend and feature, can often seem daunting because of the huge amount of information that we have to analyse in order to determine where the fish might be, or might feed. Conversely, the expanse of a large lake might seem featureless except by the shore, and is daunting only because of its comparative large size. This is a matter of scale.

In practice, rivers with any character, or non-uniformity, about them are always easier to read, because the features within a river's flow inform us where fish might hold station. Anglers quickly learn to recognize the more obvious features, such as bankside boulders or outcrops that disturb the flow, or rocks and islands, sills

A technically demanding water: the Rio Pas competition sector, European Championship, 2008.

and weedbeds out in the main river. What are less obvious are the scoops and channels caused by variations in the bedrock, or turns in the river which produce shingling or silting, or undercut banks.

Finally, the most information is usually obtained by watching the flow itself, observing where the foam and feed lanes are concentrated, the seams between different flow rates, the little kicks on the surface that tell us of generally larger boulders or obstructions amidst the river bed substrate.

Foam Lanes

Drifts of bubbles and foam offer us an excellent indication of where fish might be, or rather the invertebrates on which the fish feed. They are formed immediately downstream of a disturbed piece of water, particularly broken water on a rapid, and then are concentrated in water of fairly even flow rate. They might persist for the entire length of a pool or glide, from neck to tail. In a feeble flow, such as in drought conditions, they often broaden and disperse. On a fairly narrow river, such as the upper (trout and grayling) reaches of most British streams (up to 40m (130ft) in width), there might be only one foam lane between one bank and the other. On a broad European river (up to 150m (500ft))

such as the San (Poland) or Sava (Slovenia), or a Scandinavian immensity such as the Largen (Norway), there might be several complex currents in any short stretch, producing a multitude of foam lanes across the flow.

The foam lanes indicate where food forms might be trapped and carried, while numerous fish species such as trout and grayling are almost certain to be close to or within them, maximizing the opportunity for feeding, while also benefiting from the surface cover afforded by the turbulence and foam.

We watch the current, or rather for changes in it. Perfectly even, or laminar, flow is rare in a natural river, and might exist over very short stretches of even-depth gravel, at most. Any feature that disrupts the flow, even a few larger-than-average rocks on the river bed, will produce a degree of turbulence: non-laminar or uneven flow. This is always betrayed by the surface. Also, the shallowing and disruption of the bankside affords a greater drag on the water than out in mid-river, and this itself produces turbulence and, often, a seam effect, which is

Searching for foam lanes on a broad Eastern European river; permanent and transient features must be hunted down on big waters.

RIGHT: Intensely demanding water: broad and relatively devoid of obvious features such as islands; trout, grayling and chub might be anywhere. This is typical of wilderness waters throughout Europe and the northern United States with well spread fish populations.

BELOW: Reading large lakes: also intensely demanding, particularly away from the shore; Bohinj, beneath Triglav, Slovenia.

Reading small lakes: intimate, full of character and feature; a tarn in the Howgill Fells.

the junction between columns of water moving at different rates downstream.

Add to this the numerous features that exist on every upland river or tail water in the world, usually in startling variety, then the possibilities for uneven flow are countless. The river fly fisher watches for all the permutations, learning about the types of water flow that are likely to hold fish or afford the best presentation for his flies, pooling all experiences such that recognition of fish-holding water gradually improves and the analysis phases of a fishing session are simplified and shortened.

To read waters is not an easy skill, but it is an important one for the fly fisher to acquire. Interpreting all the micro-signals from the water's surface, and still more, being able to see into the water where the fish are, or where they hide, requires constant practice and ultimately many more fly-fishing sessions than most people can afford. On lakes it is both far more difficult and on a different scale – it is almost a *different* skill.

Invisible Currents

Only along the bank of a lake, within 30 or perhaps 40m (100 or 130ft) of the lake's shore, can we exercise significantly meaningful water-reading skills, at least in the first instance. Once afloat in a boat or float tube, we can begin to engage the larger expanse of the water, locally.

On the lake we are usually dependent on the wind, particularly its direction. Fish behaviour is strongly influenced by wind direction. Lakes are rarely particularly still, even though they are referred to as 'still' waters in order to differentiate them from the running waters of streams and rivers, or 'gradient' waters.

Wind has a very profound effect on establishing currents on a lake, with rapid movements of surface waters and slower, bulk movement of deeper-lying layers: the larger the lake the more massive the currents. They have a powerful influence on the behaviour of invertebrate life forms and bait fish, as well as the transportation and mixing of water with its dissolved nutrients and oxygen.

Apart from the wind, light intensity and water temperature have a strong influence both on food forms and the target fish. Positioning of the thermocline, the junction between warm and cold water layers, is of great significance in hot weather, particularly for trout, which require cool water for comfortable metabolism, and even for feeding. On a large lake or reservoir during prolonged periods of hot weather, most trout will be at depths greater than 6m (20ft), where the water is coolest and oxygen concentrations are reasonable. Only the wind can make the surface bearable for them, by cooling it (particularly in the turbulence of a downwind shore) and increasing oxygen concentration. Here, too, waters of different temperature are mixed, and the deeper, upwind-moving currents carry cooler, oxygenated waters to the fish. Currents in a lake are therefore temporal, ever-changing according mostly to the wind direction and strength. The fly fisher needs to know what the weather has been in previous days, as well as to interpret the current weather, in order to analyse the current, local situation.

Light Intensity

Light intensity has an immediate effect on fish behaviour. This is often suggested to be caused by their lack of eyelids, but one feels this is only a minor factor. As with a mammalian eye, the fish's eye has a pupil which contracts and dilates according to light intensity. Water itself, along with suspended matter, provides a reasonable shield, particularly from UV light, even at half a metre (18in) depth. It is far more a matter of how light affects the food forms. Plankton such as daphnia, a hugely important food form for trout and numerous cyprinids, rises and falls in the water, *en masse*, very rapidly according to light intensity; thus in dull weather the daphnia clouds can be very close to the surface, whereas in bright conditions, the bulk of daphnia can be at depths of greater than 10m (30ft), which means away from all shallows except possibly a turbulent downwind shore. Many observers have suggested that bright sunlight *per se* will drive fish away from the surface, whereas this is only a minor contributor to fish location in the water column. It is much more likely that the higher temperatures associated with sunny conditions will influence fish to seek deeper, cooler water.

It is noticeable that in the spring and autumn, even in bright weather, fish can be highly active feeding or cruising in the lake shallows, or on the surface out over deep water. The sun angles are lower at this time of year, and the surface waters are cooler, and much more likely to be enriched with planktonic food forms. Nonetheless, light intensity is a factor that we account for when we are reading the waters, analysing for possibilities of fish-holding water, in river or lake (or even saltwater). The shielding effect of tree shadows or hillsides, or rafts of surface weed, all reduce light intensity, while also reducing the temperature. Indeed, in the early spring, when the water temperature is low, we often seek the warmest areas of shallows, which are warmed up more quickly by being exposed to sunlight, rather than being in shade. Fish are usually actively hunting in these areas, eager for the plethora of food forms in the warming spring waters.

As foam lanes and food drifts are so important for fish location in a river, so are the foam lanes and calm 'slicks' that form in a fair breeze on a lake. Formed by dynamic influences of water of different temperature, and consequently density, foam lanes usually trap higher concentrations of surface food forms than elsewhere in the bulk of a lake. Rainbow and brown trout are always to be found cruising the foam lanes, feeding among the trapped larder of invertebrates. The fly fisher in a drifting boat or float tube is best able to exploit the lanes, though the shore-bound angler can often benefit by reaching a foam lane, often formed close to a promontory or across a bay. In the absence of showing fish, the observant fly fisher can pick out the foam lanes and confidently expect to find trout hunting among them.

Signs of Fish

Visible fish at least simplify the problem of their location, but the behaviour of those fish strongly influences how we should approach them. The fact that we might see them rising does not mean they are necessarily taking dry fly, or anything actually off the surface, and even if they are, we still have to identify what, and how. The surface-feeding behaviour of trout on daphnia is remarkably similar to their feeding on mature midge pupae (chironomids), or even migrating snails. Fry-chasing activity is similar to their attacking sedge pupae on the point of ecdysis. There are numerous similarities, but there are always differences, and correct analysis leads efficiently to a suitable approach.

Gleaning information from rise forms is essential to the correct presentation of surface and near-surface flies. Only experience enables the fly fisher to differentiate between the rise to buzzers, or lake olives, or sedges; or the cruise feeding – like baleen whales – adopted by trout with planktonic food forms or snails in the surface, in all the variety of conditions that confront us out there on a big lake. Yet more difficult, and requisite of long experience, is interpreting the signs or conditions that dominate the presentation of flies sub-surface, particularly at appreciable depth. From knowledge of the particular water (or similar waters from

Obvious signs and an exercise in GISS: phosphor dun on the calm flow.

memory), and interpretation of signs on the surface, the fly fisher needs to think into three-dimensional water space.

Analysis on a large lake can be hugely testing, and actually one of the great skills in watercraft and fly fishing more generally. Previous knowledge might shorten and ease the process, but special circumstances on the day can make all the difference. Wind direction and strength provide the best clues, and we are always interested in downwind shores, or waves piling up into bays or islands and across points. In particularly strong winds, when fishing along windward shores is dangerous or impossible, we search for calmer regions under the lee of the bank, where fish might be taking windfalls from the surrounding vegetation.

We must also remember that in strong winds from a constant direction deep-lying layers of water will be dragged up on to the shallows of the lee shore (from the direction the wind is blowing) and consequently mixed with the surface layers. This can have a profound effect on both invertebrates and fish. It all depends on temperature gradients in the lake in the weeks leading up to the strong winds and mixing conditions, so prior knowledge of recent weather can be essential in analysing fishing potential in various areas of the lake.

A large stillwater is multi-dimensional, and the hunter fly fisher has many variables to deal with in order to achieve consistent success. The dry fly fisher, or the river angler, or even the fly fisher on a small lake, has fewer variables to consider, or at least more information on a smaller scale with which to deal and make decisions. The very best lake fly fishermen in the world – and here we are talking about the British – achieve their success by being able to analyse large stillwaters. My loch-style England team-mate of years ago, Chris Howitt, owed his enormous success in this discipline to his consistent ability to analyse a particular area of a lake in terms of the potential it had for catchable fish. This is much more complex than it sounds, and actually a rare ability, and one that relied on many years of practice. This skill enabled Chris to engage an area of lake for the duration of a competition, while having the courage to ignore the rest. It won him internationals, including the coveted Brown Bowl, the highest individual award for a British loch-style competitor, on several occasions.

So how is it that experience, or anything else, allows us this heightened sense of watercraft? The easy answer is that it is the experience itself that makes us more sensitive to small signals, amplifying them. Signs of fish, or appropriate food forms, are sometimes enormously subtle, and more often we recognize situations as being similar to those in the recent or even distant past. We hear echoes. Perhaps we observe a few buzzer shucks in the waves and understand that there has been a hatch. We go further and register the wind direction, working out where the hatch took place, and where the adults will have drifted. We note the time of day, and work out when the next hatch will occur, reasoning that it will be in the same place as the last. We position ourselves in time and place to capitalize on this. Then again, we might be drifting the expanse of a large lake and takes are few and far between. It is a difficult day. We ease into a bay and a fish takes, but then nothing more. A few drifts later another fish takes.

We are constantly reading the signals, but wonder about what else is happening elsewhere on the lake. Fish are just starting to be accessible in this bay, but are they also beginning to

John Tyzack with grayling.

feed elsewhere, perhaps in larger shoals? The way they are taking, at what depth, and their frequency, will influence us. Chris Howitt was always brilliant at this. He could determine from only a few signals whether it was worth persisting in a certain location, or if it was time to move on and hunt elsewhere. Finally, it comes down to more than experience itself: it comes down to instinct, which is something that cannot be taught, only honed.

Fish on the surface, in river, lake or sea, give us our easiest signs, while visible fish below the surface in clear water also usually increase the odds in our favour. At least we have our targets. Nevertheless, the visible fish might not be feeding fish, or they might be extremely difficult fish to catch for a number of reasons, presenting us with a trap. Recognizing these, and avoiding the trap, is all part of the analysis phase of a fishing session. Summer grayling, for example, can be masters of springing this particular trap as they rise to nondescript tiny dry flies and emergers, or near-microscopic food forms in the surface film. I used to be caught out every time. Seeing

grayling rising relentlessly has a way of holding one's attention. You start by presenting usually successful dry flies, then scaling down into the sub-20 size region, then micro-nymphs held up on a greased leader – all to very little success excepting the usual suicidal trout in the vicinity, while the grayling continue to rise. This is hugely frustrating, but it is nearly always best to retreat as soon as possible and find fish elsewhere.

I remember my best ever lesson in this regard, when John Tyzack and I were partnering each other on the Welsh Dee in an England regional qualifier. We had both made reasonable catches when we discovered a large shoal of grayling feeding at the surface. John caught one almost immediately, while I rose a couple, but failed to hook them. It then became virtually impossible even to move a fish, while they continued to rise relentlessly. After fifteen minutes or so John said: 'We have to leave these fish; if we don't, we won't qualify.'

Reluctantly I agreed, and we moved off half a mile downstream. We found nothing like similar numbers of fish, but we proceeded to catch several more, and we both qualified in first and second place. This was a tactical move, based on experience and escaping the trap that visible (particularly rising) fish can lead us into while reading the signs on the water.

On other occasions, in clear waters such as the San in Poland, or Sava Bohinka and Baca in Slovenia, we have been entranced by big grayling and trout hovering in the depths. These have often been catchable fish, but there have also been fish that have been easier to target elsewhere, even if not so visible, or visible at all. Big fish will almost always be more challenging, even if more visible, often because of their depth.

Building Analytical Skills

Placing a fly at the correct depth is far from trivial. In Slovenia, for example, the rainbows were sometimes lying at depths of over 4m (13ft), though it looked more like 2m (7ft). In anything of a flow, presentation of a suitable fly (that is not too bulky because of heavy ballast), with reasonable indication of a take, is hugely demanding and requires exceptional skills in analysis of pace of current throughout the water column, positioning upstream of the cast delivery, and anticipation of currents all the way downstream to the target fish, as well as obstructions in the water course. Only with correct analysis, and then technical application, does it become possible, and an immensely satisfying element of tactical fly fishing.

While reading waters we observe all manner of niches and feed lanes, or currents in still-waters. We observe, or attempt to find a knowledge of the food forms, in the relevant season, and by experience and observation we see the interaction of food form, water conditions and target fish. The analytical mind takes in all these signs and indicators, assimilating them, along with the physical demands of the particular water space that is the focus of our attention. We also account for effects of light, temperature and weather, adjusting accordingly, and adapting this analysis even as we fish through a session. Building our analytical skills by experience, as well as the technical requirements, we become ever more tuned and able to employ the tactical aspects that bring the greatest rewards in our sport.

Working with the elements among the Norwegian enormity.

8 TACTICAL FLIES: TYING AND PRESENTATION

Right at the outset we should realize that there is no such thing as a panacea fly, in any situation. There is not even any one fly pattern that is the only one that will work. But there are very good fly patterns that can make a significant difference: they can make an ordinary fishing session into a spectacular one. Conversely, of course, a poor fly, or one that is inappropriate for a particular use, can severely and detrimentally affect success, even when presentation is good.

Flies do not have to be perfect. They need not be very good imitations of natural food forms, and sometimes they should not be imitations of anything at all, though there is something rather English perhaps, or something to do with the essence of the classical sport, that gives us a certain satisfaction when we are convinced that a fish has taken our imitation for an actual food form on which it is feeding. The great stillwater nymph fisherman, Arthur Cove, used to say: 'Any old bit of carpet wrapped around a hook will catch a trout; it's the presentation that matters.' He used to prove this to an extent, because he was a bit of a showman in the old days on the banks of Grafham.

The real truth is, however, that while presentation is the keystone in this sport, fly patterns and fly design do also matter. I will go so far as to say that while there is not one fly, or one presentation, that will work in any particular situation, there is always a fly and presentation in combination that will catch a fish, if that fish has not been spooked.

Very early in my own fly-fishing career I started tying my own flies. This was born of a necessity to do so, because almost at the start I discovered that most commercially available flies were not suitable. In many cases they lacked something, though I did not have the experience at the time to know exactly what this was. In those days my own tyings were mainly crude copies of traditional patterns, mostly wet flies, but I soon graduated to streamer patterns for reservoir rainbows and dressed-down salmon patterns, or sparse variants of traditional wet flies for sea trout, and nymphs and dry flies for lake trout.

My fishing was varied, and in consequence my flies were varied to suit the species and the range of waters that I fished, which was extensive. Also, I soon built in certain design features that improved the presentation of several patterns. I recall even back in the late 1970s building in lead split shot to the heads of fry-imitating lures, glued behind the hook eye, and

Cove-style Pheasant Tail Nymph, the classic stillwater nymph.

Sawyer-style Pheasant Tail Nymph, the classic river nymph.

painting these with eyeballs. They were very effective wherever I used them in rivers, estuaries and along the sea shore for trout and sea trout, and occasional salmon. This was not, I think, particularly because of the actual dressing, which generally imitated bait fish, or the painted-on eyes, but because they sank so rapidly to the feeding or cruising depth of the target fish when presented on a fairly long leader and floating line (Grafham influence). Though I did not see it then, I had in fact produced a crude tactical fly.

Arthur Cove did the same with several patterns, most famously with his variation of the Pheasant Tail Nymph (PTN), following in the tradition of another great nymph fisher, Frank Sawyer, who produced several flies for purpose, including another version of the Pheasant Tail Nymph as well as the Killer Bug and Bow-tie Buzzer, all of them tactical flies.

One thing that always struck me about several of my England team-mates was that they were as good at tying particular patterns of fly as they were at fishing them; the two skills go very much hand in hand. The same could be said of all the great teams on the World and European Cham-

pionship stage: the Czechs and Poles, the Italians and French; they are all master fly dressers. No matter what the discipline, all flies should have design features built into them that make them fit for particular purpose, and the imitation of natural food forms is only one of these features. Historically, tyers have concentrated on the imitative qualities of flies, simply because this is a feature that is so visual and obvious. I claim that there are other factors, such as the dynamic aspects, or the related ballasting or buoyancy features, which are at least as important as the attempted imitation of food forms.

Tactical Flies

I should say here that this chapter is not a manual on fly tying. It is, rather, a set of ideas that might encourage readers to explore key features of fly design, and the use of materials and hooks, such that the end result are flies better suited for purpose. These are tactical flies. A fly that has built into it dynamic features (buoyancy, streamlining, disturbance, weighting...) is a tactical fly. If further encouragement is required, I might add that I have found enormous personal success in this sport in large part due to my efforts at the fly vice, and I know several other fly anglers who could say the same, some of them even more so. I would be going too far, perhaps, to say that we have won internationals because of our work at fly design, but it is certain that success in this regard has at least in part been due to the role of fly tying.

I am a minimalist fly tyer, and have always disliked complicated patterns. In particular, fully dressed traditional salmon patterns have seemed strange to me, part of a fly-fishing world to which I do not belong. I can admire the tying techniques and the enormous skill tyers have in preparing these works of art, way beyond my skills at the vice, but they are not for me. Nor, here, are we talking about the simply stunning, highly imitative patterns tied by genius fly dressers such as Oliver Edwards. These flies are not usually what we consider to be actual 'fishing' flies: they are fabrications of extreme skill and are certainly fabulous imitations of natural food forms, but in most cases (except perhaps some of the dry patterns or nymphs) they are not the first choice to present to a target fish.

The reason for this, I suggest, is that in striving for imitative excellence, matters of ballasting and dynamics must take a secondary role, and frankly these factors must be built into tactical flies as primary features. In situations in which presentation is absolutely the most crucial component of a session, which is typical, then rather than fish a near-perfect imitation, it is better to consider the dynamic factors of a fly, and various trigger features. Perhaps it is possible to build in high imitative quality together with appropriate weighting, triggers and dynamic factors, but for the purposes of a tactical fly this is usually unnecessary.

GISS

Tactical flies, rather, fall into the category defined by what we refer to as 'General Impression of Size and Shape', or 'GISS', where it is far more important to build in a reasonable impression of key features of a food form than to strive for a high degree of imitation. We are not abandoning imitation here, merely setting a reasonable level for this factor that we find acceptable (because so do the target fish), while also incorporating other factors into a fly which make it ideal for purpose. Size and shape are important features, no question, and we might add to these colour (or hue and intensity), hardness, density, and various other features that affect not only the visually life-like qualities of the fly, but also how it will behave in the water. For most of us, after all, it is not how close a copy of a natural insect our fly is, but the features about it that allow it to be presented in a life-like way to the spot where the fish are actually feeding.

Materials

I use a lot of natural materials, probably more than synthetic. This has little to do with any misinformed (or even well informed) ideological or environmental ideas, but is mostly

Variety of fly-tying materials.

because the natural materials I employ in my fly tying have proven so effective for purpose. I would not want to be without both cock and hen pheasant tail, or rabbit, hare's mask or seal furs. Lambs' wool in various dyed colours is a wonderful dubbing material, while the coarse Pennine sheep's wool I find all over our Cumbrian fells produces the perfect 'leggy' effect that I want for numerous invertebrate imitations. Heron and peacock herls are also pretty essential to many of the flies I use, and both hen and genetic cock hackles in various colours and patterns.

Having said that, there are also some fabulous synthetic materials, most of which one can find as by-product or waste material, such as from packing. You can, for instance, develop stunning 'shell-back' or wing-case effects using old cassette tape or Quality Street toffee wrappers.

We are lucky nowadays to have such a wide range of fly-tying materials available that we can produce any effect we want, while many of these materials are free – there for the selecting from Christmas present wrappings to confectionary and crisp packets, to whatever the hunter/gatherer can find on a walk through the countryside.

But then again, I would often be lost without the services of my friend Pat Stevens, owner of the FlyTek fly-tying materials business, who so often has found for me the perfect material for

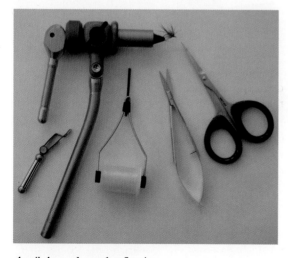

Anvil Apex, the perfect fly vice.

an effect I am seeking in a particular fly, quite apart from hooks and tools. Every dedicated fly tyer will need the services of a good materials supplier, because there are many items that are difficult or impossible to obtain elsewhere, and sometimes the free substitutes are just not as good as the 'real thing'.

Tools

First on the list of tools that you need is a good fly vice, ideally one with fine jaws and a rotary capability, with simple, reliable clamping. There are a lot to choose from. For the last five years I have used an Anvil Apex, an American design that does everything I want in a vice, is reasonably compact, and is supplied with both a pedestal base and a lightweight G-clamp for travelling purposes. It is slightly understated, and there are many others, but this is the one for me – I could not have designed one better for my personal use. Whatever you go for, make sure you are happy with it, because it is difficult to live with a fly vice, our most important tool, if there is anything about it that annoys you.

Other essential tools with which it is simply not worth compromising are bobbin holders and scissors. These are tools, after all, that will be used for any fly you tie, so top quality, which fits the user, is essential. For threads, fine ceramic tubes are essential, while for wires you can get away with steel tubular designs. A pair of scissors capable of dealing with lengths of skin or coarse fur is useful, as well as a fine-nosed pair. If the latter are the spring design, then so much the better – perfect for speed tying and fine work.

Beyond these, in terms of tools, only a good hackle pliers is (almost) essential. There are so many to choose from that it is a matter of experimentation to find the one that suits you best. I recommend a short-shanked rotary plier, with strong grips. What you don't want is an unreliable, weakly clasping plier that springs off the hackle tip too readily.

All other tools are optional, in practice, and you can survive as a fly dresser without them – certainly in fabricating tactical flies. There are a few, however, that are useful: a needle, a strip of Velcro (preferably glued to a flat wooden splint), a threader perhaps (though I very rarely use one), and even a whip-finish tool if you cannot master the finish with fingers alone (which I always recommend).

Essential Tying Techniques

There are only a few tying techniques that are important, but these few are absolutely crucial and should be mastered; they are:

- 'Yorkshire style', as Oliver Edwards calls it, using a minimum of thread that needs to be wasted (with practice this is absolutely zero).
- Winding with minimal length thread under controlled tension ('thread control', as stressed by élite fly dresser and teacher, Pat Stevens) at all stages until tying off.
- Ribbing, with graduated turns (narrow turns at the tail, broadening towards the head of the fly).
- Dubbing, particularly traditional 'laid on and turned' style, but also split thread (recommended) and/or dubbing loop (aesthetically lovely).
- Hackling, all types: head, false (or beard), palmer and parachute.

With hackling, also, as one gains experience, it becomes clear that appropriate choice of hackle, and even the way it is tied in, affects the final presentation and balance of the fly. A spider, for example, will be one thing with a partridge hackle tied in and wound from the hackle tip, and quite a different fly with the hackle tied in and wound from the stub.

Traditional winging technique with materials such as starling primaries or duck secondaries is not really important (though a beautiful technique to master) in tactical flies, but fluency of use with contemporary materials such as polypropylene and cul de canard (CDC) is vital.

With expertise in the above, and the additional dexterity to accomplish rapid whip finishes, there is little else that needs to be mastered, though many subtle aspects of fly dressing are gained with time, along with suitable materials. The application of a shell-back or wing case, with appropriate materials, calls for no extra dexterity or expertise, merely practice in combination with the fundamental tying techniques.

I should add a small caveat here concerning ballasting, or weighting. The beginner tends to overweight (and thereby add undue bulk) to a nymph or streamer, while also tying in too much low density material (and bulk again) to a buoyant fly. Experience trains us to weight appropriately, and we eventually learn just how much copper wire, or lead, or tungsten perhaps, to add to a particular fly in order to present that fly at the depth we want in any particular situation. There is a huge interest in buoyant patterns for stillwater and even saltwater use nowadays, such as poppers and particularly booby patterns. The latter can be ruined by having over-much foam in the buoyant region, completely overbalancing the fly. Big boobs? Only when conditions are very windy, thanks!

More subtly, with dry flies there is always the temptation to put in that extra bit of buoyancy, with CDC or polypropylene perhaps, or hackle, or tail; but this is almost always a mistake. Think of using the minimum of material for the effect you want, then take some away and go for it. You might then come close to a good tactical dry fly.

We should be familiar with the most common food forms of the fish we seek to catch; in fact the more familiar we are, the more easily one can apply the ideas of GISS so that we build in the appropriate features and trigger points to our flies. We do not have to be highly attuned entomologists, but familiarity and observation are the keys here. We do not need to be entrenched with detail and fine imitation, though it can be fun and satisfying, if little to do with tactical fly dressing. We are familiar with the prevalent food forms, with size, shape and colour, and we are knowledgeable about trigger features, and we build these into our flies appropriately.

Hook selection.

Hook Selection

While you might think that any fine wire hook will do for dry flies, or any heavier hook for nymphs, say, I will counter that this is not the case. I have spent too many days pursuing difficult fish, finally to have them rise to a fly only for the hook to let me down – and by too many days I mean hundreds, and quite honestly thousands of fish lost because of inadequacies in the hooks. Really, thousands! Most people would look at these flies, these hooks, and think they were suitable for the task, but very subtle features can mean that a hook is right for a particular purpose, or that it isn't.

It might be better to acquire the bargain pack of a thousand hooks in order to recycle the metal, rather than dress a thousand flies on them and risk that they repeatedly let down the user (and damage the fish). The bottom line is that you should always have in mind the fly (or streamer) that you want to create. The first consideration should be the appropriate hook for the job, in every case: if the hook is wrong,

the final fly cannot possibly be right. The tactical fly dresser therefore thinks in this order: GISS, hook, ballast, materials and construction.

A good illustration of the above point would be to consider the sort of hook that Arthur Cove employed when tying his version of the PTN. Initially Arthur wanted a sacrificial pattern, one that would sink quickly to the lake bed and even catch up in the silt or on the weed in order to allow the middle and top dropper flies to be presented properly in the mid-depths. At first, he didn't worry too much about what was dressed on the hook, but he was very concerned with the weight of the hook, and to a lesser extent its shape. He elected for the heavy wire Mustad Sealy sproat design, in a size eight, or even a six, for the purpose. We should bear in mind that Arthur did not like using lead, a dislike that he and I shared for many years; he wanted all the ballast in the fly to be in the hook itself.

'You don't need lead if you choose a proper hook and don't put too much material on it to stop it sinking,' he would say. I sometimes commented that I thought the hook was a bit big. Arthur's reply was more or less the same every time: 'Always use the biggest hook you can get away with; the hook is part of the fly, and the most important part, too!' He was right, of course, though I never really took to the idea of fishing the biggest hook possible, but rather went for the hook size, and weight, appropriate for purpose.

Nowadays we are lucky to have so many hook designs to choose from, for every conceivable purpose – far more than Arthur had when he was so actively pushing at the frontier of lake fly fishing for trout, back in the 1970s and 1980s. In fact our problem now is too much choice, because there are hooks available in most manufacturers' ranges suitable for most of the uses we will put them to. I will simply urge you not to be influenced overmuch by price: go for the

hook with the right shape and thickness of wire, and the point and eye designs that make it right for the type of fly pattern that will be dressed on it.

Ideally, use the shape of the hook in the fly itself, always remembering that a fish is never, certainly in my experience, worried one little bit about the pointy end of things. The hook point is part of the hook, just like the eye: so use it in the fly's design. It can be an attractive feature, a shuck of an ecloding midge, perhaps, or an appendage of a hatching sedge... Its purpose – our purpose – to hook the fish, has no possible meaning to the fish itself, so don't worry about it, and don't try to hide it. This is a fruitless avenue that preoccupies too many inexperienced fly tyers. Rather than list hooks here, I will give details of the hooks used in the context of each of the tactical flies described in this chapter.

The importance of hook selection and fly design – PTN variant with wild trout.

Speed Tying

I see a wonderful elegance in fly tying with speed and efficiency. Speed tying is a concept that dawned on me by watching and working with England team-mates over the years, particularly master fly fishers/fly tyers such as Stuart Crofts, Simon Robinson and John Tyzack. In some cases, you might appreciate, I have been more impressed by feats of fly tying than by actual fly fishing. Speed tying, very much a part of tying tactical flies, involves an optimum, efficient use of materials and tying techniques such that the craftsman constructs a pattern geared for specific purpose or for more general use, say in 'method' fishing. It is all done with speed so that a large number of flies are created, with minimal differences between them in terms of visual or weighting characteristics, as well as materials and hook types. Classical fly-tying techniques are honed or adapted to suit the patterns, with minimal use of tools, materials and changing between techniques. Much thought is given to this, and developmental work at the fly vice.

Speed tyers tend to be very good away from home in the sense that while the majority of their tying is at the bench at home, they have travel kits that are used to effect when travelling, when tying with efficiency and speed is a necessity, and always geared to the local situation. A travel kit should be minimalist to be most useful.

Speed tying is not a relatively new concept in the art: just look at Frank Sawyer's version of the PTN, which illustrates the idea very well. Here a classical nymph pattern has been adapted by a master fly fisher to suit a local situation. GISS has been applied, with the crucial simplification of materials to the extent that tying thread has

Pat Steven's impromptu fly-tying kit in the fishing lodge on the river bank.

been abandoned and the whole pattern has been executed using only two materials: fine copper wire (in place of the thread), and cock pheasant tail. This pattern is an outstanding example of speed tying, as is the Killer Bug, also from the Sawyer stable. I find the elegant simplicity of these patterns simply breathtaking.

Trigger Features

The idea that there are features of a fly that induce a fish to take has led us to try to build these points into a fly. There are many 'flies' today that rely on particular trigger features exclusively, rather than any imitative or dynamic quality. Many lure or streamer patterns would illustrate this, such as the infamous Blob or Booby patterns, or the slim-line glued buzzers, that have recently dominated the artificial 'put-and-take' stillwater sport in Britain. Trigger features are vital to an effective fly. If we had no trigger feature, why would a trout pick out our artificial from the thousands of naturals in a hatch of large dark olives, for instance?

There are numerous factors, often hugely subtle, in both fly architecture and presentation, which afford a fly its trigger features. There are also triggers we purposely build into our flies that have significant tactical implications. In most imitative flies it is very easy to overdo the trigger features, or to build in too many. Simplification, including the minimal, but purposeful, use of trigger points, is the way to go with imitative patterns, and to a certain extent also with what are termed 'attractor' patterns. Remember that it is very easy to overdo trigger points: if you build in too many, the result can be overkill, completely ruining the fly's effectiveness.

Threads

In most of the patterns described, as in all my tying, I recommend the use of ghost thread where appropriate, a fine, colourless, nylon monofilament fly-tying thread by the Italian producer, Benecchi. This is a wonderful mate-rial, perfect for speed tyers or for highly imitative fly dressers, for flies up to about a size 10. We use other threads in patterns for varnished buzzers, for which a thicker thread is much more useful, and in patterns for which a coloured thread is necessary, such as the water-hen bloa or Greenwell spider (primrose yellow); also for the special technique of split-thread dubbing.

Ghost thread is so fine that it can take a huge number of turns without applying any bulk to a fly, something which can ruin a fly that has otherwise been well dressed; one can therefore dress highly durable flies with no untoward bulk. This thread also takes indelible marker pen well, so that the tyer can colour appropriately, if necessary. It also takes most dubbing materials quite well (using the traditional lay-on and twist-dubbing technique), but can be hugely improved for this by a single application of cobbler's wax or beeswax, which makes it suitably tacky.

A good substitute for ghost thread, or a suitable material for building thread bodies, is a

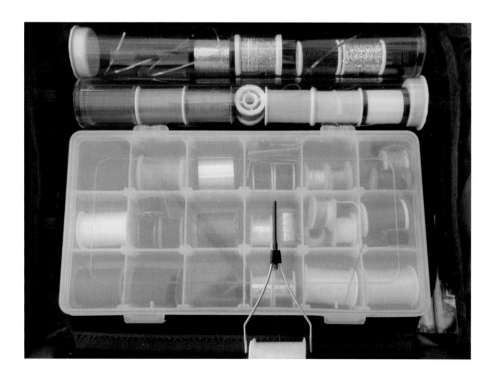

Threads and bobbins.

fine, spun thread such as that again produced by Benecchi, with a maximum thickness of 12/0 (traditional thread scale). Waxed UTC thread, manufactured in the USA, is another fine thread, unspun; it is also suitable for split thread dubbing.

Essential Patterns for Tactical Flies

I could write a whole book entirely on the subject of tactical flies and their presentation (and might do so one day); but what follows are the absolute essential patterns that I use from the stance of my tactical platform, gathered over the last forty years of fly-fishing experience, with a heavy bias towards grayling and trout species, and geared also to speed tying with its consummate efficiency and elegance. I claim very little originality. I have rather 'stood on the shoulders' of others and pooled ideas and techniques, always trying to simplify, always gearing towards creating patterns suited for purpose. I feel that I, and all others in truth, are merely nudging away at the frontier of this esoteric craft of fly tying. Also, I do not neatly differentiate patterns into those for stillwater or river use, or any other, but rather by their particular ranges of use, as should become clear.

In all the patterns listed I do not describe the basic architecture and tying procedure; these can, in any case, be gleaned from the photographs and descriptions. I do, however, give details of the hooks used for each pattern where relevant (because this is so important to their design and functionality), and give some specific dressing notes, where necessary. At each stage of dressing a fly, think of its parts and the overall visual and dynamic effects desired, such that the finished product is what was intended at the outset. And think of this: I must have tied several thousand Sawyer-style Pheasant Tail Nymph variants (for example) as described in this chapter, before I began to get every single one (well, most anyway) exactly as I wanted it. The flies made along the way, on the journey, however, were not wasted, even if they were cut

up and disassembled so as to get back to the hook starting point. Most of them taught me a little bit more about tactical fly fishing and the dressing of tactical flies – so even your mistakes are useful.

Lastly in this context, I would recommend that you avoid the rut of conforming to over-prescriptive fly tying. In most cases a slight or even a large variation from a fly recipe can actually be experimentally liberating. If a dressing calls for copper wire in a rib and you only have silver wire to hand, then go for it, with confidence. Think about the visual and dynamic effects each and all your materials will have on a fly.

I lean very much towards small copper (tungsten) beads for several fly patterns, because experience has led me towards the far greater effectiveness of these, over a broader range of conditions, compared with brass beads, say, which might have been employed in the original dressings.

You might also notice that the following list of flies does not include any nymphs in either the Czech style or Polish woven style. This is entirely intentional. Indeed, there are a lot of styles and a large number of specific patterns which I could add. I have used both the above styles a great deal, and continue to do so from time to time, but in nearly all cases, I use the nymphs described, since I regard them as tactically superior.

Let me clarify this, just to rationalize my selection. Given ideal 'seam' water (the interface between faster and slower pace water downstream of an obstruction such as a pool head) of between 0.5 and 1.5m (2 and 5ft) depth, I would actually like to have a Czech nymph set-up, probably three nymphs of appropriate ballasting according to their position on the leader, designed to fish the entire water column. In practice, however, I usually choose appropriate flies from the list below to perform exactly the same function. Now, come off that seam – that ideal water for the Czech nymph method – even a few metres, and a team of these nymphs becomes tactically less favourable,

Team competition selection of PTNs prepared for the European Championships in Spain.

whereas, say, a hare's fur bug on point, a Sawyer PTN in middle and a spider variant on top dropper, becomes significantly more versatile and effective.

Nymphs

Pheasant Tail Nymph variants are absolutely essential to my tactical fly approach. In almost any nymph-fishing situations on stillwater or river, we can cover needs with PTN variants. It amuses me a lot, because it amuses them so much, that my loch-style team-mates always comment about my trust in Cove-style pheasant tails. Even John Horsey glanced at me sideways a few years back and said, 'Surely you're not still using Coves!' Well I was, and I still am, because they still work. The trout have not changed,

after all (although this is arguable to an extent), and nor have the situations when we use the Cove variants.

Although there are probably just as excellent alternative patterns developed today, I still use Cove variant PTNs for slow nymphing methods on stillwaters, particularly from the bank, but also from a drifting boat if I can slow the retrieve down sufficiently (because buzzer-style flies, of which the Cove PTN is an example, need to be presented slowly). In those situations, in spring and summer, when you need to drop a fly deep, particularly on a long leader and floating fly line, a Cove PTN on point is unbeatable, in my view, at least when there are buzzers (chironomid pupae) active. I will go so far as to suggest that it is entirely possible to fish effectively with Cove PTNs, and its variants as below, to stillwater trout and certain other

127

species exclusively throughout the year in all nymph-fishing situations. I have actually done this on lakes as far apart as Britain and British Columbia: the Cove PTN has been supreme.

The Cove PTN and Variants

Hooks

For different visual effects and sink rates use Drennan Traditional Wet, size 8; Fulling Mill (FM) Competition Heavyweight, size 10; Fulling Mill Grub Heavyweight and Super Heavyweight, sizes 10 and 12; and Kamasan B160 sizes 8, 10, 12 and 14.

The Drennan and FM hooks above are heavy wire hooks of varying design. When Arthur Cove first showed me this pattern in the 1970s, he tied it on a heavy Mustad Sealy hook, which I never really liked, even though it was manifestly so effective. As soon as the Drennan Traditional Wet hook arrived on the scene I started using it for the Cove PTNs, dressed short on the shank. The FM Competition Heavyweight also gives a nice shape to this fly, and I like this hook for general PTN use, rather than just a heavy pattern for the point of a long leader. I also use the heavy curve shank design of the FM grub hooks, which sink even faster than the Drennan Traditional Wet and arguably give the fly a better shape (more like a chironomid pupa).

The Kamasan B160 is a lovely wide-gape, short-shank hook in a finer wire than any of the other hooks above. It yields a good shape to Cove PTN-type flies and makes them suitable for fishing on droppers, or higher in the water column than the heavyweight hooks mentioned here. This is the hook I recommend for the smaller Cove-style PTNs, fished high in the water, generally imitating the smaller midge pupae.

Materials

You will need a cock pheasant centre tail feather, as copper-coloured as possible for the standard patterns, while variously dyed feathers can be useful, particularly olive, orange and

Pheasant Tail Nymphs, size 16: TOP, black tungsten 2mm; MIDDLE, copper tungsten 2.3mm; BOTTOM, Sawyer-style on Knapek in-point.

claret (all of these will and should be dark, dyed on the unbleached feather). Only rarely have I honestly felt that there was some advantage in using dyed rather than the natural, well coloured pheasant tail, yet I never tire of attempting to build in a closer match to prevalent invertebrates, or colour triggers to most of the flies I use.

Rabbit fur is used in the thorax. Arthur Cove used to tell me to use mostly the lovely soft blue underfur, with just a few of the coarser guard hairs; nowadays I sometimes use hardly any guard hairs at all. Fine copper wire is used for the rib. Generally I use a fairly dark copper, but variously coloured wires can be used with good effect.

Tying Notes

The illustrations show the overall visual effect of several Cove PTN variants. In all cases note the sparse nature of the abdominal regions of the flies, with the ball-like effect of the slightly more bulky thoracic region. Also, for durability the copper wire rib is applied counter to the feather fibre – so if the feather strands are wound clockwise, the rib should be wound counter-clockwise. Apart from strengthening the fly against the ravages of trout's teeth, the ribbing (or segmentation) effect is more pronounced with this technique. For the heavyweight versions of this fly – for fishing deep and slow – rather than use any lead under the dressing, continue winding the rib in the thorax region, before the rabbit fur is dubbed in, producing a ball-like under-dressing of the wire. This is easier to do, and produces a denser body, with fine, tightly wound wire.

The fly is finished by taking the excess cock pheasant tail over the top of the thorax to form a wing-case effect. Note that this can be taken forwards, then backwards to be tied off so as to build up a more bulky wing-case effect, a possible trigger feature.

Cove PTN Variants

As with many nymphs, it is possible to abandon the use of tying thread entirely, and tie instead with fine copper wire. With the Cove PTN one can do this, dubbing the rabbit fur directly to a waxed length of the wire. The final product is a dense variant, with plenty of the copper wire glinting through the rabbit fur. Alternatively, one can abandon the use of dubbing fur entirely and simply build the thorax entirely with wire. The effect is particularly striking with the use of silver wire (steel), and this silver-thoraxed PTN is a very effective variant, particularly when fished within 1m (3ft) or so of the surface, where it glints in the same way as the natural buzzers starting the process of ecdysis (in which a shining layer of gas begins to disengage the emergers from their pupal shucks and also lifts them to the surface).

Another set of variations is achieved by employing different materials for the thorax.

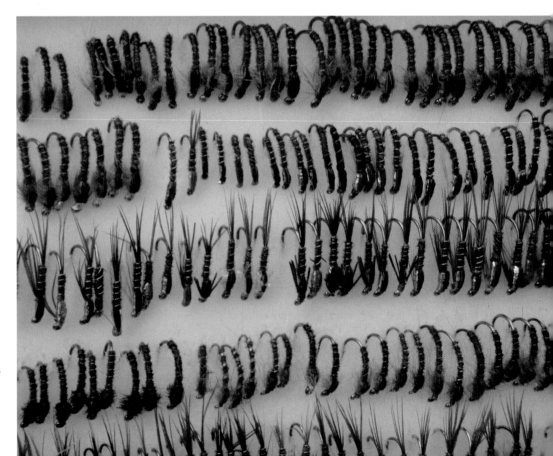

Selection of PTN variants, mostly for stillwater use.

Variously dyed seal, rabbit and hare furs yield a vast range of possibilities here. Seal fur gives a lovely translucence and the effect of invertebrate appendages, while also being stiff enough to retard the rate of fall of the fly through the water column (in the same way as sheep's wool or the guard hairs of rabbit or hare). This is a dynamic feature built into a fly for tactical purposes. The way any fly is presented to fish can be hugely affected by the choice and amount of any materials in its dressing.

Additional ballasting can be added using fine lead wire wrapped beneath the thorax, or – hugely popular now – using a tungsten bead threaded on the hook and set behind the eye. The visual and dynamic aspects of this pattern are altered considerably with the latter addition, and this has a significant tactical effect.

The Sawyer-Style PTN

This is another of the truly great patterns for both stillwater and river use, completely excelling in the latter. Without a doubt, for all nymph-fishing use, I would be completely lost without this pattern and its many variants. There are just two essential materials: cock pheasant tail and fine copper wire, with the optional use of tying thread. The illustrations show my style of dressing this pattern, which is not quite as Sawyer tied them. I try to exaggerate the thorax and wing case and – as with the Cove style – I often use dubbed rabbit fur in the thorax. This is easier when using tying thread (such as ghost thread) rather than wire.

Hooks

The outstanding Fulling Mill Competition Heavyweight or the Kamsan B175 are excellent for this pattern, but for river use I lean towards the Knapek B203 wet fly hook, barbless and in-pointed, on black, heavyweight steel. This is one of the best trout and grayling nymph hook designs of all time. The hooks are the perfect weight, with or without additional ballast, for a vast range of nymph designs, they are not over-springy, and have a superb, in-point design (on a fairly wide gape) that penetrates easily and makes for a hook-hold as secure as a barbed hook.

Dressing Notes

The general shape of this pattern and its variants is that of ephemerid nymphs, though I am quite sure the fly is taken for all manner of nymphs, including chironomids and damsels in stillwater. As such I tie in a tail of the cock pheasant fibres, winding with the rest to form the nymph abdomen, and counter-ribbing with copper wire. The stub of this feather is then used as a wing case and can be taken over the thorax once, twice or even three times to exaggerate this feature. The thorax itself can be bare windings of copper wire, cock pheasant, or dubbed materials including my personal favourite, the blue underfur of rabbit with a few guard hairs well picked out.

Variants

Variations of colour in the pheasant tail, and even using hen pheasant tail rather than cock, lead to a vast range of possibilities. I frequently use olive, pink, orange or claret-dyed cock pheasant, and also vary the thorax dubbing with variously dyed hare's mask fur.

A stunningly good variant for coloured or turbid water is achieved with tying the standard pattern (entirely with natural cock pheasant tail), but using fluorescent green or orange tying thread instead of ghost thread. Just enough of the tying thread shows through the dressing, and is exposed at the head, to provide a highly visible strike point or trigger. The addition of a very small shell-back effect over the wing case (or instead of the wing case) in pearl mylar is good, but noticeably not for spooky fish.

Absolutely the most useful variant of all, and probably my top tactical river nymph of all time, is achieved by the addition of a 2mm or 2.3mm tungsten bead at the head. Most people favour the gold-finished beads, though I prefer copper.

A Merging of Patterns

This is like coming around full circle. After so many years trapped in the school that so

Hare Fur Nymph variants.

strongly differentiates between river and lake fly patterns (and approach), it struck me that the flies really do not have to be that different. The GISS on a stillwater might lead us in a direction that is dominated by invertebrates not so common on rivers, such as several species of chironomid and damsel flies, while the river fisher will inevitably lean more towards the

ephemerids. The resultant differences in fly patterns will be obvious. And yet there are midges and damsel species in the rivers, and there are ephemerids in the lakes, and orders of invertebrates common to both environments, such as the hugely varied beetle and caddis species.

The Pheasant Tail Nymph in its Cove-style guise is very much focused on the buzzer GISS, while in Sawyer format it is oriented towards the olives; finally with very minor adaptations in dressing – mostly by adding a tail to the Sawyer, or taking the abdomen slightly around the bend of the hook in the case of the Cove – we have almost identical flies. In short, there is no reason why the Cove-style PTN should not be used on a river.

Hare Fur Nymphs

These flies are variants of the famous Gold-Ribbed Hare's Ear (GRHE), though in the contemporary form described here they are tactically superior for a broader range of use

Hare Fur Bugs, mostly for river use. Notice the Tup Wool Bugs.

than the classic fly. The consensus is that Hare Fur Nymphs are generally representative of caddis larvae and pupae, and probably gammarus shrimps, scuds and the like.

Hooks

Use either the failsafe Fulling Mill Competition Heavyweight (16–10), or the Tiemco 3761 SPBL (16–10), with its slightly longer shank than the former.

Tying Notes

A bunch of hare fur guard hairs, or red game makes a good tail, though there are several other materials worth experimenting with here – even fine strands of off-white polypropylene wool, which gives a lovely shuck-like appearance. The body needs to be gently tapered from tail to head, and counter ribbed for durability (and also to allow the ribbing to produce a more distinct segmentation effect). Fine gold mylar, pearl mylar, or gold or copper wire are used to rib.

Throat hackles are probably unnecessary, but a bunch of red game, as in the tail, looks good. Keep the whole fly sparse, in all sizes. The fur is best taken from the hare's mask, and generally I prefer the darker fur, with plenty of guard hairs with their appearance of invertebrate appendages. As with the Diawl Bach nymph (below), the addition of small jungle-cock cheeks can provide a wonderful strike point (trigger) to this pattern for aggressive, feeding trout.

Variants

The most significant variant is undoubtedly achieved by the use of a tungsten bead at the head. Most tyers go along the theme of the original GRHE and employ a gold bead; my own preference, however, is definitely towards copper (in 2mm and 2.4mm) and black (same

Winter grayling on a Tup Wool Bug.

size beads) for ultra-spooky fish. I seldom nowadays use gold or silver beads on any fly. The exceptions would be in coloured water or (contrarily) bright, sunny conditions when a small gold bead can provide a startlingly good trigger point. Also, for coloured or fast-flowing, turbid water, a small fluorescent bead can add an effective target feature to the head of the fly.

Tup Wool Bug
This is a version of the famous Killer Bug, by Sawyer, incorporating loosely dubbed sheep's wool in the perfect 'trigger' shade of pink – in fact similar to the pink found in the classic dry fly, the Tup's Indispensable. The pink is the crucial part here, apart from the density of the fly. For many years I dabbled with all shades and intensities of pink in flies for both trout and grayling, and particularly in bugs for winter grayling fishing; but I often felt that even if I had the colour right, the texture in the material was wrong.

I also frequently incorporate Pennine sheep's wool in various patterns; this wool is found all over our Cumbrian fells and elsewhere in Britain where sheep grazing is intense. I choose a mixture of lamb's wool and the coarser sheep's wool, blend them together and then dye in the colours I want. It was during experiments with dyeing that I hit on the colour I wanted – the orangey pink that was instantly recognizable as 'tup' pink. This colour is reproduced by mixing Hot Dylon Rose Pink to Veniard Hot Orange in a ratio of 9:1.

Hook
Fulling Mill Competition Heavyweight (sizes 14 and 12).

Tying Notes
Wind a fine lead wire underbody in a single layer from bend to eye, and cover it with a layer of fluorescent pink tying thread (this is one of the rare patterns for which I do not use ghost thread). A bunch of pearl mylar strands is tied in short at the tail, just a stub of material, while the wool should be fairly loosely dubbed on to fluo-

rescent pink tying thread and wound the whole length of the body. There is no rib. The wool can be brushed out a little with Velcro. The overall effect should by slightly carrot-shaped, while the fluorescent thread glows through the wool.

This is undoubtedly an intense fly, and while very effective for grayling, for which it was designed (as was Sawyer's Killer Bug), wild brown trout and rainbows love it! To be completely honest, I think this fly is often taken for a salmon egg.

Variants
I use only two variations of this fly, with and without a 2.4mm copper tungsten bead. The beaded version is used only in both sizes, on point or middle dropper, while the non-beaded variant is designed to fish higher in the water column, on middle or top dropper.

Diawl Bach Nymph
Another general nymph pattern, with perhaps a greater following for stillwater rather than river use. It might represent various invertebrates such as beetles and corixa, and olive, buzzer and damsel fly nymphs, and I feel it is also a good pin fry imitation. Whatever its likeness, it looks alive and is accepted static, on the drop or slowly 'nymphed'; I have also known it work stripped on sinking lines.

Tying Notes
I use either the failsafe Fulling Mill Competition Heavyweight (16–10) or the Tiemco 3761 SPBL (16–12) for this pattern. A bunch of fairly pale red game cock, or ginger, is good for the tail and false hackle, while a single strand of peacock herl, counter ribbed with fine copper wire, is adequate for the body, even on 12s and 10s. Go for a very slim effect. Alternative ribbing materials can be red copper wire, fine pearl mylar or fine red holographic mylar. A red or orange head provides a good trigger point. I know some people who love a fluorescent red head, but I do not, unless it is for use in particularly coloured water (though there are better flies for this).

Feral rainbow on Diawl Bach variant.

The addition of small jungle-cock cheeks or eyes adds greatly to this fly in early and mid trout season, though their efficacy falls away as the season wears on, when often a more subdued, subtler effect is more readily accepted.

Buzzers

This quintessential stillwater nymph pattern really justifies a huge section by itself – although I could say the same about other tactical flies such as the Pheasant Tail Nymph; so I will offer the following summary version. It is odd to think that such development as we have witnessed has taken place since the rudimentary buzzer pupae patterns of Frank Sawyer (the Bow-tie Buzzer) and Dr Bell of Blagdon. I am not suggesting that these historic patterns are obsolete, just that today we have more sophisticated patterns that work over a greater range of circumstances, yet there is very little fundamental difference between them all, historic and contemporary: they all represent pupae of the chironomid family. This is a very broad family,

ranging from the planktonic scale up to 2.5cm (1in) – the Grafham racehorses, as Arthur Cove used to call them.

There are two main types of buzzer I want to present here: the varnished pupae, and the slower sinking, unvarnished versions. The former are generally tied on fairly heavy wire hooks, such as the FM Competition Heavyweight or heavyweight grub hook, very sparsely, with thread bodies (abdomen and thorax), with various coloured materials as wing cases and/or wing buds; the whole is treated to several coats of varnish, either super glue, cellulose nitrate or even epoxy resin. The result is a very dense fly that sinks rapidly, particularly on thick fluorocarbon leaders, and allows presentation in a way not possible with any other type of dressing. The black version, with silver wire and an orange wing case, for example from a slip of crisp packet, is a great general variant, but there is a vast range of possibilities. The photograph shows several variations on this central theme.

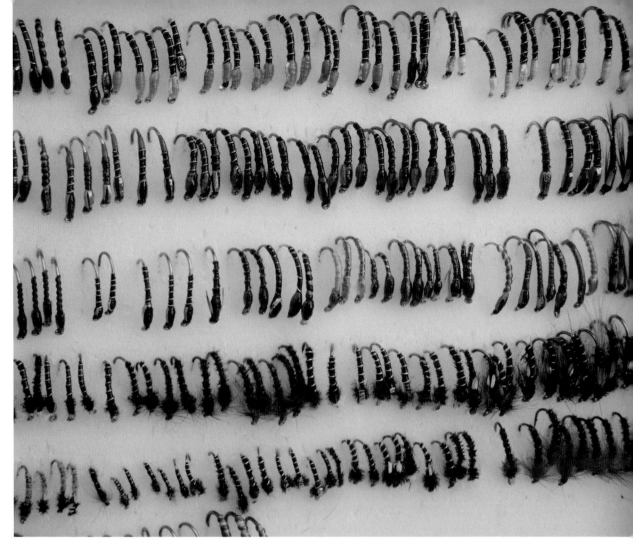

BELOW: *Buzzer teams: the upper fly is slow-sinking and is placed on top dropper; lower flies are on heavy wire hooks and placed on point.*

This is a great family of tactical patterns with a lot going for it: slimness, translucence, good GISS, good possibilities for presentation, good use of the hook as part of the design (in terms of shape), easy variation of colour, and simple target or trigger features (for example the wing case colour)... A word to the wise: do not become obsessed by building in too many trigger features to this pattern: these are very easily overdone. The coloured wing case is trigger enough beyond, of course, the general imitative shape, the segmentation effect and the translucence. Some tyers, however, like to put in a narrow collar of coloured thread (red is popular) between thorax and abdomen as a further trigger.

The second buzzer style of pattern to consider also has a vast range of possibilities on the basic theme. I believe these are generally

more useful than the former class of imitation because they have more presentation possibilities and are more suitable for a wider range of retrieve styles. The varnished buzzers, after all, certainly fish best on the drop, static, or with very slow retrieve (where they are supreme). The chief difference between the two styles is, of course, the lack of varnish in the second type, and the vast range of materials that can be used to bring out subtle imitative effects, trigger features and presentation possibilities.

The abdomen consists of tying thread or fine feather herl such as pheasant tail, or even a very fine dubbing material such as mole or lamb's fur. Another alternative is stripped peacock quill, which gives a lovely natural appearance. Rib is fine wire to bring out the segmentation effect. The thorax material can also be various materials such as feather fibres (peacock herl is a good standard), but coarse sheep's wool or seal's fur is excellent, producing a strong, 'leggy' effect. A ball of blue rabbit fur is also useful for this purpose, as in the Cove PTN.

Wing buds of goose biots or, ideally, tiny jungle-cock stubs produce a startling trigger feature, while a pearlescent material (such as pearl mylar) makes a good wing-case effect. Pearl mylar or holographic tinsel yields a very good impression of the trapped gas that is prevalent in ascending pupae as they prepare for ecdysis near the surface. This can be used as a rib, or in that wing case, or, even rather extremely, over-wrapping the entire abdominal region of the fly.

An enormous range of variety is possible, all meeting GISS criteria and trigger features, and all producing flies with tactical variety in terms of depth at which they will fish. The largest single influence on the latter will be the type of hook used and the material used in the thorax, with coarse sheep's wool or seal fur (which can be greased for semi-dry technique) giving the largest amount of drag to the sinking fly. For this style of dressing the buzzers, I most commonly use the range of hooks as for the Cove-style PTN, right down to size 20 for the micro midge imitations.

Spiders

The spider range of patterns represents a particular tying style, and beautifully incorporates the GISS idea in that the end result is a fly that is generally representative of nymphs, or pupae, in their final water-borne stage, lifting towards the surface and preparing, or undertaking, ecdysis. Spiders might also represent windblown or drowned duns. The spiders I use most frequently are the following, with subtle variations, because experience has shown me that these cover most requirements I find for this style of patterns on all the rivers and lakes I fish, throughout the world: black spider, partridge and orange, partridge and hare's mask, Greenwell spider, waterhen bloa.

In all these patterns I strongly recommend sizes 18 up to 14, with 16 being easily the most useful, unsurprisingly perhaps. I will not give specific dressings of these patterns, which are very well documented elsewhere, other than to suggest that sparseness of dressing is absolutely crucial, in my view. I would also strongly recommend the reader to look at Arthur Cove's account of the black spider (particularly in terms of the effect of different numbers of turns of hackle) in his great work, *My Way With Trout* (The Crowood Press).

Partridge and hare's mask spiders; compare the Tiemco in-point hook on the spider on the left, and the spiders dressed on FM Competition Heavyweight hooks, size 14.

Spider variants.

As with all flies, variation of materials and effect can, and should, be built into spiders for specific tactical purpose. A rib of fine pearl mylar instead of silver wire on a black spider, for instance, produces a distinctly different segmentation (and shuck-detachment) effect, while substitution of the black thread body for a dark claret dubbing such as seal fur (thus making a claret spider) transforms this pattern into something rather more urgent in terms of a trigger for aggressive trout.

When tampering with materials, however, the thoughtful tyer will be aware that the dynamics of the fly will also alter. Mylar is almost neutral density, while wire is significantly denser than water. A fly tied with the former will not sink as rapidly as one ribbed with wire. Similarly, a thread body, particularly if it is varnished, will allow a fly to sink more rapidly than a dubbed fur body, which has more drag through the water (and air). And another reminder: the choice of hook has a profound effect on any fly's dynamics, and thus its presentation.

Arthur Cove's standard dropper patterns were black spiders, and it is indicative of the man's hugely tactical mind that he altered the number of turns of hackle on his flies in order to give different dynamic features and thus affect where they fished in the water column.

Wet Flies

A list of tactical wet flies could easily be overwhelming, and it has been very difficult for me to rationalize it sufficiently, limiting the range so that it is a useful summary. The range of impressions and imitations that are covered by wet flies is truly immense, far more than any other fly type; thus a wet fly can be an immature invertebrate larva or a crustacean; it might be a nymph on the point of ecdysis, or a small fish of numerous species; it might be a windfall terrestrial or a mollusc. Then again it might represent nothing, and work simply by virtue of possessing trigger features that alert something in our target fish,

Palmers: Whickam and pink-tailed Whickam above; Soldier Palmers and Grenadier variants below.

inciting the need to investigate (with its mouth), or to feed or strike out of some predatory, aggressive or defensive instinct. Wet flies exist across the entire spectrum of the above, with an infinite gradation of variation. The spectrum might be loosely described as running from specifically to generally imitative, through to imitative/attractor combinations, to pure attractor.

As regards hooks, in all cases for wet flies I recommend either the Kamasan B175, or the Fulling Mill Scorpion Competition Heavyweight (these hooks are all made in the same factory, with slightly different finishes). The Knapek B203 barbless wet fly hook is also excellent for all these patterns.

Palmer-Style Patterns
These are generally imitative in that they tend to be most effective fairly high in the water or on the surface, giving the impression of either a wind-blown insect or a hatching fly on the point

of escape. The Soldier Palmer is supreme as such, and works very well greased so that it makes a lot of disturbance when drawn through the surface. It benefits from having a strong colour trigger, and this can be exaggerated by the addition (as in the traditional pattern) of a red wool tail. My own preference is for no tail, and I also like an orange/red or plain orange seal fur body, which converts this palmer into the famous Grenadier.

Also in this stable of palmer-hackled flies is the snatcher style of patterns incorporating a tapered, palmered hackle, wound slightly on to the bend of the hook and possessing that extraordinary trigger feature of small junglecock cheeks. As such, the Bibio Snatcher is my most outstanding variant, and is often on my team of wet flies (on middle or top) when there are buzzer pupae active near the surface of a stillwater.

The wingless Wickham (of Wickham's Fancy tradition) is another great, generally imitative, palmered pattern, with attractor features. This pattern in summer and autumn is an uncannily consistent performer in the middle dropper position of a wet fly team (or combined nymph/wet team). The gold body should glint strongly through the red game hackle, which should be fairly sparse – perhaps a maximum of four palmered turns on a size 12, and two turns on a 16. A small bunch of red game hackles in the tail adds a shuck-like appearance, while my all-time best variant is achieved by substituting the bunch of game hackles for a thin (don't overdo this) tail of fluorescent pink polypropylene wool, making the wonderful pink-tailed Wickham.

Tying Notes

The most important feature of these patterns is that palmered hackle, and this is affected by both the number of turns and the type of hackle used, whether cock or hen, stiff or soft. Remember that the stiffer the hackle and the greater the number of turns, the more buoyant

(or slower sinking) the fly will be. Soft hen hackles can be wonderfully mobile when sparse – hence their use in spider patterns – but when used in excess can easily convert a palmer into something resembling a bit of waterlogged carpet!

A very stiff cock hackle takes grease well and converts the palmer into a semi-dry pattern. Care should be taken with a stiff palmered hackle that the hook point is not shielded, or this will result in poor hook-ups. Trim the hackle if necessary to reveal the hook point.

In all cases, selection of an appropriately sized hackle is important – one too large for the hook simply looks out of balance. It is easy enough to judge by eye. However, fly-dressing perfectionists can take this a little too far; I often purposefully choose a hackle that is (to the perfectionist) too small for the hook and the overall dressing, simply because it gives me the effect I seek. Such flies will not win fly-tying competitions, but they are very often tactically superior in actual fishing.

Trout on Bibio Snatcher, the perfect palmer pattern for upland waters; Cow Green Wild Brown Trout Fishery, north Pennines.

Silver Invicta variants; a great standard pattern, easily varied as here, generally imitating a wide range of near-surface invertebrates as well as small fry.

Winged Generally Imitative Wets

The addition of a wing to a palmered (or spider) pattern significantly alters its appearance and its dynamics. Though traditionally the wing was added in order to imitate the actual wings of various insects, I do not believe that this really holds up in contemporary wet-fly fishing. Unless the fly is imitating a windfall or drowned insect, the actual insects in the water do not have wings in any case.

The wing is much more like any nymphal appendage or collection of appendages, or some other part of the nymph body, or perhaps the back of a fish fry. Some feather materials such as bronze mallard shoulder or the striking barred effect of teal duck, lend themselves to the latter impression. Top of my list in this category are the mallard and claret, with the famous Connemara black and silver Invicta

close behind. All three of these, with their variants, are generally imitative of a huge range of trout food forms, from buzzers and sedges to fish fry.

Dabbler-Style Patterns

These are hybrid wet-fly patterns, owing much to palmers and winged wets, as well as to Irish Bumbles, with generally imitative features. For me, a variant of the claret Dabbler is first choice, and usually on the top dropper position of a loch-style team. I like to 'chase' this pattern, with more attractor-style wets, nymphs or even a streamer on point, working the Dabbler close to and across the surface. It has been as successful for rainbows and brown trout as for sea trout.

My version of the claret Dabbler is tied on a size 12 or a 10 (for a big wave), has a wispy tail

Claret Dabbler; my own most favoured top dropper of a loch-style team of flies, combining the virtues of the traditional mallard and claret, and the more broken outline of palmer patterns, highly suggestive of hatching, or drowned flies at, or close to, the surface.

BELOW: *Dunkeld – the perfect attractor wet fly for all trout species and salmon. This pattern has caught me trout from all over the world. If I limited myself to just one attractor wet fly, this would be it.*

of bronze mallard or wood duck (six to ten strands) and a well picked-out (Velcro), dubbed body of claret seal fur. A palmered hackle of soft red game cock (or furnace or Greenwell) is ribbed with fine holographic red mylar or red copper wire. The head hackle (actually a cloak of feather fibres) is bronze mallard (or grouse) tied in like a traditional wet fly wing, but spread down the sides of the dressing as well as the top – that is, three-quarters of the way round the head of the fly. A small, varnished head of red mylar creates a good trigger feature.

Attractor-Style Patterns

Without a doubt the addition of pure attractors to a wet-fly team of flies, or sometimes a hybrid wet-fly/nymph team, can give a distinct performance advantage. Even if the attractor does not hook the fish, it can bring the more imitative flies on the team to the attention of fish. It is so common for brown trout and rainbows to follow an attractor over long distances, then turn away to take a nymph. There are countless attractors out there, including the infamous blob variants, but my all-time perfect fly for this function is a version of the Dunkeld.

I use this pattern in two sizes, always using either the Fulling Mill Competition Heavyweight or Knapek B203, in sizes 12 and 14. The main pattern is virtually the traditional, dressed-down salmon pattern, though I use a hot orange-dyed hen hackle palmered on the body, which is gold mylar, ribbed with fine gold wire. A further head hackle of the same material is added, either one or two turns, before the wing (rolled bronze mallard) is tied in, just longer than the hook. Jungle-cock cheeks really set off this pattern.

The variant I most use is different only in the tail. In the original Dunkeld, golden pheasant crest is used, which indeed gives a beautiful effect and is what I like for wild brown trout, but if this is substituted for a tail of chartreuse or lime-green fluorescent floss, the effect is dazzling and produces an outstanding rainbow trout pattern.

You can use this pattern at pace, from a nymphed retrieve all the way to a fast strip. Although I use it occasionally in appropriate circumstances for river rainbows, and sometimes browns, this startling fly is my first line of attack when I want to give lake trout a wake-up call.

Streamers/Lures

Fry Patterns

These are very well covered by the mink or rabbit-fur style of streamer. I use both, mostly natural, but sometimes dyed to suit the bait fish colours, and generally prefer just natural rabbit (which is a very good colour match for most bait fish species such as roach, bream, perch).

Tying Notes

A long shank, heavy wire hook is essential, such as the Kamasan B803 or the Tiemco 3671 SPBL size 10. Dressing is very simple and relies mostly on obtaining the right strip of rabbit fur – which includes the skin; this should be about 3 to 4mm thick. Tie in the body material first, which can simply be dubbed rabbit fur, but might include some pearlescent material such as glister, and some silver wire which will be the rib. At the head, dub in a little more rabbit fur or alternatively a hen hackle in dull orange or

Fry pattern with rabbit fur – in the Minkie style.

red (perfect for perch and roach fry imitations), before tying in the top of the rabbit strip. The strip is laid over the back of the fly and fastened down using the wire in wide, open turns, taking care not to catch in or flatten the fur (you have to tease the fur out of the way so that the wire bites down only on to the skin). There should be an appreciable length of the strip protruding from the tail.

If used on a floating line, this streamer benefits from a little weighting, and this can be incorporated via an underbody of a single layer of fine lead wire, super-glued to prevent slipping, or alternatively (or additionally) by applying a tungsten bead at the head. A word of caution: these patterns tend to fish more effectively (and certainly cast more easily) with only minimal weighting, such as the layer of fine lead.

In recent years, streamer fishing is becoming more popular in rivers in Britain. The main bait species here is the minnow, and a superb variant of the above pattern to achieve a good minnow imitation substitutes the rabbit fur with butter yellow dubbing fur, or the ginger fur from a hare pelt.

A black version of this streamer (using dyed black or natural black rabbit fur) is superb as a leech imitation. Many people do not realize that both lake and river trout feed on leeches.

Tadpole Style

I class this style of streamer under the 'tadpole' banner, simply because it has this general shape.

Tadpole variants (black and green; white and green). The path leading towards the ideal compromise streamer patterns has been long.

Feral rainbow on black and green tadpole; Wet Cel intermediate line with 9ft #5 Streamflex and Vision Koma reel.

I usually use the Fulling Mill Competition Heavyweight for this pattern, in both 10 and 12, though the Knapek heavy wet-fly in-points are also superb. The top colour combination is certainly the black and green, though one wonders if this is because it is used so much, and is bound therefore to catch so many trout. There is a tail of black marabou, with an abdominal region dubbed with the same material, and ribbed with silver wire. A black hen hackle (one to two turns) is tied in at this point, leaving sufficient room to finish with a light dubbing of fluorescent lime green SLF or similar. A strip of pearl mylar is taken over the dubbing.

The overall effect is similar to the Montana-style 'nymph' (which was originally designed to imitate a stone fly nymph), but with the lovely mobility of marabou. The fly is very versatile in terms of weighting, and I should add that with six to eight turns of fine or medium lead under the thorax region it is an outstanding searching pattern, having that inducing fall and rise in the water column, sinking quickly, head first, with the tail wafting behind, and then rising on the retrieve...

Other colour combinations that have been very successful include the above with a fluorescent pink thorax, and the white and green combination, as in the ubiquitous cat's whisker. Sunbust orange marabou in combination with a hot orange hen hackle and a fluorescent orange SLF dubbing at the head produce a startling combination, which has proved effective with steelhead and plankton-feeding rainbows.

Cat booby.

Black hopper booby; a great pattern fished on point of a washing-line rig on a 'nymphed' retrieve.

Buoyant Patterns

Through the 1990s, and continuing to this day, buoyant patterns have had a tremendous influence on the development of, particularly, the stillwater sport for trout (and to a lesser extent and in a different context, carp). From a starting point of semi-buoyant patterns such as the Muddler Minnow, which in its original form remains a very good surface 'disturbance' pattern, we have evolved to flies such as the 'booby', which have revolutionized our fishing. I still use Muddlers from time to time; in the autumn, when fry feeding is intense, I often put up a Muddler, densely tied with deer hair for good buoyancy. Just as people remark about the Cove PTN, so they are dismissive of the Muddler, but as a floating fry imitation, or as a stripped pattern to switch on surface-feeding rainbows, this pattern remains effective. This being said, there are other flies that have probably usurped the Muddler, in terms of design, function and effectiveness, most notably the ubiquitous booby and its many variants.

The washing-line technique incorporating a booby on point is remarkably effective for the presentation of nymphs. Sometimes the booby actually takes most of the fish, while at other times the nymphs score more heavily. There are countless booby variants out there nowadays, though I focus on just four. The cat's whisker, in white and green, is a remarkably consistent performer, though the black hopper-style booby is a pattern I use much more than the cat version with this technique, while another remarkably effective pattern has been the black marabou with red holographic body variant. For all these patterns I use the FM Competition Heavyweight in 10 down to 14.

In my experience, the classic mistake, particularly as the season matures, is to continue using boobies that are too large, while 12s and 14s become progressively more effective. Indeed, the best booby I have ever found is the silver Invicta variant, in a 14. This fly is dressed as a traditional silver Invicta wet fly, but instead of the wing of hen pheasant, a few tufts of white

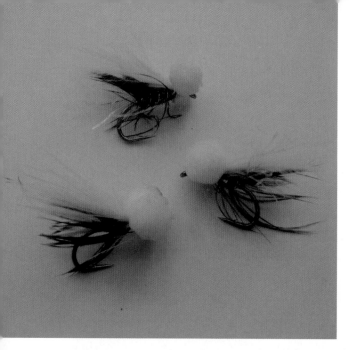

Silver Invicta or pin fry booby, my number one buoyant fry pattern.

tail. The V shape should be fairly open; this aids stability of the fly on the surface and helps prevent it keeling over.

Stuart ties these paraduns with either dark olive, light olive or buff-coloured fine SLF or similar (for example, hare's fur blends). The buff colour produces the ideal pale watery version, in 18 and 20, while the other two cover most other common ephemerid duns, such as blue winged, olive, olive upright and large dark olive. Probably the most useful general size in either the light olive or dark olive is a 16, though a 14 or even a 12 can be useful when any of the larger mayflies are about, such as the LDO.

Interestingly, I very seldom bother with specific imitations of the danica mayfly duns,

marabou are used, before the addition of the booby eyes. The booby in this guise has probably been my most successful washing-line rig pattern over recent years, with the black hopper version a close second.

Dry Flies

Paraduns in shades of olive are remarkable performers as imitations of both general and more specific ephemerid duns and spinners. My friend Stuart Minnikin, an APGAI level guide endorsed by the Hardy/Greys Academy, and one-time England river team member (2004), designed what for me is the perfect paradun for tactical use.

A delightfully simple pattern, it has proved its worth on rivers all over Europe. Its greatest feature is the way it sits down on the surface (something that is more easily attained with the parachute style of hackling) and has the ideal 'footprint'. A pale blue dun polypropylene is used for the wing post, and a similar shade of blue dun for the hackle. A few strands of this same hackle (good quality cock hackle, fairly stiff) are tied in the familiar 'V' format at the

ABOVE: Dark olive paradun; Stuart Minnikin version, tied by Fulling Mill.

BELOW: Pale watery paradun; Stuart Minnikin version, tied by Fulling Mill.

Brown trout on a pale olive paradun.

largely because on most of the rivers I fish the grayling completely ignore the adults, while the trout are seldom particularly preoccupied with them (on the other hand, there are lakes that I fish, such as Ullswater, where the wild trout certainly do get locked on to mayfly duns). I used to use a large Adams when targeting trout that were obviously tuned into the danica hatch, though nowadays I tend to use a large (14 or 12) light olive paradun. It is extraordinary how fish will pick this out, even among rafts of (larger) naturals. For the hook of the paradun I always use the FM all-purpose fine wire SPBL, offsetting them slightly in the fly vice, which improves their hooking capability.

Orange Polyprop

This polyprop is my number one tactical dry fly. It is a simply remarkable performer, having everything I demand of a dry pattern for a range of applications on river and even still-water. It has completely usurped the Klink-hamer (which I always found unsatisfactory except in 'bouncy' water), and even most Muller variants (which I have written about elsewhere, for example in *Fly Fishing & Fly Tying* maga-zine). I tie this pattern in 18 up to 12, with by far the most useful sizes being 16 and 14, again on the delightful FM all-purpose fine wire SPBL. Good alternatives to this hook are the Knapek HMD (dry fly design) and the Tiemco 902BL.

Trout on an orange polyprop.

All these hooks have in common a fairly long shank, which is necessary for this fly. Moreover, you will need to perform a small operation on the hook before tying the fly. Kink the hook shank by about 30 degrees, about one third of the way down the shank from the hook eye. This is very easy to do by gripping firmly with needle-nose pliers; the photograph shows the effect. The purpose is to allow greater stability of the fly on the surface, with the pattern sitting down nicely on its parachute hackle and creating a distinct footprint, while also projecting the hook point and bend below the surface – absolutely crucial for grayling.

I would not recommend the use of the (currently) commercially available Klinkhamer hook for this pattern (or any other); they are very poor performers, being short-pointed, too

long in the (curved) shank, and very springy, all of which results in poor hooking qualities and 'bouncing' fish on the take.

The abdomen is dubbed hare's mask fur (blended), with plenty of exposed guard hairs, ribbed with stretched pearl mylar (fine), or with no rib at all. Orange polypropylene is used as a wing post, tied in on the hook kink. The hackle is tied in, but not wound at this point, and the thorax (of the same material as the abdomen) is then dubbed and wound. The hackle is ideally a genetic cree, though grizzle is a reasonable substitute (I prefer a low-grade version of the latter, rather than a very well marked high-grade feather). Take as many turns as are necessary for the desired effect and use; this might be a single turn in an 18 for single dry-fly use on flat water, and up to eight turns on a 14 for lively water or for duo/trio use.

CDC upwing; note the use of Coq de Lion fibres in the tail, and mole fur on yellow thread for the body.

Size 20 CDC variants in F-Fly style; note the wave-bend hooks and the use of pink CDC.

CDC Variants

CDC has had a huge effect on our dry-fly fishing, for trout and grayling in particular. This feather allows the construction of highly imitative, suitably buoyant dry patterns, without the use of hackle in some cases. The three styles used, namely F-fly, upwing and shuttlecock, produce different effects via the different profiles. The F-wing has a 'flat over the back', rather sedge-like appearance, while the upwing is just that, typical of the ephemerid dun shape, while the shuttlecock is representative of all manner of emergers, including the chironomids or midges. The different CDC architectures therefore provide a whole range of imitative possibilities for surface-bound flies.

I invariably tie these variants on the Tiemco 103BL, though the shuttlecocks are ideal for the FM all-purpose light (as midge imitations). I also like the comparatively new Varivas curve-shanked 2210, right down to #24 for both the shuttlecock style, and also F-fly style for aphid imitations. The bodies of these flies are made of thread in a suitable colour, heron herl or cock pheasant tail (sometimes dyed), or fine hare fur (ideally from the ear), counter-ribbed if necessary for durability with ghost thread. I use single CDC plume tips for all flies up to 16/17, and double plume tips for 14/15. For the 12 I use double plume tips, plus some of the stalk fibres.

The photos show some of my most commonly used variants. For the larger shuttlecock style patterns I also dub in a tiny ball of CDC (from the stalk) at the thorax, which gives added buoyancy (in the right place) as well as a lovely 'leggy' effect. Pink CDC produces a hugely effective trigger in low light intensity conditions.

'Hopper-Style' Patterns

The strangely named 'hoppers' had a huge effect on stillwater dry-fly fishing throughout Britain and Europe in the 1990s. They are nothing to do with grasshoppers and the hopper patterns used in the US. Their imitative qualities lean rather towards the chironomids, and more particularly to windfall insects such as the hawthorn and heather flies and the crane flies ('daddy long legs'). For big winds on the lakes a size 10 is useful, though for all other conditions 12 and 14 cover one's needs. The FM all-purpose light is the ideal hook, slightly off-set (or kinked, as for the orange polyprop described above).

Dubbed seal fur or SLF, or hare's mask fur, make up the bulk of the fly, abdomen and

ABOVE: Rainbow on a pink hopper.

BELOW: The pink hopper, an outstanding stillwater dry pattern. Note how the Turle knot forces perfect 'in-line' presentation.

thorax, and this is ribbed with stretched pearl mylar (fine silver or gold mylar is often used by some tyers). Four knotted cock pheasant tail fibres are tied in to yield that crane fly-like appearance, and the head is finished with two or three turns of variously marked cock hackle. Red game is good (Rhode Island), while Greenwell, Furnace or ginger all give suitable colouring for specific requirements. I do not use genetic, stiff hackles for this pattern.

One needs buoyancy, but not excessively so. Gink or other non-viscous floatant, worked a little into the hackle, legs and dubbed fur, affords the ideal level of buoyancy of this pattern (on the fine wire hook). In any case, hoppers work very well while drowned, and even retrieved on sunk lines, although their primary tactical purpose is as all-round, generally imitative dry patterns.

The main variation is achieved by changing the body colour, and to a lesser extent the head hackle. Most of my successful colours are shown in the photographs. Note that the black version gives a very good hawthorn imitation.

In Conclusion

To finish this summary of tactical flies I will add that the collected patterns described here are the result of the past forty years of fly fishing, mostly for rainbow trout, brown trout, sea trout and grayling, for me heavily influenced by many others with whom I have fished or competed. I have, or have had, I don't know how many thousands of other patterns. The above are what I have with me for sessions on rivers and stillwaters, for the above species, anywhere in the world. I also, obviously, have more specific patterns for particular waters and fish species.

When out on a campaign, an international, the above (and many others) come with me, and it is similar with most of my team-mates. I always try to reduce the variables, and lock on to favoured patterns of the moment, based as always on a tactical approach. We derive a 'match' or 'competition' box, developed and tuned by the practice sessions and team briefings.

What you need out there in the hostility and loneliness of the sessions, is as simple a selection as you can get. What you do not want is to be staring at rows and columns of thousands of flies, because out there, this makes no sense at all and is entirely counterproductive.

What you need is to take control of the situation, and tactical flies are part of this control. You have to be both pragmatic and aggressive, and must think in terms firstly of presentation, and secondly of imitation.

9 TACTICAL STRATEGIES

This is my favourite chapter of this book because it expresses the essence of my approach. Almost everything in this sport for me, now, is based on the tactical aspects, and although it may not be everything I love about fly fishing, it is my driving passion in the sport. It has been drummed into me relentlessly in my many years of England team representation, and now I simply cannot get away from it. From the moment I scent and sight the water I feel myself excited, switched to a heightened state of awareness, analysing, and going tactical.

I have been quite 'effective' as a fly fisher, particularly for the various trout species and grayling, and no matter what attention I pay to the analytical and technical aspects – which are themselves hugely significant – my most relevant personal achievements (the ones that matter to me) are due to the way the tactical approach consumes me, and allows me to

engage in a fly-fishing session. I realize now that when I was a boy, my minor successes were largely due to a nascent tactical awareness, and this has actually intensified and become highly motivational as I grow older. Furthermore there are no signs of it diminishing, even though physical abilities are very much called into play, and it is inevitable, sadly, that there comes a time for all of us when we begin to lose the latter, and therefore also the tactical improvisation that lifts one's personal game.

When I look at all the truly outstanding performers in this sport, I recognize exactly what it is that does it for them. The intensity and concentration is in their every movement; they are tactically maximizing their potential. We say that the Czechs attack a river, and they are, without a doubt, the world masters of river fly fishing. 'Attack' is not an inappropriate word: as I say, you have to be aggressive.

Where you have to be tactical; European Championship, San river, Poland, 2005.

It is also a matter of temperament. Some people simply do not have the personality that allows a tactical approach, and in fly fishing they must exploit other aspects if they are to be personally successful. In competitive fly fishing, at international level, tactical ability and awareness are absolutely critical; but I suggest that one can reach an advanced level of ability in the non-competitive sport without it, or at least with only minimal tactical ability. In this case, however, analytical power and technical ability must be very highly developed.

Part of this is adjusting appropriately to the particular situation, working with the prevalent conditions. Beyond this is the need to think ahead, like the moves to follow in a chess game. Imagine you are at the beginning of a session on a freestone river (though the principles apply to a stillwater, or even the sea shore): you analyse the water, working out from the currents and weedbeds, rocks and overhangs, even the bankside vegetation and features – anything and everything that might indicate where trout might be located or feeding. The conditions of wind and waterflow, of light intensity and clarity of water, all lead you to choosing the right equipment and technical approach.

There are no fish showing on the surface, so you adopt a searching approach, with double nymph on a 3m (10ft) leader and greased line tip. The point fly is heavier than the fly on a dropper so that you can search down to a depth of at least a metre, while the dropper nymph will be much closer to the surface. This rig can be adjusted very quickly, even by changing the nymph on the dropper for a dry fly as an indicator or controller for the nymph on point, or perhaps for an effective dry pattern if fish start moving on the surface. It is thus a tactical rig.

The analysis phase continues even as you ease into the water, having chosen the starting point. Part of the tactical approach is the ability to adjust according to constant analysis. Reading the water is essential throughout a fishing session, not just at the start. Already, wading in ankle-deep water, the section of river looks different to how it appears when standing

Wojtek Gibinski nymphing in fast water.

higher on the bank, and the features close at hand are better defined, giving more information. The first tentative, exploratory casts are put in short, under 6m (20ft), in places where there could be fish, but anyway where you expect to be wading as you search the water beyond.

You remember the mantra 'Never wade in water where you have not first put your flies': think of fish close in to your starting point as a bonus, and they are very welcome indeed. Information is pouring in all the time, whether or not you move fish. Your stare sweeps the whole water, in and out of range, in those moments when you dare not watch the line tip. Any sign – flies on the surface, a rising fish, a flash in the flow, a kick of current or a line of foam – can be used to effect. And all the while you are placing your nymphs in new water as you explore, now fishing consistently and methodically at the 6m range, where control in a river is always at its best.

Effective Fishing at Range

Effective tactical fly fishing is dependent on approach and presentation, and this requires knowledge of the target, the fish, and how to induce it to take the presented fly. The range to the target is thus an important feature, and is at least as important as the angle a fly fisher has on that target. While having an instinctive component, accurate range finding with a fly rod is something that comes only with a lot of practice. It is more than learning to cast accurately: it is about casting with an appropriate style of cast, such as an overhead, side cast or Spey, while moving, such that the range between you and the fish changes. It includes moving one's feet and shifting body attitude as much as the casting stroke itself, constantly being aware of the position of the target and exactly where you need to cast the fly, which are not the same thing.

A fish lying on station at 0.5m (18in) depth will need the fly to enter the water a distance upstream, such that it sinks close to the fish's depth and position. If that fish is feeding, however, it might be that it will rise to the surface, but even so a dry fly will still need to be placed a certain distance upstream: casting directly over a rising fish is missing the range, because by the time the fish has reacted, the fly is downstream and lost. At worst a fly cast in a fish's rising position will spook it. Anticipation of current, drift or wind-induced surface flow on a lake is an essential part of fishing at the correct range: this is range finding.

Fishing at the correct range is also about achieving proper control. This can hardly be absolute, of course, but it can be nearly so, most of the time. Continuing with the river theme, where line control and fly presentation is at its most critical because of currents and the effects of non-laminar flow, we soon learn the importance of range. Every beginner tries to cast too far on a river, unless it is a very small stream. Holes and pockets are indistinctly seen out across the river, or even rising fish, and the angler is naturally keen to put his flies out there, where fish cannot perhaps be seen, rather than in the immediately accessible water,

Out goes a long cast, spooking everything between angler and the far bank, while the fly alights, even if gently, somewhere close to where the angler intended – only to be ripped away in moments by the effect on the line of the mishmash of currents. It really does happen all the time. It happened to me for more years than I care to admit, yet I cannot think of a single circumstance or situation when it was not better to wade closer to the attractive lies – after fishing the inside line, of course – and cast a short line at them. This is effective fishing at range, and it is tactical fly fishing.

Paul Craig netting a trout on the shallows, having steered it away from fish-holding water.

Stuart Crofts on Rio Gandara, having crossed the river downstream to give him a good presentation angle on the pool run-in.

The Ideal Range

Six metres is a very good range. I mean by this that after a lot of years developing an understanding of effective range fishing on rivers, I have come to the conclusion that 6m (20ft) is somewhere close to the ideal. This needs to be defined and qualified. The range I am discussing is that between the angler's body and the fish. The actual length of line cast will vary in order to present the flies accurately at this range. Even the angler's posture makes a difference here. If very upright, the casting length is significantly more (at least 0.5m (18ft)) than an angler who is leaning forwards, heron-like in the approach. The amount of slack line on the water, and the angle and elevation of the rod, also make a difference. The angler will probably be in motion, working towards the target area, shortening and shifting the range. Of course too close, under 6m, and the approach can be compromised, the fish alerted, and also the presentation adversely affected. On any scale of river above a very small beck or locally constricted river space, 6m really is the ideal range. If the angler can maintain this, then tactically he is adopting the best compromise between presentation and control.

It is almost always better to wade towards a fish and then cast at short range, than it is to cast beyond comfortable control range. Think of the currents in a fast-moving upland river, or boisterous tail water: as soon as a fly line touches down on these currents it will be affected by them, ultimately interfering with the intended travel of the fly or flies. This is most pronounced with dry fly, though also important with nymph presentation. The current interfering with a reasonably 'tight' fly line will almost immediately cause drag. If the angler puts in a wiggle cast, or upstream mend, to set slack into a cast, then this usually results in decreased accuracy and loss of control. Conversely, if the angler is able to wade up to a fish, ideally to the 6m range, then there is far less current to interfere with the line and fly. Control, and contact with the fly, are drastically improved.

It is not reasonable, however, to expect to be able to achieve a consistent short range on our fish. The obstacles in the river, the severity of the current or the depth of water, can all mean that we need to cast at longer range, for the sake of comfort, or even safety. We have to accept this, but also that control exponentially drops off with increasing range to the target fish. Beyond 10m (30ft), on fast-flowing or unevenly flowing water both presentation and control are hopelessly compromised. It is always worth attempting to find an option which allows you to approach within short range of a fish (preferably from downstream) before casting beyond the 10m range.

Consider this: the Czech team masters, each and every one of them, will have no hesitation (at least in competition) in swimming across the river if necessary, in order to reach fish on the far bank, even if these fish could be reached with, say, a 20m (65ft) cast. I have seen them do this on numerous occasions, even on cold, glacier-fed torrents in Norway. This might be extreme fly fishing, but the principle of shortening the range is the point here. There are always options, tactical options, and it is you who takes the choice.

The Angle of Presentation

After range come other aspects of control: we think about the angle and the presentation. You are still on that river working up on a fish you can see; it is rising now, a good brown trout close to the far bank beneath a foam lane, feeding on olives. You can put in casts upstream, away from this sighted fish, just to make sure there is nothing lying there, unseen, while you wade up, trying to achieve that ideal angle on the target fish. This angle is somewhere around 45 degrees: that is to say, the angle between the axis defined by the length of the fish, facing the stream, and the position of the angler, is 45 degrees. This allows a reasonable length of dead drift as well as presentation of the fly, rather than leader or fly line, over the target fish's position.

Too acute an angle, or presentation from directly downstream, will compromise presentation, in that the fish will see the leader or, worse, the fly line: it will be 'lined', particularly if it is near the surface. An angle too square (90 degrees) will allow only a short dead-drift phase and will induce drag of a dry fly, or loss of control of a nymph, too early in the drift. The latter situation will be exaggerated with increasing range and with the complexity of currents between the angler and the fish. It has often struck me that the selection of the correct angle between us and the fish is the reason our sport generally is referred to as 'angling'.

The river sport is dominated by a compromise between range and angle. These factors are hugely more important than, say, choice of fly pattern. The shorter the range – ideally 6m –

Paul Sharman making a good angle on a crease at ten metres.

Paul Fear tactically fishing through 360 degrees on open water in drought conditions.

and the nearer the angle to 45 degrees, the more perfect the control and the presentation. On stillwater or in the ocean, matters are different. For me, I will always choose an angle to the wind, or the current or tide, if at all possible. Sometimes it is not, and we have the choice of either taking the chance with a poor, compromised presentation, or abandoning the cast and the opportunity. This is down to the individual. Nearly everyone will take the chance, compromise, and cast at the fish and hope. Very few will walk away, wondering what might have been. After all, sometimes there is no choice of presentation – sometimes there is only one feasible position from which to cast, particularly on rivers, and frankly very few of us can walk away without casting at all. We cannot abandon the chance. The little boy working, skill-less, on the pond side, or the octogenarian presenting upstream dry – neither finds it easy to walk away from the chance, however limited the odds.

What we do is force the angle, and close the range. The best river fishers in the world will always do this, and saltwater fly fishers, or those devoted to the stillwater sport, can gain a lot by attempting the same. It is all a matter of scale, and then analysis of the currents and microniches between angler and fish. Because it

works so well on rivers, where the chaos of currents makes it so important in terms of presentation, should actually at least hint at its importance on stillwater or saltwater. Fish usually face the current, and anything which can give us an angle to the fish and its position relative to the flow, can be used to our advantage.

So we are focused on 6m, with a maximum of 10m on flowing waters; then 20m on stillwater, extending outwards from this, to 30m (100ft) from the bank of a large lake perhaps, and beyond even this, into territory where the fly fisher with single-handed fly rod is on the limit of control; the 30m + range. Those among us who love casting, with either accuracy or range, or both, will always push the boundaries, simply because they exist and we have a need for exploring them and beyond.

Finally, beyond 30m on a stillwater, and the fly fisher has very little control. At this range we are on the ragged edge, simply hoping for the best, hoping that out there, if a fish strikes, it will hook itself. Control is minimal, yet we seek this: we need to be able to cast to this range. Frankly, it looks and feels good – it impresses, even if only the inner man, and I would be the last to say that this is pointless. I would suggest only that we have very little contact with, or control over, our flies beyond 30m on a stillwater. Really, we are casting out there mostly only because we find satisfaction in laying out a long line over the waters. This itself is a thrill, something removed from the need to reach our target fish at range. We do it because we can, or want to, not because we need to in order to catch our fish. The latter will be achieved with a better strategy: a tactical approach.

There are a few exceptions to the above. Drift fishermen will know all too well that a long-range cast, downwind (or in flat calm conditions) is often necessary, even if only to present flies to cruising fish before one's boat partner can do it: tactical loch-style. Also, with fish lying at depth where we are presenting flies on fast-sinking lines from drifting boats, long casts are often necessary in order to compensate for the distance drifted while the flies are sinking to the feeding depth. If we cast to fifteen metres, say, the boat might have drifted over the flies by the time they are at the desired depth.

Stuart Crofts; wading technique is most crucial on broad rivers.

The Importance of Wading Technique

The very best river fly fishers catch a lot of their fish because they wade easily, rapidly closing the range and making an angle on their target fish. This might seem obvious in the light of what is written above, but I have found increasingly over the years that the aspect of fly fishing (particularly on rivers) that most interferes with one's success is the ability to wade with confidence, and appropriately. I go so far as to say that provided one's casting is adequate, wading technique is the next most important feature leading to good presentation and control. Neither is this compromising safety. I am not necessarily talking about deep wading, or wading on rapids; I am considering *appropriate* wading in fishable water. Indeed, having confidence and practice with one's wading technique will improve safety.

I will always advise any wading fly fisher to use a wading stick and a life jacket, though have to admit that I use neither. It could be argued, actually, that having a wading stick will lead to a false sense of security, encouraging an angler to wade when he is too far out, or in water too fast for safety. Better by far to practise wading and fishing within limits known or discovered by the individual as being safe. Even so, the river fisher will inevitably fall in from time to time, and the shock of cold water can be incredibly disorientating and cause immediate panic; this is when the life jacket is important, keeping the head above water while the panic subsides.

There are rules that should be summarized as follows. First, know your limits; if you feel insecure, then you should back off. Never wade into water from which there is not at least one obvious means of escape. This might not be the way you enter (for example wading downstream on a fast-water gravel bar, from which the escape is very likely to be across the current rather than against it).

Related to the above is recognition of depth and flow rate. If you cannot see the river bed because of turbid or fast water, then you should be very alert because that water might be deep

Lawrence Greasley in hugely demanding wading water; the River Tees.

or the current too ferocious to hold against. Understanding the nature of water is all part of the analytical approach. You read the waters, mapping them out, even while you set up the tackle at the river's edge. Subconsciously, it seems, a mental image builds of areas in which you expect to be standing and moving through, in the same sort of detail and attention as those places where you expect to be presenting a fly. It comes naturally after a while, but until it does, the thinking angler must make every conscious effort to create this mind map of the waiting waters.

Wading with both legs facing the current is both unstable and tiring; it is always better to have one leg behind the other, in other words to move sideways up, down or across the flow. It is also much more stable to spread one's feet reasonably far apart; this effectively lowers the angler's centre of gravity while also lowering the body and head positions, so giving greater possibility of more closely approaching a target fish – that is, closing the range.

It is very noticeable that beginners, or tentative waders, constantly look at the river bed in front of them before every step is taken, and this is ultimately sensible, of course. It is just as noticeable, however, that an experienced wader will pre-map the water before even entering the river, only visually checking from time to time (typically while actually casting) as he moves through the water, though he is constantly feeling the river bed with his feet. More information is assimilated by this feeling process than by visual signals. The angler 'feels' his way through the river, prowling across the stream like a cat through grass, mentally locked on to the target, but aware of everything in the local environment.

If there is a tide rip scouring the shore gravels, or a criss-cross of currents on the river and our target fish lie among these, or on the far side, we simply have to become tactical in our approach, and wading technique will be central to this. Even the wind blowing across a lake shore will force us to react accordingly if we want to present a fly properly to a feeding fish. In every case the thinking fly fisher must choose a position from which to cast and find a *compromise* position, in order to present an appropriate fly in an appropriate way, maximizing the chances that a fish will strike and the hook be set.

It is an impossible situation, actually, achieving this perfection of presentation, a solution, in every case. It is something akin to Fermat's 'Last Theorem' in mathematics, or the Heisenberg 'Uncertainty Principle' in quantum physics. You can present a fly to a bass in the sea, or a trout in the river, almost every time as well as you think is possible, but you will not catch every fish you cast at, no matter how good you get at this. There is not the perfect solution to everything, or if there is, we cannot always find it.

So you must say to yourself that you can cast as well as you can, with excellent wading technique, and you can learn everything you can about the reaction of fish, at all depths, to food forms or to attractors, but finally you will make mistakes, no matter how experienced you become. Nearly forty-five years as a fly fisher has taught me this much, which is why I cannot approach any fly-fishing option without going tactical, searching for that elusive solution. Yet good presentation, with appropriate wading, closing the range and optimizing the angle, will drastically increase the odds of success, in every situation.

Crucially, this does not necessarily mean wading (or casting) directly towards your target fish; it is much more likely that it is better to wade or move more strategically. Consider the diagram, which illustrates a fish located at point X with an angler at point Y, out of range and at an inappropriate angle for good presentation. If the current is strong between the angler and fish, wading directly towards the fish will be noisy, uncomfortable, slow and even dangerous. It will be far better to follow the path shown in order to assume the optimum range and angle. It will also be faster, in that although not a straight line approach, it will avoid beating up directly against the current.

Range and angle might be the most important aspects of good, tactical presentation, but the depth of the target fish is also an important factor. This is where leader and fly design become more significant. Tactical flies are dealt

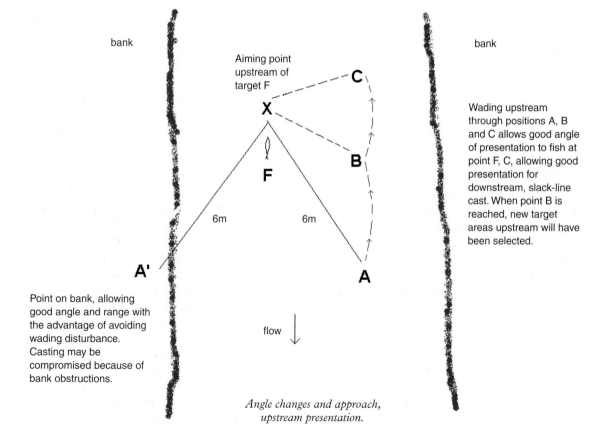

bank

Aiming point upstream of target F

Point on bank, allowing good angle and range with the advantage of avoiding wading disturbance. Casting may be compromised because of bank obstructions.

flow

bank

Wading upstream through positions A, B and C allows good angle of presentation to fish at point F, C, allowing good presentation for downstream, slack-line cast. When point B is reached, new target areas upstream will have been selected.

Angle changes and approach, upstream presentation.

with in the fly-tying chapter of this book, and it should suffice here to say that for fish not feeding on the surface, an appropriately ballasted fly should be chosen in order to present at the desired depth. Actually, apart from weighting, another factor to consider here is the streamlined nature of the fly. A 'fuzzy', bulky fly, with poor hydrodynamics, sinks much more slowly than an equivalently weighted, sparse, streamlined fly. Think of it like this: drop a feather and a pin, each weighing the same... Drag through the air, drag through water – it is the same principle.

The importance of appropriately weighted and designed nymphs becomes more important as target depth increases, so much so that we enter here the territory of 'sacrificial' patterns designed to take imitative flies down to an appropriate depth. This is entirely analogous to the bait angler's use of weights on the line in order to present a bait at the appropriate feeding depth. Some argue that the use of sacrificial weighting is not, strictly speaking, 'fly' fishing, but I think this is not so. It might not be classical fly fishing (whatever that is – upstream dry fly, perhaps?), but it is a necessary tactical adaptation in order to present flies at depth.

Weighting the line, or weighting the flies, or a mixture of both, offers varied means of depth control and presentation. Most of us will choose to weight flies directly and to employ teams of these flies on appropriately designed leaders, wherever possible, rather than use sacrificial weighting. I believe this stems from a desire to achieve better (or simpler) presentation than to fulfil some antiquated or anachronistic view of the perception of what is fly fishing. In any case, this book is not about fly fishing, it is about tactical fly fishing, and the two are not necessarily the same.

Fishing tactically is fishing multi-dimensionally, the three spatial dimensions in terms of the angler's and the fish's reference points, but also the need for anticipation of the drift of the fly, or movement of the fish. We should seldom cast directly at fish, but cast our fly to a point from which it will drift and fall to the target fish's position in the water. This is always simplest with dry fly presentation, of course, because there is no adjustment required for depth, merely drift.

Presentation

The keystone of successful fly fishing is presentation, and we finally come to this as we learn to put together the aspects of range, angle and control; the latter being a multitude of factors including depth control and the movement of the fly at the target depth. As I guide people, particularly in the river disciplines, it strikes me that where guiding becomes most important or useful is in terms of teaching about correct presentation, and being able to adapt with every step taken, because rivers change as you move through them, particularly upland, rain-fed streams.

With fly choice I am always satisfied with something close to imitating basic, prevalent food forms, and much more concerned with the dynamic requirements of the fly, especially nymphs required for fishing at specific depths. Then our attention must immediately turn to presentation requirements, and we must focus on the dynamics of everything that follows – range, angle, control – in order to achieve the desired result: the fish accepting the fly.

It is simple to say, and might seem trivial to the reader, but you really cannot be successful in this sport unless you can get close to consistent, appropriate presentation in all disciplines, but perhaps most so in river nymph presentation (though I do not want to belittle in any way the need for presentation in saltwater or stillwater, or dry fly on the stream). No matter how good the fly you have on the end of the line, a policy of 'chuck and chance it' will never produce more than a tiny fraction of the true potential of any fishing situation: this is just random casting. Thinking through the aspects considered here will improve results, they always do. The choice is yours, but then you would not be reading so far unless you had

John Horsey, outstanding loch-style tactician and to date the most capped England international of all time.

There are many situations, probably mostly in competition, when there is simply too much information, or too complicated a reach of water, or simply not enough time, that we must compromise to the extent that we are effectively 'method' fishing, going through routines of method that will give us a percentage of success. We do little more than select a presentation method, adjusting a little to nuances of presentation requirements as we move through a reach of water, and accept whatever return we achieve from this approach. It is comfort-zone fishing, not requiring overmuch effort, but it is always a compromise. Give that extra bit of effort, take the chance of improving presentation, searching for a better solution, and we will always learn more and, finally, achieve better results.

All of us, however, will go for this percentage approach from time to time. Some people do it almost all the time, and enjoy a certain percentage success: gamblers working the numbers, the odds, the chances. I have known a lot of national team members who adopt this approach in internationals (particularly in loch-style). They

addressed this. The secrets in our sport lie not with special flies or panacea methods, and still less with high-performance tackle, but with presentation.

John Tyzack; the ultimate river tactician.

Speed Fishing

This concept is an approach that is really encompassed almost entirely within competitive rather than advanced fly fishing *per se*. The analytical, technical and tactical approach to fly fishing inevitably leads to those 'purple patches'; periods in a fishing session in which fish come in fast and absolutely everything is working well. Naturally, the more you practise the art and the more attention one pays to detail, the more frequent and of longer duration these periods become, and the luckier you get. Sometimes it is the difference between a fish spilling the hook on one side of the net rim or the other. Then it might be the choice of angle while nymph fishing in a river, one producing good hook-holds and the other resulting in pricking or losing the fish.

Often it is a sense – no more than this – that the fish are suddenly up close to the surface, feeding hard on emergers, say, and that an appropriate fly change and leader rig will afford that perfect presentation. One moves then, with good timing and stealth through the water, utterly confident that the next cast will produce another take, that the hook-hold will be firm and the fish will come tumbling to the correctly positioned net. A rhythm sets in and an unusual, euphoric sense of command of the entire situation, a state of engagement with the fish and the environment: it is achievable only when all the analytical, technical and tactical considerations are perfectly tuned to the situation and remain unchanged for a period of time, or, conversely and more rarely, the angler can adjust as these components change. It is a state of grace.

Speed fishing really is about fine-tuning for efficiency. In the appropriate context of rivers or stillwaters it also very much involves wading technique and boat control (particularly with drifting as opposed to anchored boats).

The author; concentration and engagement.

Inexperienced river fishers remain relatively static while wading, tending either to wade or fish, seldom simultaneously. Yet wading is fully inclusive of the fishing process; it is a huge part of catching the fish. It is crucial to presentation, to shortening the range and adopting the angle.

The advanced level river fisher uses his feet as much as the cast to catch a fish. When I guide people I always find myself encouraging them to use their feet to place themselves closer to the fish, or to obtain a better angle, rather than forcing the issue with an inappropriately long cast. The confidence to move smoothly in varying depths of water, the ability to feel one's way across a river rather than to spend too long peering into the depths to find good foot-falls, is all crucial to successful river fishing: it is, absolutely, also about speed fishing.

rigorously stick to a particular method and locations which have proven effective in team practice sessions, and work entirely within this comfort zone. It is a strategic approach rather than tactical, and is something I have rarely done myself, though I completely understand the approach. It might not win matches, but it will usually result in a solid performance for the team. In so far as this is the case, one applauds this approach. It requires a certain mind-set and control, particularly when things go wrong and it does not work. The feeling of being marooned out there, doing something which is simply not working, is simply ghastly. No matter how long the international (loch-styles in Britain are usually eight hours), you feel you are running out of time so fast. You simply cannot decide whether or not to continue with the method approach, hoping that the fish will respond, or play the wild card and engage the tactical mind.

When it has happened to me, my nerve has usually given way and I have broken free from the team approach and fished as an individual. In this case, one faces the extremes: the abandoned method approach results in disaster or fantastic success if the tactical approach brings in the desired result, or better. Finally, it is as much a feature of personality as anything else. One can compete for the team, or as an individual. Sometimes these are the same, but usually they are not.

While it might horrify one or two team managers or captains I have had, they have all known that I will more often than not play the wild card. Though a team player, I feel that my best service to the team (after the preparation phase of a campaign) is to achieve whatever I can as an individual out there – even if this means abandoning the general team approach of a percentage method and acknowledged area (in a lake event), for the sake of following one's instinct. This is dangerous, however, and in truth I know that I have got it wrong on some occasions and have therefore effectively let down the team, though I think more often it has been advantageous to the England team cause.

Finally, it must come down to the individual, and it is his or her own choice. How strong is your instinct, and what is the depth of your experience, that pulls you away from the team strategy? Are you really able to go tactical to the extent that you can go it alone and change the course of a championship? Believe me, get it right and you are a hero for a short while, and will enjoy a Zen-like state of euphoria and well-being; but get it wrong, and you will be in utter despair, and your standing will crash in the estimation of your team-mates. Follow the team approach and you will probably know neither of these extremes; but the choice is yours alone.

Wild card fishing might be better described in terms of situation tactics, be it in competitive fly fishing or fly fishing more generally. It involves very much adjustment to the specific needs of the prevalent conditions and fish behaviour: the situation of the moment.

Boat Control

Much more than just an ability to set a drift in the right place so that the boat will be carried towards or through a target area, boat control is part of the skill leading to good fly presentation. Boats seldom drift truly beam on to the wind. Allowing a boat to drift as it will is seldom good practice. It is the lazy way, and it rarely leads to good catches. It makes tactical sense to take control of the drift, so far as this is possible. Changing weight distribution within the boat makes a difference, though by far the best way is the use of a drogue, which does more than slow down the rate of drift – it can significantly alter the angle of drift, benefiting one or both (assuming two) anglers in the boat.

There are other drift-controlling devices, even those that will allow a drift with the axis of the boat in the wind direction, necessitating side casting – the so-called 'Northampton style' in Britain. Also, the traditional way of controlling drift by oars works particularly well in heavy wooden drift boats. This can even be done by a sole angler fishing one-handed, with occasional touches of the oar to subtly control the angle of drift. I used to do this a great deal on the sea

Study in boat control; European Championship, Norway, 2007.

trout and brown trout lochs of northern Scotland and Norway, where the boats tend to be heavy. You leave both oars overboard, tethered or fixed at the rowlock, and occasionally work whichever one is appropriate to give the boat the necessary angle change. Working a short line, loch-style, can be done smoothly one-handed, allowing the other hand to fine-tune with an oar, or if necessary to make adjustments to a drogue.

Finally, in the context of the purely tactical, it is necessary to know the nature of the type of fish one is targeting in order to know one's target. There are usually differences between wild and stocked fish, which has implications on how best to catch them, and always different demands when targeting specimen or large fish rather than the average size for a particular water. Specimen hunters have a completely different ethos of approach to that of the speed fisherman or the competitor. The artistry and technical requirements of any type of fly fisher are comparable, but according to the nature of the fish, the technical and tactical demands of approach differ appreciably. It is a matter of focus, and what enthuses you in this all-consuming sport.

10 MAKING THE FRAME

Coaching and Training

An angler will improve every time he or she goes out on the water. It is one of the clichés in our sport that we learn something every time, but it is true nonetheless. On some days we learn more than on others, but no matter how experienced we become, and whatever pool of experiences we have with which to compare, there is always more to be taken on board. It is sad, I think, if someone reaches a personal limit and decides there is nowhere left to go – though I wonder if this can even happen in our sport. Without a doubt, however, an individual, fishing alone, will not develop as fast towards advanced abilities as when being coached, or sharing experiences with others. View it like this: if one wishes to achieve anything like the potential offered by a new water, in a location perhaps rather different to those within one's realm of personal experience, you can only really do this by being guided appropriately.

Other than in competition there is no better way to develop skills than to be guided by someone who is more skilled than you, in specific, defined ways. Even in competition, though one can hone skills and fish-catching ability, it is all too easy (indeed inevitable) that faults become entrenched and actually compensated for in all sorts of aspects of fly fishing, particularly cast-

The Game Angling Instructors Association (GAIA)

Maybe the days of being coached or helped by friendly anglers on the water will never leave us. We should hope that they last, because so many of us learned in this way, and developed at least beyond the rudimentary demands of the sport, and fly fishing does enjoy that sort of patronage and charm. Yet for the sake of developing advanced fly-fishing skills, there is no substitute for professional help. In Britain, the Game Angling Instructors Association (GAIA) is the main body that trains and organizes a nationwide team of qualified instructors. There are other ways to find professional, qualified guides in your particular area, such as via the Hardy/Greys Academy, or the network of Orvis-endorsed guides – but really one cannot go wrong by taking the GAIA route, finding an instructor from the web-based register in all areas of the country.

Mike Roden, top-level APGAI instructor.

Howard Croston,
England team reserve,
Poland, 2005.

ing. I persisted for too many years, even during the height of my competitive endeavours, with faults in my casting and presentation (related, but not the same) before I had these corrected by skilled professional casting instructors. And it took some of the best in the business to iron out these problems, because they were so deeply ingrained.

There is absolutely no one who cannot benefit from properly geared or personalized coaching. Even at national team level – indeed, especially at this level – we benefit hugely from master class and coaching sessions. Several of the European national teams have coaches permanently working with them.

The important thing, when climbing from intermediate to advanced level in any particular area, is to be clear about what one is trying to achieve. This must be clear to the coach and the person being coached. For instance, presentation on rivers is strongly dependent on the casting strategy. In a range of casting scenarios there will be choices, good and less good. A skilled coach will be able to identify these and to convey the need for selection of the appropriate cast, and then to teach it. The coach should identify the possibilities, which might, say, be

multiple single Speys or a simple switch cast, and then demonstrate these, teach both if necessary, and correct faults; all such that the angler more naturally and correctly selects the appropriate cast and commensurate presentation in future, similar situations.

Add to this the vast range of permutations involved in casting and presentation just in the river discipline, and one might begin to appreciate how professional guidance can drastically shorten the developmental process. This is what we call skills analysis. Many people at the so-called intermediate level often go to a coach with unclear aims; often the stated objective is to improve fish-catching ability but with little idea of the procedure. Nearly always this will involve help with casting, and it will also require work on wading technique (in rivers), presentation and even reading the water. While most guides are very good casting instructors, and will do this naturally, it is less common to find those who will quickly focus on other issues, unless directed to do so by the angler.

The best coaching sessions are always when a strong relationship and understanding have been formed between both parties. One-off coaching sessions for specific needs can also be valuable, however, for instance in addressing defined casting issues with a good casting instructor, or food-form identification with a first-rate entomologist, such as my England International team-mate Stuart Crofts.

One should not confuse the roles of guide and instructor, though it is possible to have both simultaneously. A guide shows his guests those areas of the fishery (with which he or she is intimately familiar) where the fish are most likely to be caught, in any particular season, and will be able to help with fly selection and presentation. An instructor will coach in specific general requirements of fly casting and fly fishing, suitable for a range of waters.

In competitive fly fishing there are structures in most countries, and all the top performing countries, throughout the spectrum of competition levels for training and development. This is fairly rudimentary at club level, of course, and really relies on the momentum and enterprise of the club teams, though most clubs I have encountered in Britain and Europe have had acknowledged experts in certain areas who have managed to pass on this expertise, with varying levels of success, to their team-mates.

As the level of competition rises, so the more formal and focused the training becomes. Team captains, managers and coaches all take on developmental roles, with the captains more concerned with tactical considerations, while the managers and coaches deal with strategic and general issues of team development. In any team, whether at club or national level, every team member has a responsibility to convey specific knowledge and skills analysis to team-mates, though it is the role of the management of a team to direct this pool of expertise to the team in various strategic (long-term) and tactical ways.

I have fished in England teams in which we have had manager and captain, but no coach, and others in which we also had a coach. The latter has seemed like a luxury, and was certainly more common twenty years ago when costs for internationals were not so great. Nowadays there are again signs that the team coaching role is returning as a separate role to

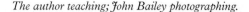

The author teaching; John Bailey photographing.

the manager's. The coach is an expert teacher in specific, defined ways. The effective coach will be able to convey this expertise to individuals in order to strategically strengthen the team. On the other hand, without a doubt, in an international event the manager has the most crucial role to play, and can define success or failure more than any other team entity.

So what does a good manager do? This stems from both an understanding of the individuals in the team, and the overall aim of the team in a campaign. He (or she) understands each member, the needs of the individuals, the moods, the skills, and the reaction of any of the individuals to the adverse conditions of an international campaign. It is a hugely demanding role. I think back to the problems I have given my managers, knowing that they have had other, different problems to deal with from others in the team, all the while nudging us towards our ultimate goal, and one understands then just how vital the manager is to a consistently high-performing team.

Physical and Mental Preparations

Physical and mental preparations go hand in hand, though we can undertake them separately. Fitness is always an issue, at any level in the sport, perhaps most so for rivers and saltwater fishing from the shore, although long sessions in a boat (perhaps up to eight hours) call for a lot of endurance. Within all disciplines it is the wading in large freestone rivers that has perhaps the most requirement on fitness. With experience, wading technique and confidence improve, but taking on strong flows cannot properly, or safely, be done unless the fly fisher is fit. I have always found middle-distance and long-distance running to be a great preparation for this area of demand in fly fishing, because it builds up stamina and cardio-vascular fitness, so crucial to long periods in fast-flowing water.

Even so, I strongly recall times when I have been in a river competition, when each fish caught had to be netted and taken for measure-

ment to one's controller, when I have been struggling for breath after numerous forays to and fro across powerful flows and unstable river beds. I have known too, the need for swimming in order to reach fish on the far bank of wide rivers; not to be recommended, perhaps, but it is certainly a part of advanced competitive and extreme fly fishing. Three hours of that sort of activity can have very fit men literally on their knees with exhaustion.

While running does it for me, I also find long periods of gardening and light building work useful for tuning the body towards the sort of fly fishing I most usually encounter. Some of my team-mates have done the same, while others spend long hours on more formal circuit or weights training. Walking or biking over reasonable distances are also great for fitness, and rather less damaging to the back and knees than heavy work in the garden or running. This latter problem (knees and backs are typically the most common physical problems that adversely affect a fly fisher's performance) should be stressed. Believe me, if your knees or, particularly, your back are injured, this can be so incapacitating as to completely preclude the possibility of even shallow water or stillwater wading, let alone casting. As such, one might recommend swimming as one of the best ways of tuning the body for the demands of advanced fly fishing, though it is surprising that very few of the top fly fishers I have known spend very much time actually swimming, for training or leisure.

The Analytical Approach

Without a doubt, it has been the analytical approach that has best prepared me for any particular fly-fishing session, properly tuning the mind to the demands of the situation. It is almost entirely subconscious nowadays, as it was when I was young. Thus I do not approach a water and tell myself to start the analysis process, because this is done involuntarily: I cannot prevent myself doing it, even if I am not fishing or about to fish – one automatically goes

To take on water like this you have to be fit, alert, and have good analytical skills; one of my competition sectors in the European Championship, Spain, 2008. It gets hardly more demanding than this.

into analytical mode. I do, however, verbally express the analytical approach, and thus consciously acknowledge this component of preparation for fly fishing, to those who I am guiding or coaching. Indeed, it has been my guiding that has brought the analytical (as well as the technical) aspects of fly fishing to the core of my approach to advanced fly fishing, while it has been international competition that has honed the tactical aspects of this overall approach. And it is always analytical, technical, tactical, in that order, and intimately inter-woven, which are the components leading along the path towards advanced fly-fishing ability.

It is the competitive mind that sharpens these components, and not necessarily the exposure to any formal competition. Many fly fishers are simply naturally competitive without ever actually competing. It may be an unstated match with a boat partner, or a will to catch more than the fisherman upstream, or the need to take more bass than another regular to your beach – anything that alerts the competitive mind. It might, after all, be simply the need to overcome the problems presented by a particular fish lie,

therefore competition with the fish and its element, and no other person involved. And the most profound aspect of all this is the development of the tactical mind.

On the water it is relatively easy to engage the tactical issues necessary for success. Everything is so immediate that all the signs are quickly read (analysis), and the fisherman has adopted the appropriate fly (or flies) with the optimum angle and range (technical), such that the final execution of the presentation (tactical) is dealt with appropriately. If the latter is not properly addressed, the analytical and technical aspects of the situation are wasted. Time on the water provides the depth of experience such that all aspects of the overall approach are shortened and honed; nevertheless, time off the water is also valuable.

Advancement Away from the Water

I have discussed elsewhere how important fly tying is to the actual fly-fishing success of an individual, and there is no doubt that the success of many international competitors is due in large part to time spent at the fly vice, or even in preparing for a competition, or training session, away from the water. The success of professional casters, guides or instructors is also due in some degree to preparation time away from actual fishing, or casting. Frankly, in fly fishing generally, of any type and at whatever level, there must be much advancement gained for all of us during those times we spend away from the water. This is not simply 'down time' (though this is important, too); it is much more a period in which those aspects of our sport which are not sufficiently addressed while we are actually fishing, may be dealt with and developed. Imagine the long-distance runner, waiting at the start before the race, mentally mapping out the course, rehearsing the hills ahead, planning the sections where energy must be conserved…

The therapy of another sport, and the benefit this has to our fly fishing, should not be undervalued. Long-distance running, say, might be wildly dissimilar to fishing, and yet even this activity can be complementary to an individ-

ual's progress; and there are others that are much more closely related, sometimes even surprisingly so. Target shooting, for example, particularly at short range, has curious parallels with fly fishing. The Olympic-style 10m air-pistol and air-rifle disciplines, for example, or hunter field target, are all undertaken at the ranges we seek to control and present flies. Just think of the importance of focusing on 10m in the river discipline – precisely the range at which the air-gun disciplines are shot at Olympic Games.

There is also (though not an Olympic category) a 6m (actually 6yd) range shot in air-pistol discipline in many countries, to national and international championship level – and this leads to an extraordinary comparison here with the absolutely perfect range for control and presentation for single-handed fly-rod discipline in rivers. I have absolutely no doubt whatsoever that my own limited work with a target air pistol has gradually improved my control at short-range (appropriate range) river fly fishing. I cannot explain this sufficiently, but I suspect it has something to do with the training of the

The author demonstrating tactical dry fly in deep, slow-moving water. (Courtesy Andy Smith)

Engage or walk away? The author observing the myriad of possibilities for trout and grayling on island water at Appleby, Eden.

mind to focus on these particular ranges and to exercise control, albeit in different ways. Discipline of body and mind: advanced fly fishing demands it just as any other sport.

Sometimes it is valuable just to be able to walk away from the sport, to have some real down-time and to exercise the mind in ways completely divorced from fly fishing. We can become too attached to it, too focused, too intense, and this drains us. None of us can exist with a permanent adrenalin rush; if we were in tactical mode all the time we would simply burn up, and the enthusiasm would wane. If this begins to happen, walk away, do something completely different. The sport is so deeply entrenched in so many of us, so important to our very being, that the enthusiasm will return,

and quite naturally we will find ourselves drawn again to the water. Many times in my long fly-fishing career I have had to do this, sometimes for months at a time, and always I have returned with fresh enthusiasm, a better sportsman for the rest period. Curiously, it takes very little time to build up to the former, established skill levels, but with fresh focus and new targets. Be in the wilderness a while, and you will return with new understanding and aspiration.

Advancing in Stages

In our route towards advanced fly-fishing skills there are recognizable stages that indicate success. It is always worth having these stages, or targets, towards which to strive because there is tremendous satisfaction to be derived from achieving each stage – although there is also huge frustration should we miss the mark. The stages can be simple or complex, specific or varied. We might determine to better recognize invertebrate activity during a particular season, or perhaps to choose from among the range of Spey casts – or change of direction, roll-based casts – the ideal for the situation, and to execute this perfectly. We might have a simple target number of fish to catch in a given period of time, or, more subtly, the capture of a specific fish from a difficult lie in the river.

Towards the more demanding end of the training/practice region of the spectrum, we might choose a given stretch of river (with complexity and variety of fish-holding water) and fish it with a range of methods, choosing angle, range and presentation suitable for each target area; all of this reworked and, ideally, following other expert anglers through the same beat. There is little more exacting than this, and indeed this has formed the basis of masterclass training sessions for the England European Championship team in recent years. Imagine following river master John Tyzack up a techni-cally demanding river beat in high summer and low water! Yet in international competition this is exactly what you have to be prepared to do. Rarely is the fishing easy, and usually one is fish-ing water that has already been covered by other

Away from competition, in the wilderness; big trout going back.

international level competitors. This is why such anglers tend to be tactically supreme.

We can develop a training programme with defined stages of development and achievement. From personal goals based on analytical and technical achievements through to tactical excellence, such practice is the best way possible, along with a degree of coaching by exponents in particular, defined fields of expertise, to reaching the grail of advanced fly-fishing skills.

The Demands of Competition

Competitive fly fishing has a passionate following in Britain and many other countries in Europe, and elsewhere. In most countries the number of fly fishers who seriously compete is not that great, but in most cases the standard of competition is high because those who do take part do so seriously and reach an advanced standard. Competition is fierce. I feel that many advanced-level anglers are actually put off from competing simply because of the very high standard out there, and the sheer competitiveness of this sector of the sport. No matter how skilled and experienced the angler, there will always be others who can reach the same standard, or better, on any particular day. Yet one should never fear competition: this is healthy, and leads to significant developments in the sport at large; nevertheless it does put off a lot of people from entering the fray.

Realistically, a newcomer cannot expect to go out there and win, or even consistently to make the top ten. The occasional win or high placing is reasonable to expect, and personally wonderful to achieve, but a realistic approach will encompass the necessity of developing within the sport, as with the (larger) non-competitive sector. One cannot, for instance, expect to become an outstanding river presentation caster without putting in hundreds of hours of casting on a range of river environments.

It is all about developing, as with any sport. From the rudimentary requirements of basic skills and an outright desire to do well, one can acquire the ability to be competitive. Entering the local and friendly competitions organized by clubs and associations can provide a sound introduction, and can help an individual decide whether or not competition is for him, or her, and whether or not to go on to the next level. Most of the clubs and associations in Britain have teams that fish various boat- and bank-based competitions either on their local still-water, or even nationally on various fisheries through the year.

River competitive fly fishing is much more popular in continental Europe than in Britain, where the 'entry level' is mostly via the CEFF regional qualifiers. Realistically, this is far too high a level to be introductory for this discipline, and it is no surprise, given this current situation, that many of the European teams are significantly ahead of the British in terms of river competitiveness. Conversely, the British have developed so far as to have become virtually unbeatable in the stillwater disciplines.

Individuals and teams need to develop by practice and exposure to the disciplines in which they seek to be competitive. The British boat and cycling team successes at the 2008 Olympics were a direct result of the focus on achieving success through a long developmental process. Fly fishing is no different in this sense.

We all have different ways of learning and developing in our sport. Broadly, we might do well as individuals, with some one-to-one coaching perhaps, or we might perform much better within the more nebulous structure of a club or team. Most of us like a mixture of both, enjoying a personal competition on the river one day – just the fly fisher, the trout and a wild place – and then being part of a loch-style team event on a large stillwater venue, all the while developing ideas and skills. Whether fishing as an individual or as part of a team, there are several differing demands, and it is best to have these clearly understood. Fishing to a team plan and strategy will almost always differ from the approach of an individual; the agendas are different, and the nature of the competition is different.

Some of my team return to the boat beach at Menteith on practice day before the autumn international, where I was England captain, 2005; Martin Dixon and Julie Emerson in the foreground.

Achieving Personal Goals

In a team, be it a local club team or all the way to the national team, the abilities of the collective are more than the sum of the individual skills and experiences. A good team makes optimum use of the characteristics of the team members via the team's captain, coach or manager. Each individual will have a role, and this is all a part of the team's structure. Stray from this role, and the team's fortunes might be severely affected. A team has a strategic position, and the team members are tactically deployed in order to meet this strategy. It is tactical competitive sport generally, and tactical fly fishing specifically, at the extreme. This needs team management skills, whereas the individual needs only the much simpler, personal tactical approach. I write about some

great team and individual performances, and what made them great, in the appropriate place in this book; here I am focusing on setting and achieving personal goals.

I believe it is best to have targets. In order to be competitive one needs to be able to focus on particular issues, be they skills development or a particular competition or event. They may very well stem from the type of fishery most known to the individual. My own happened to be Bewl Water, as described in the introduction to this book, and several years fishing in the European Open Championships. The fishery and the events happened to coincide with other stages in my personal and fly-fishing life, so giving me a focus. It transpired that the series of events which followed brought me a high degree of personal success, though it might not have happened that way. I might not have done very well at all in the competition – from exactly the same level of skills that I had at that time, and with whatever was happening with timing and circumstances, I might have failed to catch even a single trout. Or I might have caught just two or three and been nowhere near 'making the frame', as we say. It happens, and the individual walks away with his own perspective and reasoning. If you cannot assimilate, or come to terms with, the levels of success and failure that will be encountered, then you have no place in the competition.

Similarly, if we cannot walk away from any fly-fishing session without a rational measure of what has happened, then there is something lacking and we have missed the point. Even a blank session should not be destructive. We can, and should, be dissatisfied, perhaps, with a longing to work out what went wrong and how to improve on the situation, but it should not eat away at us. This is not what the sport is about, competitive or otherwise.

At the very highest level, however, in the harsh glare of an international campaign, I should admit that the demands on individual and team are ferocious. There is no hiding here. With the glory of success comes the certainty that failure will tear you to bits, emotionally and in the estimation of your team-mates and manager. It can destroy you, so be aware of this before you embark on a personal ambition to fly-fish for your country. This has given me, after all, the highest possible euphoria in the glow of success, and the most awful, utter despair that I have experienced in sport. But we can go a very long way before we have to expose ourselves to such risk.

Sharpening Tactical Ability

Through the early developmental stage of an individual's competitive career, it quickly becomes apparent how well one's tactical abilities are tuned. There are four major disciplines in competitive fly fishing terms: stillwater from the bank, stillwater boat fishing at anchor, still-water drift fishing (loch-style) and river fishing (with wading). There are others, such as various saltwater events and anchored boats in rivers, though these are not significant in any modern FIPS-Mouche championship events. The skills in any of these particular disciplines must be acquired first, though not necessarily honed; but in order to succeed competitively, they must be applied tactically. The tactical mind just has to be sharpened.

Think of it like this: imagine you are fishing loch-style and the fish are swimming up to a metre subsurface, nosing into the wind and feeding on buzzer pupae, rising to hatch at the surface. In loch-style you effectively have the sector available for your fishing, as shown in the diagram opposite. Few boats, even under controlling drogue, can be made to drift absolutely beam on to the wind, and will inevitably slip slightly across the wind. Indeed, this can be exaggerated by setting the drogue or distribution of weight in the boat, even by turning the engine propeller blades face on or across the drift direction. We can use this tactically, slanting the drift direction towards one or other angler in the boat (loch-style competitions have two anglers in a boat, with or without a non-fishing boatman). It is much easier for this angler to reach those cruising fish first, earlier than his disadvantaged boat partner.

If this is the case and you allow this to happen to you, then you have lost the tactical battle and it is game over. I have known cases where an angler using very subtle drift-controlling tactics has outperformed his boat partner by ten to one. Indeed I have done it myself, and in the early days of my competitive career I have had it done to me. This is not unscrupulous, and it is not breaking the rules, even the prime one of 'conducting oneself in the best traditions of the sport'; this is fishing tactically, in a competitive sense. It is always the prerogative of the competitor to say if he is feeling disadvantaged or unfairly positioned. We are, for instance, perfectly entitled to change boat ends with our partner at least once in any competition session, and also to reasonably correct drift direction.

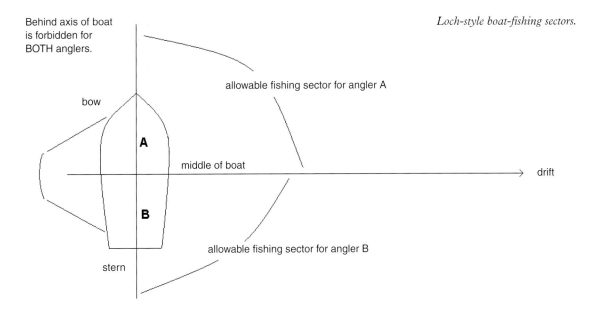

Loch-style boat-fishing sectors.

Behind axis of boat is forbidden for BOTH anglers.

allowable fishing sector for angler A

bow

A

middle of boat

drift

B

allowable fishing sector for angler B

stern

There are general fishing tactics, closely related to the particular methods employed in any discipline, and there are competitive tactics, and the two are not necessarily the same. The former are naturally important to the development towards advanced level in our sport, while the latter are absolutely crucial to consistent competitive success. This is considered a little more in the chapter concerning masters and masterclasses.

National Team Selection

Without a doubt it is qualification to one's national team that brings the peak of euphoria, if not the summit of achievement in the sport (which is probably reserved for winning an international championship). The very first time you achieve this, it completely changes your perception of the world – which suddenly seems a better place. I remember so well, one late September evening at Rutland Water, almost two decades ago: the wind had come up through the late afternoon and it was cold. I had caught four good trout on dry fly. It was the English National Final, from which the loch-style team for the following year was being selected. When the results were announced, outside in the fading light, and I had made it to the team, I almost wept. My friend, John White (who had also qualified) and I felt as if we would float back home, and this feeling did not leave me for weeks. Every morning I woke with a sort of internal glow and, I'm sure, a smile on my face. I went off to work without caring about the tedium and the journey, and the problems; I was in the England fly-fishing team, and I was so extraordinarily happy.

I have spoken to a lot of my team-mates about this over the years since then, and all recount similar feelings. Although I don't think subsequent qualification for the team reaches quite the same level of euphoria, it is, for sure, not too far removed. Only this year, in 2008, as I write this, I have qualified again for my cherished England team place. Our sport brings joy in many ways, but qualifying for the national team is right up there at the summit. I have won European championships, world team championships, international loch-style and rivers championships, but I would not swap my England team qualifications – not a single one of them – for *anything* else in the sport.

England silver medal European Championship team 2007, in Norway; LEFT TO RIGHT: John Kaasa (team guide), Vince Brooks, Stuart Crofts, Ian Barr, Mike Tinnion, Paul Page (manager), Simon Kidd, the author.

I know several people who have campaigned long and hard without yet making the frame, some for a decade or more. I will just say that you must stay with it, keep the faith, keep trying to qualify. As each year passes, you become more experienced; with each attempt you learn more. Every chance is a fresh opportunity, so go for it: every single chance that presents itself. If you want it enough, it can happen, and then the sacrifices you have made and all the failed attempts will be as nothing against your supreme achievement.

It is curious that currently the number of competitors is actually falling in both loch-style and rivers competition in Britain, while increasing elsewhere in Europe. And yet the competition itself is so strong, throughout almost every country in Europe at the very least. It is probably a function of the age and experience of the competitors still participating. We do not have enough youth coming through at the roots. Even in FIPS-Mouche World and European Championships – the supreme competitive events in the sport – the average age of competitors is currently somewhere in the forties.

It is about progress, through club and regional levels up to national level and beyond. There is so much to pick up along the way, and one must guard against becoming blinkered, or having one's sport spoiled by competition, which certainly can happen; while to others the sport *is* competition. We all find out whether or not it suits us, and if it does not, there are always other routes that lead to personal achievement, improvement and ultimate enjoyment in the sport.

11 MASTERS AND MASTERCLASSES

This chapter is a collective of the many places, people and fly-fishing episodes that have influenced my own development in the sport, and I know they have also had a profound effect on others. It will become apparent that there are many people and places that I have not mentioned. Frankly, this chapter could be a book in itself, because there is so much that I am forced to leave out, and yet it all deserves a mention, and more, even, exploring in depth. Of course, the lessons learnt, the lakes, rivers and shorelines of great waters, the fly-fishing times and events I have lived through, the brilliant fly fishers I have known and accompanied on the water, have all shaped me.

It has been a privilege to have experienced and witnessed so much in this, my treasured sport. Place, to me, once came before men, because I was a raw young angler lucky enough to visit astonishing waters that were to be so formative, before I met the men who were to continue the shaping process and pass some of their skills to me. Yet I remember so happily the help of the late Charles McLaren of Altnaharra, when we fished Loch Hope and lovely Maree for the big sea-trout. Then there was Grafham – always Grafham – and the astonishing, radical influence of Arthur Cove.

In the pages that follow you will see that I concentrate on the competitive fly-fishing

Arthur Cove, stillwater nymph-fishing master. (The Crowood Press archive)

masters and their craft, and in so doing I do not want to create the impression that I belittle in any way the great work and examples of non-competitive masters. Indeed, I believe that Arthur Cove, and before him Frank Sawyer (and of course I could go on differentiating and dissecting the sport further, and highlighting other great masters) had such a penetrating influence, greater even than the competitive practitioners I discuss here. No apologies for this: after all, Cove's and Sawyer's work have been very well documented by themselves and other observers, whereas the skills and achievements of many of the international competitors are nothing like so well documented.

Masters

Although fisheries have their own special influence on one's fly-fishing approach, we always learn most by studying the approach and performance of masters on those particular waters. Over at least the last twenty years I have learnt and discovered most by being a member of various England teams and taking part in international championships (European and World Championships, as well as river and loch-style internationals), and various qualifying competitions that led to England team representation. The campaigns leading up to these always involve one's team-mates and considerable practice together, and the events themselves often teach us aspects of our craft in a most impressive – indeed indelible – way. I cannot hope to translate this completely, or even reasonably well, within the confines of the printed page, but I can convey some aspects of these great lessons learnt, at least enough to inspire others on a similar path of development.

I have known and fished with most of the top British competitive fly fishers, and quite a few of the acknowledged Europeans, going right back at least as far as the Tony Pawson era, when he became one of the first World Champions in Spain in 1984. Though I often say that there is vastly more in advanced fly fishing than compe-

tition, it is without doubt this sector and these exponents who have had the greatest influence on my analytical, technical and tactical approach to the sport over the last two decades. In single-handed fly-rod fishing, I suggest that most of the significant developments have been inspired by competitive fly fishing – actually from the extreme hunger of competitors to find and develop a performance edge in the harsh glare of a championship. In the last instance, you see, out there in a session you are without the comfort of your team-mates, or friends or family. You are alone, and you perform or you go under. You are everything or you are nothing (within the confines of our sport) – and this really does bring about great performances.

Sporting success is defined by consistency imbued with spectacular periods of the exceptional, even brilliance, albeit these might be mere moments. As such, this success can be achieved only after considerable practice and development. When I look back at all the great performances I have witnessed, they have without exception been produced by very experienced anglers, though not necessarily particularly old. Many young anglers have demonstrated exceptional skill, although this is restricted to well defined areas of expertise, rather than all-round, multi-disciplinary excellence. Indeed, competitive fly fishing in Britain is increasingly a younger person's game, because it has physical and emotional demands that are better suited to young bodies and minds.

Simon Robinson

Themes that seem to be common to all the performances described here are that one is only as good (or successful) as the last competition, and also that the most important fish is the next one. The latter point is extolled by my team-mate Simon Robinson, arguably the best English all-round international competitor to date, so I will start with a description of this relatively young competitor's brilliance.

It was the Lake of Menteith in Scotland, in the Autumn International of 2005, and I was England team captain at the close of a year in

A Note of Caution

A word of warning: having been so intensely involved with the England team for so long, I know that this has changed me considerably as a fly fisher, while also significantly affecting my own personality. Several of my friends tell me that they often do not like what they see in me when out there on a campaign. I think, sometimes, about what I have become, and still more, what I will do when it is time to retire from England selection, or worse, when I am no longer able to 'make the frame'.

I have personal experience of this: although fairly fit, I collapsed during the 2008 European Championship, in Spain, after the first day's double sessions; I woke up in Santander A&E, where I was told that I was suffering from exhaustion. It was a gruelling championship, wading and fishing in white-water torrents under a blazing sun, but ten years ago I would not have been so worn down by the effort. As a result of this, the CEFF (the international selection committee) dropped me from the 2009 World/European squads – and they were right to do so, forcing me to fight for my treasured England team place again through the established qualification process in order to

What lies beyond? The wild water of a mountain lake.

prove my fitness at this level. Fortunately for me, I managed to regain my eligibility by qualifying from the 2008 English National Final to the 2009 England loch-style team. This allows me to decide when I should retire, rather than having the decision forced upon me by others.

I hope I will have the sense, at least, to know when the time is right for this, and to walk away before it destroys my spirit. But I wonder what lies beyond, on the other side of those waters…

which I had been involved in four internationals, including this one (two loch-style internationals, a river international and the European Championship; an individual record of caps in one year in English competitive circles). Team practice had been fair, and without a doubt we had learned a lot about the lake, even though I thought my team a little preoccupied with booby patterns. A lot of fish were caught on these, especially a yellow-eyed, pale pink variant, but I suspected this was only because so many of my team had fished them. This is quite common in loch-style internationals: if a successful fly begins to shine, it is fished exhaustively through the practice days, and I think this

is often counterproductive on the actual match day, because there are a lot of wary fish that have already been exposed to the favoured fly pattern(s); furthermore anglers can become blinkered, unable to see outside the confines of team practice.

I had noticed in conversations and team briefings that Simon did not appear to be very confident, and certainly had not caught many fish in practice. I talked with him about it on the eve of the international, and picked up a certain diffidence: 'I really don't know what to do tomorrow, or where to go. Frankly, I haven't got a Scooby!' Yet I saw him the following morning, as we collected by the boats after a final brief-

The England team being piped to the boats at the beginning of an international on the Lake of Menteith; at this moment, representing your country in your chosen sport, emotion is overwhelming. On the left is Stuart Wardle, then CEFF chairman; and on the right, Mike Childs, team manager.

ing, and I sensed that we were on the brink of a special performance. There was nothing I could put my finger on, and anyway, as captain I had other concerns for other members of my team; but I knew that Simon, veteran of numerous loch-style internationals, would be all right out there and did not need me fussing over him.

And indeed he was, coming in with twelve fish, when the average catch was four, to comfortably win the coveted Brown Bowl (the award for the individual international champion) and the Grafham Trophy (top England rod). 'I played hit and run!' he told me. 'Wherever I persuaded my boat partner to stop, we were immediately into fish; the trick was not to stop too long in one place, because the fish spooked very quickly, particularly if you showed them a booby!'

Simon Robinson with the Brown Bowl and the Grafham Trophy (top England rod) at Menteith, 2005.

This was nerve, playing the wild card and disengaging with the team approach. It is something that I always encourage anglers who are 'on form' to do – though it takes courage and enormous self-confidence to break away from the team map, method and approach, quite apart from the proven fly patterns. But this is part of what makes Simon Robinson a truly world class competitor.

Chris Howitt

Much earlier, back in 1991 on Loch Leven, another outstanding competitor, now retired, was very central to England's gold medal performance in that particular year's Autumn International. Chris Howitt and I travelled up to famous Leven together, not exactly relishing the prospect of the very dour fishing we knew to expect. The most famous of Scotland's lowland lochs had suffered too many years of gross

nitrate and phosphate pollution, and in truth was on borrowed time in its existence as a wild brown trout fishery. It was badly eutrophied, and survived only because of stocking with indigenous strain trout and, of course, its dazzling historic reputation.

Team practice confirmed our fears to the extent that some team members caught no fish whatsoever throughout either the practice, or the international itself. It was extremely hard work and hugely disillusioning: when an angler applies all his skills and knowledge for up to eight hours, for not even a single take, the spirit wanes and confidence disintegrates. I managed an average of two trout a day through practice, and I recall that Chris enjoyed the same.

It was not a confident England team that met for the final briefing, though there was one small gem of information, ignored by almost everyone, that was to prove significant. Up near

Guiding and masterclass on San.

the North Quoitch (a small inlet), one of our team-mates had hooked and lost a big trout, caught one smaller, and had at least one more trout take, along with several perch. There were, in fact, vast shoals of small perch in the loch, particularly in this area, and Chris and I both wondered if trout were collecting here, not just to feed on the best protein source for a predator that the water provided – the young perch – but in preparation for the spawning run up the feeder streams in a month or so. It was not much to go on, and I think most competitors disregarded this information, preferring to concentrate on the deep water marks such as off the east shore of St Serfs' Island.

On the day of the international, after being 'piped' down to the jetty and into the boats (as is traditional in Scottish internationals), we were off, and indeed most boats, including mine, headed off to the deep water drifts. I spent the morning fishing deep, with a Hi-D line, using a Peter Ross on the top dropper. This had been my most successful fly in practice, being generally imitative of coarse fish fry. The other two flies on the team were a Dunkeld (another essentially fry-like pattern) on point and a Pheasant Tail Nymph on the middle dropper.

For three hours neither my Scots boat partner nor I had a single take, and we did not observe any trout rising or being caught in any of the nearby boats. It was desperate: Loch Leven in the foulest of moods. Then I remembered the North Quoitch, and knowing that Chris would be in that area, following the team briefing, decided to persuade my boat partner that we might head off that way. He was strangely reluctant, but at a little past 2pm, when control of the boat was passed to me, we made the long journey (20 minutes) across the loch.

Sure enough there was Chris Howitt's boat, along with Chris Ogborne's, drifting a couple of hundred metres the other side of the stream inlet. There were also two or three other boats in the same general area. I set our drift, way out over the deep water, drifting approximately towards the inlet, 400 metres down-drift, with instructions for our boatman to do no more

than an occasional stroke on the oars to keep us drifting more or less beam to the wind.

There we remained, drifting through the remainder of the international, and on one of those drifts an immense trout appeared behind the Peter Ross, snatching it away as I roll-cast on the surface. I hooked the fish and immediately regretted the size of it – it was easily the biggest trout I had ever seen in the loch. In an international you really want sizable fish (above the minimum size limit), but not so big that there is every chance of losing them. We estimated this fish at somewhere around 5lb.

After initially boring deep, it took off in the most spectacular runs, twice stripping off backing almost down to the reel knot. I have never had a fight with a loch trout like that one. At the end of both runs the monster approached first Chris Howitt's boat, and then Chris Ogborne's, so they both had a good sight of the fish. Finally, of course, the hook-hold gave way and the fish was gone, leaving me with more than 70m (230ft) of fly line and backing to reel in, while I very nearly sobbed: I had lost the fish that would have won me both the Brown Bowl and the Grafham Trophy, as well as the Emir Lewis trophy for the biggest fish of the international.

Chris Howitt, however, was faring rather better, though he too had hooked and lost two or three very large, predatory trout. He told me afterwards that he was praying all day for a small trout to take the fly, because every time he hooked one of the larger fish it tore off on a long run and actually opened out the hooks. Chris was using three buoyant fry patterns on a Hi-D line, concentrating where he could on the edge of the perch shoal, which he gradually 'mapped' through the day. He found that if he cast into the midst of the shoal he would catch only the perch. The fry patterns needed to be in clear water, suspended close to the loch bed and close to the shoals. This was where the predators lurked, prowling near the perch fry, and occasionally scything in among them on a hunting and feeding foray. We guessed later that most of the large trout in Loch Leven would have been there at that time, though they were very difficult to catch. Chris had it absolutely right, and with a brilliant performance netted three good trout, easily enough to give him the Grafham Trophy for top England rod (yes, just three trout), and he was instrumental in winning England the gold medals.

This was, in my view, the culmination of a dazzling Home International career for Chris (though he carried on competing successfully for several years after this). I think his greatest strength in competition was his uncanny ability to map the water, to read the signs, and estimate not only the fish-holding potential of this water, but also the ideal technique to catch them. I don't think I ever knew anyone who could do this so consistently well as Chris. Though I could not put a description or words to it at the time, I now know that it was a highly personal and highly attuned blend of the analytical, technical and tactical approach which drives the top competitive fly fishers in the world.

Brian Leadbetter

At the time of Chris Howitt's outstanding performances in Home Internationals and other top competitions of the era, such as the European Open competitions (held on stillwater venues in England, France and Belgium), and the Benson & Hedges (now Anglian Water Club International events), Brian Leadbetter, England's most successful world class performer to date, was also at the pinnacle of his career. Brian actually achieved almost the impossible, twice winning the most demanding and coveted title of all, the FIPS-Mouche World Championship, and doing this once in Britain (England) and once abroad, which is certainly more testing for a British angler.

Brian, now retired from competition and enjoying playing golf more than fishing, was a hugely instinctive fly fisher, right up there with Chris Howitt and Simon Robinson, and I hope he will not mind me saying that he relied on his instinctive approach much more than any technical ability he possessed. He was an out-and-out stillwater fly fisher, coming, as many did, from a background of coarse fishing in the

English Midlands, and taking up fly fishing at the start of the stillwater boom in the 1970s. His command of this discipline was staggering, borne of long hours spent on the drift and also fishing from the bank of mostly the larger reservoirs.

He was hugely pragmatic, adapting the loch-style, lure and nymph-fishing methods in highly functional ways in order to maximize his catch rate. He was a speed fisherman, quickly adapting his method in order to rake through shoals of fish and build a bag. If there were fresh stockies or shoaled wild brown trout to be caught he would capitalize on them to the extent that he would sweep aside the competition.

I remember his performance in the World Championship in England, when out on Rutland Water he completely annihilated the field by coming in with an enormous catch of thirty-six trout in a single three-hour session. Even in the victorious England team there was no one who could get close to this, not even John Pawson, who was one of the most ferocious competitors I ever knew.

I think it was Brian who was the first ever to be considered as a speed fisherman. It was this, coupled with the fact that he was one of the few stillwater specialists who managed to adjust successfully to the competitive river situation – particularly with heavy Czech-style nymphing – to the level of excellence which was to contribute to him winning his second World Champion title. I fished with and watched Brian a lot in the early 1990s, and often came away stunned by the level of performance with which he could at times lift his game. In the modern era we might have some great competitors, and non competitors with supreme technical skill, but it was Brian Leadbetter who set the benchmark of excellence in terms of the analytical and tactical aspects of fly fishing with his utterly instinctive approach.

Chris Ogborne

Chris Ogborne was also one of the all-time competitive greats; a Brown Bowl winner, a World Championship team gold medallist, and

Chris Ogborne, concentrating and in tactical mode, on the River Camel, Cornwall.

unable to sleep and eat, leading up to a big competition. I have even known some who needed to be helped into the boat on the morning of the big match.

Chris was always so calm and focused, and I envied him these qualities, because I always tended towards the other pole, and continue to be like that – undoubtedly a weakness in my competitiveness, and which also certainly contributed to my collapse during the 2008 European Championship in Spain. Chris is also a highly versatile angler, and he was certainly able to adjust to the river discipline at the highest level, an attribute that launched him into several years of management of the England World Championship team. Also illustrating his versatility, Chris now concentrates on fishing in the surf of his beloved Cornish coast, and has provided a classic contribution in this book on saltwater fly fishing (*see* Chapter 5).

Iain Barr

Bringing us right back up into the modern era are two anglers who between them define the most advanced level of stillwater and river fishing in Britain: Iain Barr in the former, and John Tyzack the latter. Iain, or 'Barny' to his team-mates, is a vastly successful competitive fly fisher who is at the very top of the tree in the stillwater discipline, while John Tyzack, as five times English Rivers National Champion, is certainly the most aggressively successful river fisherman I have known.

Barny is a stillwater specialist who has managed, with surprisingly little practice, to translate enough of his fish-catching abilities to the river discipline in order to make him a world class competitor. It is his ability on stillwater, however, that is simply breathtaking. His mind is hyperactive. He verges on the cusp of sanity, and something that lies beyond – it might be genius. His supreme skill is his distance casting and accuracy, and this is married with an ability to read the water. He has a reputation for fishing lure patterns with a fast strip, and he can undoubtedly do this when required – in fact his skill here is very impressive. He has wonderful

perhaps most significantly, so enormously consistent over a long period of time, particularly in the testing loch-style internationals. Chris and I have been team-mates in both loch-style Home Internationals and World Championships, and what always struck me most was his even, almost laid-back approach, a confidence in his own ability and experience. This, too, is rare. I think of other great international competitors, and notice that in spite of their great skills, and personal knowledge of those skills and abilities, they are anything but confident on the morning of an international: witness Simon Robinson's nervousness in the description above. Indeed, I have seen competitors being sick with fear and trepidation, completely

skill, however, in far more delicate techniques, even with dry fly on the stream.

I recall his (and his controller's) description of a session in Spain (the European Championship, 2008) in which he was drawn on a difficult section with very few trout present, and those had already been caught, or at least fished for, in previous sessions. For over an hour and a half he worked the stream with nymph and duo for absolutely nothing, not even a take. Rather than panic, he retreated to a vantage point from which he could watch most of the beat. For twenty minutes (in a three-hour session) he watched.

There was a kick lane off a cliff face which was a natural food lane, and right on the edge of this Iain noticed a small dimpling rise. The first time he saw it he thought he had imagined it, but when the fish rose a second time he knew that here was his big chance. The most impressive aspect of the whole episode, however, was the way in which Iain worked out a strategy for catching this fish, which was of course in an incredibly difficult lie to approach, being on the far side of the kick lane which would certainly produce almost immediate drag to a dry fly.

Hard-fished Spanish trout are completely unforgiving. You get one chance only, at best, and the shadow of a fly line over the water, even the spray off a false cast, will put them down. Yet Iain had to figure how to present a dry fly (a JT olive – general ephemerid dun imitation) without drag for long enough for this fish to rise at it. Just think of the real pressure here: this was effectively a blank saver, with virtually no possibility of catching another fish on this section, and it was lying at extreme range (for minimal control) from any casting point.

Iain finally elected for a casting position that was a little over 15m (50ft) from the fish, with a mixture of curling current and slack water in between. Control at this range is verging on the impossible; even with perfect delivery, with multiple line mends, you have perhaps a metre of drift, and up to three seconds before drag inevitably sets in – and you will have only the one cast. If the first cast is wrong (unless it is

Iain Barr, double silver medallist, European Championship, Norway, 2007.

very short and off-line from the target), the fish will spook, no question.

There were now just minutes to the end of the session. Iain had seen the fish rising three times, even though numerous olives had passed over its head.

The controller, crouching low on the bank, watched the whole performance. He told me later that Ian was like a cat, and when at last he made his cast, it was probably the most perfect cast he had ever seen, placing the fly right on the kick lane where it would drift over the fish's head. And up came the trout to suck it down. Barny hit the fish at 15m and spent the next four minutes playing it to the net. With just a few minutes left in the session he finally netted what was one of the largest trout caught in the river sessions of the competition, and certainly one of the most important, being a blank saver and a fish that was to help secure a top ten place in the championship.

A year before the above, this time during the European Championships in Norway, Iain again faced a difficult river session, but in rather different circumstances. This time he had caught two trout on the near bank of his section and time was again running out when he noticed trout rising on the far bank, 35m (115ft) across the river. There were two options. The first, which would have been very costly of time as well as being dangerous, involved a swim across the cold water (it was a glacier-fed river) in order to reach the trout with a short-range controlled cast, and then a swim back to the controller on the near bank with any fish caught. Surprisingly perhaps, this option is often taken by some teams, notably the Czechs, who will never hesitate to deep wade or swim if this gives them a tactical advantage.

The other option was a long cast with commensurate loss of control. This option is actually much more risky in terms of catching a fish, though obviously less risky to the individual's safety. To Iain's mind, however, it was the best option for catching a trout in the dying minutes of the competition. Again, it required supreme accuracy in placing the flies very close to the rising fish, while wading 5m (16ft) off the near bank (the limit before the water overflowed into the top of Iain's waders) and casting a full 30m (100ft) to the target area. Drag was almost instant, but with the point fly being a wet fly, Iain was able to incorporate this drag into a diving sweep to induce the fish to take. And this was only the beginning of the problem, because a fish hooked at such range, with a very powerful flow between angler and fish, will always be difficult to bring to the net.

The perfection and rarity of utterly wild Spanish brown trout; the author on a Cantabrian mountain river.

John Tyzack teaching before the 2006 Home River International on the Wear.

Iain anticipated the take (which was almost instant on delivery), and stripped into the fish, continuing to strip as the fish was dragged across and down the stream, and not stopping until the trout hit the net. With just minutes to go before the end of the session, Iain then chanced his arm and repeated the whole process, again achieving the near impossible in the circumstances and successfully netting another measurable trout. This performance was crucial in winning the individual silver medal, as well as the England team silver medal, and was the summit of Iain Barr's career to date. Yet people say that Iain Barr is a stillwater 'blob' puller and has a liking for lead in his flies. Yes, all right; but you can take it from me, and all his team-mates who know him well, that he is an outstanding, world class performer, and a brilliant tactical fly fisher.

John Tyzack

I once called John Tyzack ('JT') a tactical genius. It was on a mild November day on the Welsh Dee in a North-West qualifier for the English National River Final, when we were partnering each other. We had both had a good start with early grayling to the net, and were moving well over the water, 'hit and run' fishing, which we both enjoy, until we came to a pool tail in which grayling were showing, rising to aphids and pale wateries. These fish proved to be challenging: John caught one of them, and I rose two or three, but missed them all.

Now, up to that point I felt we both had the tactical measure of the match, but I was abruptly, metaphorically brought to my knees by these grayling, even though I have met this sort of behaviour before. It is all too easy to be seduced by rising fish, and very difficult to tear yourself away; after all, we all instinctively feel that a showing, feeding fish is a catchable fish. This is not always the case with grayling, however. An hour passed, and I was becoming more frustrated, but equally infuriated enough to want to catch one or more of these fish. I estimated that there were at least a dozen sizable grayling within casting range.

My tactical sense had deserted me by the time John said: 'We have to leave these fish.'

'How so,' I replied; 'how can we leave this many fish? Just look at them all!'

'If we stay here we will not qualify.'

With huge reluctance, thinking that we were throwing away the opportunity to qualify with ease if we could just crack the problem and get these grayling to take, I agreed to move away and search elsewhere in the river. We waded and walked (jogged, actually) a long way before we saw one or two fish rising again on a long glide. Suspicious that they were trout (which did not count in the competition, because they were out of season) I questioned John. 'Trust me,' he

said, 'there are enough grayling here to walk us through.' And there were. In the last hour of the match we each caught enough grayling on dry fly to give us first and second place to qualify us to the National Final. If we had not left the difficult fish that had preoccupied my attention, we would both have missed out.

This was the first of several episodes that have fascinated me about this enigmatic competitor. I have often talked to John about his approach, and his attitude to fly fishing, probing for the reasons for his great success. His response is usually the same, something like, 'I don't do anything different from anyone else...' But he does, with an intensity and a tactical awareness that are unparalleled.

Masterclasses

Places, great waters, always produce great performances. Some of them essentially become schools, where a lot of us push up against the

John Tyzack presentation casting on the San river.

Tail water on the San at Lukawica.

frontier of knowledge and skill within our esoteric sport. Historically, waters have been so important to the development of the sport, and this continues to this day, though they change naturally, along with fashion, emphasis, excellence and environmental influences. At one time the River Test was the best in the world for dry fly fishing for trout, and Loch Leven the traditional heartland of the beautiful loch-style method – but the situation is completely different today. The Test is now almost completely artificial in terms of trout fishing, as well as being biologically degraded, while Leven, considering that it was the source of the brown trout that stocked the New World with this species, is a travesty of its former self, savaged by pollution. Similarly Loch Maree once represented the best possible for sea trout in the Old World – but we won't go there in this book.

Great waters still exist all over the world, waters that have made brilliant fly fishers. Grafham is a great water: since the late 1960s it has swept us all along and become the model for all large, stillwater trout fisheries; it is where Tom Ivens, Cyril Inwood and the master nymph fisher, Arthur Cove, reinvented stillwater fly fishing for us all, producing a leap in understanding of what was possible and setting completely new standards in our sport.

There are many others, though none quite matching the fame and influence of Grafham. Even the earlier reservoir fisheries, beautiful Blagdon and Ravensthorpe, never swept us and the sport quite so far along as did Grafham; nor did the great waters that have opened their shores to us more recently – Rutland, Chew, Bewl, Eyebrook, Pitsford, Draycote, Stocks… Nor even did the natural lochs and lakes of Britain provide us with such development, although they remain traditionally and historically important to us, and at the foundation of the British school of fly fishing. Indeed, these natural stillwaters and our rivers, so numerous and various, provide such an enormous wealth of opportunity that it is no surprise that Britain still maintains its status as a leading nation in this proliferating and ever-evolving sport.

In spite of this, however, the river discipline owes much of its recent development, right up to the frontier, to the great European rivers, particularly in the east of the continent. I will go so far as to say that what Loch Maree was to the world of sea-trout fishing, and Leven to great brown trout lochs, and Grafham to the enormous stillwater boom, so Poland's San river is now at the pinnacle of river fishing for brown trout and, most particularly, grayling.

Among all the world's great fly-fishing venues, San was selected for the FIPS-Mouche European Championship in 2005, and also for the World Championship in 2010; yet it must be said that while it deserves such a world class status and certainly has delivered us to extraordinary heights of excellence in the river disciplines, the San river is dying, just as Maree and Leven and the hallowed Test, and so many others have died and are no longer great waters. Gross over-fishing has done for this river, and its sheer scale cannot protect it, any more than a huge stocking programme. San, even as it opens up the frontier of the sport, is slipping away from us to join too many other great fly fisheries of history. It is, finally, the combination of person and place – and perhaps circumstances – that makes for development in the sport.

My England teams of recent years have evolved masterclass sessions during practice periods which have certainly opened our eyes to what is possible in a developmental sense. We have selected sections of rivers and lakes and undertaken short sessions during which each team member fishes while under the attentive eye of the rest of the team. It is a very testing experience, and we each learn aspects of approach and presentation that are not possible even within championship sessions or briefing/debriefing team sessions. The national

Walking up an enormous dry-fly flat on the San at Padjiernik.

Stuart Crofts on the Welsh Dee; Home River International, 2005.

team members are, after all, the acknowledged 'masters of the moment', the fly fishers who are most on top of their game, for however long they can maintain it.

By watching in hyperfine detail their performance, dissecting it and reducing it to its elements, we learn and develop. We improve – and the more we undertake this process, on a greater variety of waters and conditions, the more we learn. Actually, we learn at a surprising and accelerating rate. It was the inspiration of England European team manager, Paul Page, who came up with the masterclass idea, along with my great friend and fly-fishing 'brother', Stuart 'Skippy' Crofts.

Stuart Crofts

Stuart was with me during four consecutive European Championships, as well as a Home River International on the Welsh Dee. We travelled together to Poland, Slovenia, Norway and Spain, with numerous practice sessions on a wide variety of rivers in all those countries and in England. Paul Page was there on all of them, always pushing us to learn from each other and the rest of our team-mates. In the river discipline I am sure I learnt more by watching and fishing with Stuart than with anyone. It was rather like going back to my formative stillwater days with Arthur Cove.

When, after the Spanish European in 2008, Stuart announced his retirement and withdrawal from England team selection, I felt marooned, because apart from learning so very much from him, he had always been my great ally in the river sport. His entomological knowledge is world famous and simply staggering, and his analytical and tactical approach to managing a river session is simply the best I have ever observed, better even than the great European river masters such as Pascal Cognard of France, Piotr Koneiczny of Poland or, frankly, the entire, outstanding Czech national team.

Stuart Crofts in the European Championship, Poland, 2005.

This unassuming, generous angler, always so willing to help others, is more a river specialist even than John Tyzack. Stillwaters simply do not interest him as a fly fisher, though they do as an entomologist. In any river that holds trout and grayling, Stuart is the perfect fly fisher. His analysis is so rapid and yet methodical. He misses nothing, always maximizing the chances of catching whatever fish exist in a beat.

I recall fishing with him following a team masterclass session on the Sava Dolinka in Slovenia, leading up to the European Championships in 2006. He and I selected a particular beat of this alpine blue water river, while other team pairs ventured elsewhere. It was a fascinating beat, about a mile in extent, though we concentrated on a 500m (1,640ft) length on a pronounced S-bend, full of diverse features. It

was quite unlike anything we had fished elsewhere in Slovenia. The water was particularly fast, consisting of heavy mountain rain and snowmelt, and very difficult to wade. There were a few sedges about, quickly identified by Stuart, but almost no other fly life.

I had a very good start on this river, catching two brown trout almost immediately, while Stuart was still watching and analysing the beat. This gave me a somewhat false impression of Dolinka, however, as I had caught these fish using what I had assumed to be the most appropriate method in the fast, turbid flow – an across and downstream streamer (single fly by rule) on a short line. Actually, the early success proved to be a freak event, because this method was absolutely not the optimum for this river in these conditions. Stuart read it better than I had

ABOVE: Very demanding competition water on Sava Dolinka, Slovenia.

RIGHT: Stuart Crofts, silver medallist, European Championship, Norway, 2007.

done in my haste. Fishing on for another half an hour for nothing, I then climbed out of the river to watch him work at it his way.

Stuart crept along the river margins, concentrating on the slither-like seam of water between the bankside stones and the blue-white turbidity of the rushing stream. It really was very narrow, but along with a few calmer pockets further out, behind boulders and other features affecting the massive flow, represented by far the most likely areas that trout would be holding station. Electing to fish it upstream, Stuart alternated between a weighted nymph (a generic caddis larvae imitation), and a dry 'Skippy' sedge for

Dry sedge tied in a masterclass by England team guide Louis Otano Perez.

those sections where the water was smooth enough to justify dry presentation. His analysis of about 200m (650ft) of the river had been painstaking, taking at least half an hour while I had been fishing downstream, and his approach was now methodical and precise.

Watching Stuart was a humbling experience for me, because I realized that I would not otherwise have had the confidence that one could sufficiently control a nymph or dry fly in such a ferocious current as this. The natural tendency of almost everyone would have been to fish as I had done initially: downstream, with a short dead drift, swing and pronounced hang close to the bank. This was the simplest, 'percentage' way to fish such a torrent.

Stuart's approach was considerably more demanding. He stole very slowly upstream, placing his fly in minute pockets in the flow, mostly close to the bank, all in the ideal control window around 6m (20ft), so that when trout snatched at the fly, he hooked every one. In an hour he rose seven fish and netted six of them – beautiful, wild Slovenian rainbows, all taken

from places that most anglers would have over-looked. The effect this had on me was such that when I fished my championship session on the Dolinka a few days later, I was able to approach it as Stuart had shown me in his masterclass, rather than with the percentage, downstream approach, and managed to achieve a sixteen-fish catch in three hours, and a section win.

Louis Otano Perez

Two years after this, in the Europeans in Spain, the England team was guided by Louis Otano Perez, one of the first division of Spanish competitive fly fishers, from which their national team is selected. This is a harsh school actually, because generally the fly fishing in the northern Spanish (and Portuguese) rivers is hugely demanding because of intense fishing pressure, virtually no stocking, and a largely catch-and-kill approach by the large number of bait fishermen in the region. The top Spanish fly fishers, like Louis, have therefore honed their skills much more than most, as I was to learn when one day Louis guided me on the upper reaches of the Pas, another mountain torrent (after heavy rain) with frequent gorges and a jungle of bankside foliage.

Alternating between duo and single nymph or dry fly, as circumstances dictated, finesse presentation was demanded. Louis demonstrated to me the ultimate in stealth approach for these ultra-wary trout. We used first his own 11ft three-weight, with long (18ft/5.5m) indicator leader, and then adapted this rig to my own 10ft Streamflex (slightly shortening the leader down to 15ft/4.5m), and stole up together through the rock pools.

For an hour or more I simply followed on behind Louis, watching his every move, his consummate skill in threading his line and fly through the undergrowth; a prowling cat of a fly fisher, with every step, every footfall and cast inch-perfect, his attention fixed on fly or indicator (the fluorescent, fine coil of monofilament), though undoubtedly scanning the river upstream between casts, completely absorbed in the fishing process.

The most impressive aspect of all this was the casting. There was seldom the possibility of a straightforward short-range overhead, and each potential fish-holding spot had to be cast to from often uncomfortable angles, constricted by current, rocks or shrubbery. Some of the river was in narrow gorges. Dealing with such river space while using the necessary long leader and short (variable) length of fly line, with consistent good presentation, is challenging in the extreme. I watched as Louis put in curve casts, stun and side casts, snap rolls and Spey variants, and frankly all manner of indescribable means of delivering his fly, with precision.

On hard-fished, wild waters this is how it has to be: this is advanced, tactical fly fishing, by necessity. In England we rarely have to go to such extremes, but in the waters of northern Spain, savaged by ruthless, pragmatic bait fishers catching trout for the table, the fly fishers learn to exist on the ragged edge of what is possible. They learn to be supreme fish hunters.

Louis Otano Perez stalking in complex, rapid water on the Rio Miera.

Appleby Water on Eden.

Louis showed me how to take on these wild mountain waters, at least enough such that in my championship sessions I did manage to save the blank, catching at least one trout, in every case, from water which might otherwise have left me perplexed and frustrated. It was a testing, redefining fly-fishing experience, a Spanish masterclass that demonstrated new limits in our sport.

The Author on Appleby Water

I could write on and on about my team-mates, and others I have known; about the great skills and performances I have been lucky enough to observe and from which to learn – and even then I would miss out a great deal. In a rich fishing life, there is much more that is worth the telling than I have space and time to relate. So I will close this chapter with the following master-

class, where I feel most in control and most excited: in the cool upland waters of a freestone river, among mixed brown trout and grayling. I have written about it already, really, reducing it all to the analytical and technical parts, and drawing most attention to the tactical approach. It is this that suffuses my whole being as a fly fisher: the tactical that still draws me out into the flowing waters, where I am now. It is the very tail of a long, broken glide on the Appleby Water of my beloved Eden, as the waters fine down after a week of early autumn spate.

Trout are right on the lip of the tail, mopping up blue-winged olive duns before they are lost in the rapid below. I have mapped out the whole glide from the tail right up to the rapid run-in, either side of an island a hundred metres upstream. Indeed, I am so familiar with this beat that I know it intimately. While walking down I have seen rising fish and so have set up with single dry fly, a size 18 heron herl CDC shuttlecock, on a 10ft leader consisting of 4ft of taper and 6ft of tippet at 6X, all set on the 8.5ft Streamflex four-weight. Even while walking down, I have greased the line tip to prevent drowning the tippet and fly on snap rolls or when the dry fly drops downstream of my position, and rubbed sticky Fuller's Earth along the tippet.

There is almost no wind. With dry fly I have three options at the tail. I can either approach from the rapid below, almost right up to the lip, and cast up into the smooth water, slightly upstream of the trout; however this runs the risk of lining the fish, and also, unless a long rod and short cast are used, the accelerating water will catch the line and cause almost immediate drag. Alternatively, I can approach from upstream and drop the fly down to the fish, but this risks disturbing the pool tail excessively at this stage, before the trout have been properly targeted. The ideal is to approach from the side, placing the dry fly 1m (39in) upstream of the rising trout, with a slight upstream mend in the line so as to avoid drag for the crucial 2m (6.5ft) of drift that I need.

I first target the fish lying closest to my kneeling position on the bank, so as not to line or spook them while going for the fish further away. The range is nicely down to 6m (20ft) and a fish is fairly regularly showing, completely unperturbed by my low profile and slow-motion approach. The first cast is in short, and away upstream – a 'sighter' cast – and the second puts the fly exactly on the fish's drift lane, 1m upstream. I notice already how the CDC plume completely matches the wings of the BWOs in colour and size.

Brown trout from Appleby Water, Eden.

Wild trout perfection.

A sip, and the fly is gone, the hook is set and the trout turns into the bank as I immediately apply pressure so as to bring it away from the others farther out in the stream. With practice (and at this range) you can do this, such that fish smaller than about 35cm (14in) seem almost not to wake up to being hooked. You can steer them straight into the net. The trick is to keep applying that pressure even as the hook is being set. The fish's first turn is towards the bank, and you should keep it coming in that direction. With fish of this size, or sometimes even larger, it is mostly a matter of having the nerve to do it.

Now I can stand, though stooping slightly, and with feet well apart so as to keep that low profile, and I begin to wade out into the stream,

picking out the new targets as I work out and up, always attempting to close the range to each fish, so that I can maintain that ideal 6m control, never more than 10m, or a risky 11m (36ft) or 12m (40ft) on smooth water, from potential targets. Larger fish, in the 30–50cm (12–20in) bracket, cannot be brought immediately to hand (or net). They will need to be played out, but we always attempt to bring them away from the feed lanes, ideally into the shallows away from other fish, and upstream of our position. Even so, there is never any need to exhaust them.

Good fishing practice is to bring them to hand, or beach or net them, in the shortest possible time. It is strange how their splashing on the surface does not spook nearby fish, particularly grayling, though if they slip the hook, or, much worse, break free (though with an appropriate soft rod and control up to 10m that should never happen), they will then certainly cause alarm among other fish. A trick that works every time with trout, though never with grayling, is to slide them to hand and then flip them over on to their backs. Even large trout (including rainbows) will keep perfectly still when you do this, as soon as they are on their backs. I have no idea why they do this, or why it does not work with grayling, but you can easily then remove the fly and slip them back into the water while you line up your next target. Grayling are much more difficult to deal with once brought to hand, or netted for that matter.

Gradually working upstream I can pick off fish at will. This is not a misdirected over-confidence; this is how it is if you analyse properly, and if you have the technique right. Then it is

only a matter of good wading technique and dealing with each fish appropriately, with the tactical attitude of the most important fish being the next one. Even when casting at a particular target, one's mind is already beginning to plot out the next. You are thinking as if in the flow of a chess game, working with the three dimensions of water space in front of you. As soon as the hook is set, the wading position is altering as the next angle and range is settled.

When fish are preoccupied on surface feeding, it is often the case that they will rise downstream of your position, even when you have fished up through them. Those you have missed on the way up will often quickly recover from being spooked and come back on the feed. The tactical mind should be alert to this, considering the whole 360 degrees surrounding the fly-fisher. Many bonus fish are acquired by putting

Brown trout on dry fly, the Eden system.

in a downstream cast, even with dry fly. Presentation is completely different, however, to fishing up and across, and we have to be very alert to drag. A fish facing the angler will spook very easily, and drag will be absolutely fatal.

A fish rises at 10m, across and downstream. I turn to face it, dropping 1m downstream, allowing the current to push me down. In the windless conditions I can put in a stun cast (a parachute cast with the rod tip held high at the forward stop point) and alight the fly a couple of metres upstream of the fish's position. The fly falls away downstream as I lower the rod tip to avoid drag. Again the fly is sipped away and the hook is set into a 42cm (17in) cock grayling. This is luxury, really, because I can play out the fish downstream, on water that has already been fished though, without disturbing the water upstream, and so resting it while I deal with the big grayling. Turning back to face the flow, I again work up towards the island. Fish are rising in all the places I expect them to be: shoaled grayling over the shallower gravels and larger

fish on the seams and clearly defined foam and feed lanes.

If this were a competition session I would systematically work through these fish and try not to miss a single one, but it is not and I begin to wonder what it is I am doing now. Perhaps, after another fish or two, I should tear myself away from this place and go hunting elsewhere, perhaps for the giant grayling that inhabit the waters hereabouts. To stay here, on a glide I know so very well, with the fish completely focused on the BWO hatch, I am at best just consolidating skills and experience, and not moving on.

When you have everything right – the analytical, the technical and the tactical, and the river is fished through – one wonders if there is a better feeling in our sport. We are enthused, yet humbled. We have known nature at her best – to us – and we have caught beautiful fish. We must know when to stop. We are at a good place in our journey, a waypoint that seems like a state of fly-fishing grace.

Brown trout going back.

12 DIRECTIONS IN THE FUTURE OF FLY FISHING

One wonders where fly fishing, that multi-directional, contemporary sport, is going now. The answer, of course, is that it will go wherever the practising angler wants: it depends on place, the nature of the fishery, the personal tastes of the angler, affordability, conservation issues, and many factors that are beyond our personal control. In terms of advanced fly fishing, we can look at the various disciplines that exist within the sport and extrapolate each one in order to glimpse where it is heading. Most of all, however, it will be as it has always been: given direction by those of us who have a passion for this esoteric sporting activity.

The Commercial Fishery

The rise of the commercial 'put-and-take' fly fishery – mostly lakes, and strongly dependent on stocked rainbow trout – has been astonishing since the 1970s in Britain, and stocking has become extensive throughout most of Europe towards the end of the last millennium. Even rivers (though comparatively few in Britain) have been stocked with rainbows to supplement actual numbers, or what have been perceived to be dwindling stocks of wild fish. Much of the Slovenian and northern Italian fishing, for example, would barely exist without the large-scale stocking of the alpine rivers with rainbow trout. In countries or areas where there is very limited wild trout fishing, such as Belgium, almost all the fly fishing relies on stocking. It is reasonable to assume that while the introduction of other sporting fish, such as carp, to pools and lakes, specifically for fly fishing, will continue to develop, it will always be rainbow

trout that dominate in this regard, even over brown trout.

The commercial trout fishery represents collectively an enormous range of sporting opportunity, from small pond to length of river, all the way to enormous reservoir or lake where there may be wild trout as well as stocked fish. In this regard they might be considered as 'managed' fisheries, as opposed to purely 'commercial' or indeed wild fisheries. The majority of fisheries throughout the world might be considered managed to some extent, whether or not they are stocked.

There is a strong move nowadays towards minimizing or preventing stocking with fish, particularly non-indigenous trout, and particularly in rivers. It is fairly reasonable to assume, however, that in stillwaters where there is isolation from rivers in terms of fish migration, the sporting fly fishery will persist, and possibly even proliferate further, and that this will be dominated by rainbow trout, with limited brown trout and other salmonids. As such, the commercial fishery services a huge demand. Such fisheries are very good for beginners to learn the skills of fly fishing, even up to an advanced level, and they also provide access to the sport for the more senior element (expert or otherwise), who require a relatively easy entry to the water side and possibly the stable platform of boats, giving a greater range of access to the available fishing.

The managed fisheries will also continue to develop, as will the sport as a whole. Economic and animal husbandry issues, as well as matters of sporting development, will always force these fisheries to move with the times, or collapse. There are many factors that actually force

A stocked rainbow.

change. For example, the amazing growth of cormorant populations throughout much of Europe because of their protected status, has resulted in far-reaching constraints on wild and managed trout and grayling fisheries. In areas where there are any number of these birds, fishery managers have had to take measures to protect their stocks either via constant vigilance, or by stocking with very large trout, which are significantly less vulnerable than the sub-kilo fish that hitherto formed the bulk of stock to commercial put-and-take fisheries.

The expense of such measures, and the inevitable loss of stock to predation, brings ever

greater pressure on the profitability of commercial fisheries of all types. Perhaps the time might come when the problem will be resolved by the removal of the protected status, or by more limited protection of cormorants, so that fishery managers could conserve their stock. If they were designated as farms, rather than fisheries, one suspects this would be the case in contemporary Europe where the agricultural lobby is so enormously powerful. Politics aside, however, the cormorant issue is just one of many concerns largely or wholly beyond the control of individuals, that will influence the development of all fisheries, though probably more the trout and grayling fisheries of the world.

One thing is for sure: supply and demand will mean that there will always be sufficient access to 'put and take' fly fisheries as long as we want them. And even in this world which is (as I write

OPPOSITE: Sava Bohinka in Slovenia: idyllic, though the fishing is maintained only by stocking with brown and rainbow trout; the grayling are wild.

ABOVE: Magnificent naturalized rainbow, 8lb 11oz, Bewl Water, for John White, with Seven Pound Creek in the background.

LEFT: Blue trout: a rainbow sub-species that is very successful as a stocked trout in managed stillwaters.

this) in such financial flux, if not disaster, one imagines that people will continue to indulge their sporting and recreational needs so far as this is possible. It would be a very dull, bland world if this were not the case. Of course there must be a balance between affordability, conservation and sporting quality, but there is every indication that demand for fly fishing is increasing throughout the developed world.

One guards against those who indulge in wild fish and wild fisheries to the detriment or downgrading of stocked fisheries. I believe this does a great disservice to the sport as a whole. Without a doubt the sport would be considerably weaker without the development of the commercial fishery. Frankly, in most parts of the world there are not sufficient wild fishery resources to feed the fly-fishing demand. Without the develop-

ment of, particularly, stillwater stocked fisheries, there simply would not be anywhere near the fly-fishing population that now exists.

Also, some people suggest, or believe, that a wild fish is always better than a stocked fish, in some way. This is simply not the case, other than perhaps freshly stocked fish, of any species, that really should be left well alone until they have acclimatized and adopted natural behaviour. The rainbow trout is one of the world's great sporting fish, stocked or wild, and those who suggest otherwise are speaking from a position of ignorance. We might prefer to catch a wild brown trout rising to dry fly on the stream, but for all those for whom the pinnacle of the sport is the rainbow scything through plankton on a large lake, this is no lesser a sport and no less challenging a quarry.

Wild rainbow from an upland, limestone lake; lean and very fast moving when hooked or hunting in shallow water.

Feral rainbow from a fishery with a very low stocking density.

The commercial fisheries that exist today are the most likely to change according to fly-fishing demands. Numbered are the days when small lakes are overstocked with triploid rainbows simply to provide what is perceived to be good sport, which usually means not too demanding. This type of fishery generally does a disservice to the fly-fishing public, because it does not provide sport that is indicative of the classical pursuit, and neither does it offer any scope for development. At best the intensively managed commercial fishery provides table fish and perhaps the most basic of introduction to the new fly fisher. Such fisheries, being intensively stocked, are also very expensive to maintain.

Rainbow trout, or any stock fish, are steadily becoming more expensive, and this is likely to continue to increase. Even grade three rainbows, the equivalent of the battery hen, bred and grown for table purposes, have more than doubled in price within the last few years, and

the trend is ever upwards. Grade one rainbows – and even more so, top quality brown trout – for sporting fishery purposes will always command high prices, and the cost of stocking these will obviously have to be reflected in the price of fishery tickets.

For the small fishery manager the way ahead is limited stocking with these high quality fish, with a sensitive balance between brown trout and rainbow trout species, and restricting fishing pressure on the water to reasonable levels, incorporating a degree of catch and release. For the large lakes and reservoirs, trickle stocking with high quality fish is already the norm, but here too the stocking density must be carefully managed. There is something offensive in our sport about stocking with more fish than a water can sustain in terms of adequate natural feed. Smaller upland waters with large stocks of ravenous triploid rainbows are essentially intensive farming units, where the owner is exploiting a water system and animals for personal profit.

The fish in these waters actually fall away in condition and lose weight from the day they are introduced, and the angler visiting such waters is deluding himself if he thinks otherwise. Such fisheries bring the sport into disrepute, fuelling the anti-fishing debate, and the thinking angler would have to support the views of the antis. More limited stocking, with reduced fishing pressure and a lower kill rate solves the issue at a stroke, and the less skilled angler simply has to up his game if he is to improve and catch fish with consistency. The sport benefits all round.

The Environment Under Threat

My love of this sport runs deep, and as you have seen, focuses on grayling and wild brown trout, and freestone rivers some distance from the sea where the flows are strong and clear; but I enjoy all its aspects, at least with single-handed fly rod, and see that they all have a place, and meaning, for all of us. The carp gulping down a deer-hair buoyant pattern from the surface of a lake, to the steelhead rainbow ripping across a torrent, hooked on a salmon egg imitation, are as treasured a part of our sport as stroking a big

The perfection of wild river brown trout – River Eden.

The perfection of wild lake trout – tarn in the Howgill Fells.

bait fish streamer close to weedbeds where pike wait in ambush, or the big grayling sipping down a size 22 CDC, the indigenous chalk stream brown trout, or even the rare Loch Leven fish so close to the core history of this magical sport.

In truth, we have lost so much. We have lost the special strain of giant Loch Maree sea trout (these will never return) because of intensive salmon farming (agriculture again) in the system. We are losing much of our pristine, temperate-zone freshwater environments throughout Europe and the rest of the world through urbanization and particularly agricultural damage. We have even lost Loch Leven as a wild brown trout fishery (though this could be recovered), as well as the hallowed Test and Itchen chalk spring rivers, now travesties in comparison with the perfect wild trout and grayling fisheries of just a few decades ago.

Central and Eastern Europe – Slovenia and southern Poland: now we must consider what

was here, and what is being engulfed by change so rapidly. The Sava system, the Soca, the wonderful, awe-inspiring San river are places of dreams, pristine rivers until so recently, certainly until the recent years of my own fly-fishing career. What we have done to these places is simply obscene. The fishing pressure is grotesque, and they survive only because of stocking (though much of this is hidden, invisible, undisclosed). There are many who suspect that the wild brown trout is extinct in most Slovenian river systems! And the San in terms of brown trout is no different.

Nor should we really deceive ourselves about those 'feral' rainbows, even though they provide such wonderful sport. We are all to blame for this, because we demand the fishing, apparently at all costs, or at least to the cost of the wild fish these rivers possess. As a consequence, we have an obligation to protect them, to retrace our steps and begin to remanage, to reassess our demands, to conserve the natural environment

ABOVE: Grayling spawning on the San river. BELOW: *The path inevitably leads me here: tail water on the San.*

LEFT: Nymphing on stepped shallows.

BELOW: The sun sets over the river at Lesko.

and the species it naturally supports. As advanced fly fishers we should do no more than perturb nature as we pass through; if we do more damage than this we are out of place, out of phase.

I worry, for example, about the tactical fly fisher wading through pristine river. I know we do a great deal of damage to the substrate and the invertebrates for which this environmental niche is home. And yet, can I stop myself wading out there, stealing the best that a river can give to the hunter with fly rod? I think, even when my England team days are behind me – if ever it will be out of my system – perhaps I will not be able to hold myself back, and pass over those endless opportunities as the tactical fly

fisher's mind is engaged. It will, finally, be only physical restraints that end the day.

Pushing at the Frontiers

As we conserve the places we fish, so we can conserve, and develop, our fly-fishing skills. The evolution of tackle, rig and fly, along with levels of skill in all disciplines, is bound to continue, and in some areas it will escalate. As the Angling Trust in Britain seeks to unify the pursuit of angling and increase participation, the CEFF, working with the Angling Development Board and the Game Angling Instructors Association, will concentrate on the development of English

Wild trout on Tup Wool Bug.

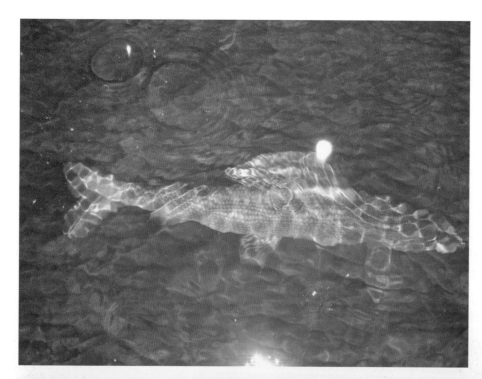

LEFT: Summer grayling.

BELOW: Pike on the fly. (Courtesy Andy Smith)

Tail water on the San.

competitive fly fishing, while similar organizations throughout most of the world are on a similar path. The great showcase championships organized by FIPS-Mouche, the annual European and World Fly Fishing Championships, are also bound to develop.

We have already made strides towards adopting the Olympic ideal, and many of us hope for Olympic events involving fly fishing, or fly casting at the very least. While we have target air rifle and air pistol shooting, for example, as Olympic category events, where the live animal is replaced with a target, so the extrapolation to fly casting, in terms of inanimate targets rather than fish, is obvious – though it is the fish, live and hunting out there in the cold waters, that truly engages the tactical fly fisher's mind.

With the Countryside Alliance, Grayling Society, Wild Trout Trust, and other initiatives in Britain and beyond, such as the Angling Trust, we work towards a certain parity among field sports, protecting and developing them all, on an equal basis. We learn that to downgrade one damages all, or the support of one strengthens all. It is at the edges, however, the extremes, where the advancement occurs (from the healthy base of the field sport); and it is extreme fly fishing that captures the imagination in this context.

This is where we push at the frontier of our sport, where we represent our countries within the national teams, where we hunt down the specimen fish, or perfect casting technique, or target-specific presentation, or evolve imitative fly design. This is where we climb towards the river sources into upland regions, to discover just how high trout will venture, or how far up the feeder streams the nomadic grayling will penetrate, or perhaps where we search the surf and tide for bass, or mysterious weedbeds of great lakes for ambushing pike. This is where we interact with the last wilderness places.

And this is where the tactical mind explores, right up on the frontier of this extraordinary, multi-faceted sport. It is, finally, a state of mind, and if the passion for it is in you, the journey is inevitable: it is only a matter of going along with it. I feel now that we are somewhere like advanced base camp, probing an assault of the summit. With our skills developed, in tune with our tastes and needs in the sport, and sufficient experience gained, the problem is only in defining the summit, because we cannot yet see it. It is somewhere up there, obscured by cloud.

Perhaps as individuals we see it. Your summit, after all, is different from mine, which is differ-

ent again from each and every fly fisher out there. Mine involves trout and grayling and international competition at the highest level. Or perhaps there is a row of summits out there for each of us, like dangerous teeth reaching up on the horizon. We can only hope this is the case, because as we venture out from base camp on an attempt to perhaps make our personal peak, it would be nice to know that there was something else to go for, something worthwhile and beyond.

My Own Frontier

When my days are done for my cherished England team place, when I can no longer make the frame and have the chance of the summit of international performance, I would dearly love to think that there could still be purpose for me,

The frontier: Norwegian lake on the west coast.

The frontier: the San river, south-east Poland.

and development, and tactical prowess, in my sport, or my place in my sport.

I would hate to turn away and leave it all behind, to go backwards, knowing that there could be nothing to match this, ever again for me. In the end it will be just a collection of memories, but I hope not lost. I hope that it makes a special mark on this occupation we love. First we must reach our peak, leave our mark, and then look beyond for the next. The most important fish is the next one.

My team-mate of the past, Simon Robinson, said to me earlier this year, before a particularly gruelling river qualifier, that he would not like to be going through that sort of physical and mental stress when he was my age. I laughed, of course, but the comment bit deep down inside me. I knew then, and I know now, that I am right out on the ragged edge of my journey and at least my physical ability; probing out from my advanced base camp with time running out for the final assault. But I am not ready just yet to stop the journey and start retracing steps, receding into the distance of lower altitude and slower flows; not just yet. The peak is still out there, the frontier, and I can see it, almost in my grasp: it is only a matter of going.

I am more aware, in this book, of not what I have written about, but what I have left out. There are two things in my life that are overwhelmingly important to me, among all the flotsam and jetsam of the life we lead: my family and close friends, and tactical fly fishing. I

ABOVE: The frontier: Baca, Slovenia.

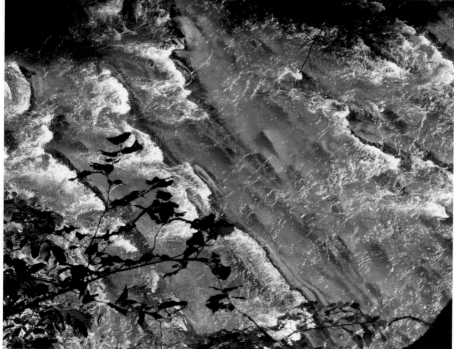

LEFT: The frontier: deep in the wilderness, a river in Poland where the SS, Red Army and partisans met in 1944.

would be utterly lost without these – though there will come a time, no matter what, when I have to do without the latter, because of physical and perhaps mental constraints.

I have been up there on the frontier of the sport, in what I can only describe as a state of grace. It has been a wonderful collection of adventures, a journey to some of the most beautiful places on our planet. My generation achieved so much and lost so much, and we are not quite through. We are still out there on our journey. My journey with single-handed fly rod is, God willing, far from over. Maybe I will get the chance to revise and add to what I have written here, and advance a little bit more along the waters that run off that line of peaks defining the frontier.

It is a question of which frontier. You have glimpsed mine here, and the one to which some of my England team-mates aspire. Yours might be completely different to mine, with different goals and aspirations, but just as valuable because it is yours. What we fly fishers all try to do is to satisfy that fragment of the hunter within our deep-seated personalities. It is ultimately an emotional journey, but for me it has passed through the analytical and technical phases and rested very much in the inescapable aspects of a tactical approach. I marry this with trout and grayling and the lovely places in the world where I find them. The apparent contrast of two worlds – international competition and wilderness – tactical fly fishing has afforded me some of the best of both these frontiers.

The frontier: the author and WG in grayling paradise, the San river, No Kill sector.

APPENDIX

Some recommendations and data for leader and tippet material, and leader and fly treatments (all data approximate).

Fluorocarbon:
Ideal for sinking leader applications. It is slightly denser than water.

5X is equivalent to a diameter of 0.16mm; BS approximately 3lb (1.4kg)
4X is equivalent to a diameter of 0.18mm; BS approximately 4lb (1.8kg)
2X is equivalent to a diameter of 0.22mm; BS approximately 6lb (2.7kg)
1X is equivalent to a diameter of 0.33mm; BS approximately 8lb (3.5kg)

Fulling Mill World Class, Hardy or Greys Greylon are strongly recommended.

Conventional nylon monofilament:
4X is equivalent to a diameter of 0.18mm; BS approximately 3lb

The best leader material of this type is produced by the German company Bayer and is marketed variously as Bayer Perlon, Drennan sub-surface green and Kamasan. It is strongly recommended as an all-purpose leader and tippet material with consistent knot strength and abrasion resistance. Although conventional mono has the weakest breaking strain for any given diameter compared with other types of leader material, it is very reliable and has excellent knot strength. Several top anglers persist in using this material.

Fluorescent nylon monofilament for indicator sections:
The company Stren produces ideal material for this, for example in 0.2mm, 6–7lb (2.7–3.2kg). In continental Europe there is a very good material of this specification found branded as ASSO Diamonds.

Pre-stretched, PTFE treated, nylon monofilament:
Stroft is recommended for delicate presentation in rivers or stillwaters, with micro dry fly and nymph. 0.08mm has a BS of approximately 2.2lb (1kg) and is the equivalent of 7X. Probably the most useful fine presentation tippet material of all is the 0.1mm, 3lb (1.4kg). The only down-side of this material is the shiny surface, which is common to all pre-stretched and treated monofilaments, and copolymer.

Copolymer:
Hardy copolymer and Fulling Mill World Class cp are strongly recommended. Try to avoid the very commonly available shiny products that are available in this category.

7X is 0.1mm with a B.S of 2.2lb (1kg)
6X is 0.13mm with a B.S of 3lb (1.4kg)

Probably the most useful over a broad range of dry fly, nymph and spider applications is the 5X, which is 0.15mm with a BS of 4.2lb (1.9kg). The 4X or 3X is recommended for heavier applications, such as for dry fly or nymph where the fish might be expected to be commonly in excess of 2.2lb (1kg) in weight. 4X is 0.18mm, 6.4lb (2.9kg); 3X is 0.2mm, 7.9lb (3.6kg).

Use good quality snips to cut leader material, most especially when you need to make an angled cut in order to thread the material through the eye of a small hook. Degreasing leader material to aid sinking is best achieved using soft clay, but a Fuller's Earth/glycerine/detergent mix to the consistency of putty is also good. Thick Silicone Mucilin is perfect for treating leaders, braids, furls and the tips of fly lines to aid buoyancy.

Gink or equivalent low-temperature melting grease is good for treating dry flies, though use very sparingly to avoid clogging fibres, and all oils and greases should be kept away from *cul de canard* (CDC), which floats by virtue of its filigree structure rather than the oil it contains. CDC is best dried by using soft tissue or amadou, and the application of a silicon oxide dessicant.

On heavier grades of fluorocarbon and conventional nylon monofilament, an excellent way to make droppers stand out more from the main line of the leader is to put in a single overhand knot after the three- or four-turn water knot. The dropper length then stands out at about 90 degrees to the leader. It has the added virtue of 'clicking' over when a fish has taken, which informs the angler which fly has been taken (if the fish is not actually hooked) among those on a team of flies. Do not try this with copolymer.

If you are using droppers, start the day with them at about 6in (15cm) long. This will give you enough room for three or four fly changes if this becomes necessary.

Some leader material is better than others in untangling and clearing kinks. Fluorocarbon and conventional nylon monofilament are best in this regard, kinks being stretched out with minimal loss of leader strength. Stretch slowly with good grip, preferably by gripping between something like leather.

Don't hurry knots, and damp them before drawing tight; this prevents friction-damaging. There is never a good reason to break on a fish. Set yourself challenges: get through a session without a break. Then go for a whole week, a season. Then really mean it and determine never to break again. And don't just cut leader material up and dump it. Fluorocarbon will never decompose. Dispose of it with care.

INDEX